EUGENE ROUSSEAU:
WITH CASUAL BRILLIANCE

by
THOMAS LILEY

North American Saxophone Alliance

Also in this series:

Larry Teal: There Will Never Be Another You
by Mary Teal

EUGENE ROUSSEAU: WITH CASUAL BRILLIANCE. Copyright © 2011 by the North American Saxophone Alliance. All rights reserved. Printed in the United States of America. No part of this book may be used or reproduced in any manner whatsoever without written permission, except in the case of brief quotations embodied in critical articles and reviews.

CONTENTS

Foreword by Steven Stusek   v

Preface   vii

Biography

1. Blue Island   1
2. Chicago Musical College   8
3. Northwestern University   12
4. Military Service   16
5. Luther College   19
6. University of Iowa   23
7. Fulbright Study   28
8. Central Missouri State College   37
9. Indiana University   42
10. University of Minnesota   68

Teaching

Introduction   99

11. Tone Production   103
12. Tuning   109
13. Technique   112
14. Articulation   116
15. High Tones   118

16.	The Other Saxophones	122
17.	Performance	125
18.	Wit and Wisdom	129
Conclusions		135

APPENDICES
A —	Works by Eugene Rousseau	146
B —	Works written for Eugene Rousseau	148
C —	Recordings by Eugene Rousseau	150
D —	Programs by Eugene Rousseau	155
E —	Students of Eugene Rousseau	200
F —	Family	205

NOTES	206
BIBLIOGRAPHY	211
INDEX	217

Illustrations appear on pages 83-98 and 138-145

FOREWORD

I remember the first time I met Dr. Rousseau. It was July 1976, the summer after my freshman year in high school. I was attending the Indianhead Center Jazz Camp in Shell Lake, Wisconsin and the first saxophone class was about to begin. Dr. Rousseau breezed into the room, asking if we wanted to see his fingering for altissimo D, which he then demonstrated in a brief burst of pure tone. I've been under his spell since that day, but not for the perfection of his high note; it was for his spontaneous charm, humor, and intelligence. Even as kids, we knew we were in the presence of someone special.

In a sense, I met Dr. Rousseau the year before I attended camp. My high school band director had been trying to find a saxophone teacher for me. When this search failed he said to me, "Here is your new teacher" as he handed me a stack of recordings. Included were three of Dr. Rousseau's LPs: *The Virtuoso Saxophone*, volumes 1 and 2, and *Saxophone Concertos*. I had never heard "classical" saxophone before and it was a revelation. Who knew the saxophone could be so beautiful? Whenever I listen to Rousseau's recording of the Dubois *Concerto* I am taken back to the first time I heard it.

Well into his 70s, Dr. Rousseau remains a force of nature. He continues to travel, teach, perform, and record. James Brown might call him the hardest working saxophonist in the business. Dr. Rousseau is such an influential current musician that one is apt to forget how large a role he has played in the saxophone's history. He gave the first classical saxophone recital at New York's Carnegie Hall, as well as the first full saxophone recitals in London and Paris. He has made more recordings than any other classical saxophonist, including the first LP entirely of saxophone concertos (Deutsche Grammophon) and the first saxophone recording released on compact disc (*Saxophone Colors*). He was a founding member of both the World Saxophone Congress (1969) and the North American Saxophone Alliance and his *Rousseau Saxophone Workshop* has been held each summer in Shell Lake, Wisconsin for more than three decades. He continues to design popular mouthpieces and reeds, and he was a driving force in the development of Yamaha's current line of saxophones. Need one mention the dozens of works he has inspired? The story of Eugene Rousseau is the story of the modern saxophone.

Yet as anyone who knows Dr. Rousseau will tell you, it's not his accomplishments that are important, it is the man himself. I had the good fortune to study with Dr. Rousseau for seven years while earning two degrees. As I was re-reading my lesson notes I realized that, in all those lessons, Dr. Rousseau never gave me an assignment. Not once. Without ever telling me what to do, Dr. Rousseau managed to communicate how to do something. I learned something new every time I met with him. I had a good time studying with him, and I often laughed.

But what makes Dr. Rousseau a great teacher? He is passionate about the saxophone and he instills that passion in his students. He believes the saxophone the equal of the great classical instruments of the world. He is always striving to better himself. How often have his students heard him use the words of his own teacher, Marcel Mule: *"On n'arrive jamais?"* One never arrives. Finally, Dr. Rousseau loves people. He pays attention to them. He remembers them. If you have met him even briefly, you have felt this.

Years ago, after having finished my undergraduate degree at Indiana, I had the opportunity to study in Paris. While I was there Dr. Rousseau "dropped in" to give a recital. The house was packed that night with brash young saxophonists like me, all ready to remark on the smallest mistake. During his performance Dr. Rousseau suddenly stopped playing. With an apologetic look, he turned to us and charmingly (and in perfect French) remarked that he had missed the repeat. Laughing with him and then applauding, we were his for the rest of the evening. I left his concert having learned something great about art and about life — again.

Dr. Steven Stusek
Professor of Saxophone
University of North Carolina-Greensboro

PREFACE

In the summer of 1968 I was on the staff of the Midwestern Music and Art Camp at the University of Kansas, which was my summer employment for several years. The Camp was then at its peak, serving more than 2000 students in several divisions; the music portion of the Camp was eight weeks of rehearsals with concerts by the bands, orchestras, and choruses every Sunday. The Camp was founded in 1935 by Russell Wiley,[1] Director of Bands at the University, and he oversaw every detail of the huge operation while relying on current and former band students and public school band and orchestra directors to make certain that housing, rehearsals, and activities ran smoothly. It was a tremendous opportunity to have many far-reaching musical experiences and I, as one of his current band students, was excited to be a part of it.

Mr. Wiley brought guest conductors to the Camp for each week's concerts, including Colonel Arnald Gabriel of the U.S. Air Force Band, retired Commander Charles Brendler of the U.S. Navy Band, Sir Vivian Dunn of Her Majesty's Royal Marine Band, Harry John Brown of the Milwaukee Symphony, and William Smith, Associate Conductor of the Philadelphia Orchestra. On the other hand, it was unusual to have a guest soloist and therefore I was intrigued when Mr. Wiley told me that saxophonists Sigurd Rascher and Eugene Rousseau both would be there that July.

I had met Rascher the previous summer for a three-hour lesson and the opportunity to spend other time with the internationally famous artist. He and his daughter Carina arrived first at the Camp and we renewed our acquaintance. Although he did not perform with any of the bands or orchestras, Rascher did present a recital. Typical of his programs, the first half consisted of transcriptions of baroque literature and the second half was all music which had been written for him.

Beyond the fact that he was on the faculty of Indiana University, Eugene Rousseau was almost unknown to me. I was told that he had taught somewhere in Missouri for a while and hadn't been at Indiana for very long. I did have an idea, however, of the kind of person to expect. I had mentioned to Jack Wells, an executive at the largest chain of music stores in Kansas City, that I would meet Rousseau. He responded, "At the end of the world when they make a list of the truly nice people who have ever lived, the list won't be very long but Eugene Rousseau's name will be on it." More than forty years later, I have no doubt that prediction is correct.

---

[1] Russell Wiley (1904–1991) was Director of Bands from 1936 to 1968 and of the Camp until 1974. In addition, he conducted the University Orchestra from 1943 to 1957. A person of great personal integrity whose career impacted thousands of students, he is considered by many to have built the University of Kansas Department of Music and Dance.

Rousseau arrived a week after Rascher's departure. He greeted me cordially and he was pleased that we shared an interest in the saxophone. Having played only tenor saxophone to that time, I had recently purchased an alto and he helped me to begin on that instrument. There were no secrets; he was more than willing to share with me his experience and insights about the saxophone and its literature. He was thorough in his knowledge and patient in his explanations. Rousseau presented a recital (Granados, Tcherepnine, Bentzon, Handel, Chopin, and Bonneau) and performed Maurice Whitney's *Introduction and Samba* with the symphonic band, conducted by Mr. Wiley. It was a different approach to the instrument than Rascher's and I now had two models to emulate.

I next saw Rousseau at the First World Saxophone Congress, held in Chicago in December of 1969. I had written to Rousseau that fall, asking him to verify that what I had read about the Congress was correct. His enthusiastic response to my letter insured that I would be there. Arriving the day before the Congress, he warmly welcomed me and introduced me to many of the participants. I was thrilled when he asked me to turn the pianist's pages for Cecil Leeson, Jean-Marie Londeix, and Daniel Deffayet. Later, we talked briefly about the possibility of graduate work at Indiana University.

After another visit by Rousseau to the Midwestern Music and Art Camp in 1970, our paths did not cross for several years until 1977 at a regional meeting of the North American Saxophone Alliance. The conference took place at Central Missouri State University, that "somewhere in Missouri" where he had taught before going to Indiana. Rousseau presented a recital and a pair of clinics. Over the course of the next several months, we talked again about the possibility of graduate study, now complicated by home ownership and my full-time position as a junior high school band director. Rousseau mentioned his Saxophone Workshop, held each August at Shell Lake in Wisconsin. It seemed like a good idea to observe him, work with him, and investigate his teaching methods in detail before selling my house and resigning my position. I knew that such a decision would be life-changing but I had no idea how much or in what ways.

The five days at Shell Lake in July of 1978 were completely convincing. Rousseau had ideas that made sense and solutions that worked, all of them delivered with kindness and good humor. Several of his students visited the Workshop and he introduced me to Dennis Bamber, Kenneth Fischer, and Fumiyoshi Maezawa; I began to feel as though I was already a part of his family of students. When I later was invited to be one of his Associate Instructors at Indiana there was no question that I would accept the offer.

Since then my relationship with Gene Rousseau has progressed from one of student and teacher to that of close friends. It is a privilege to write this book about a true gentleman who is one of the most important figures in the history of the saxophone. The book is comprised in large part from primary sources, including notes from lessons, clinics, workshops, and master classes dating back to

1977, interviews conducted in February and March of 2007, and numerous materials generously loaned by ER. All quotations are from Eugene Rousseau unless otherwise noted.

The title comes from a review by the *Weiner Zeitung* perfectly describing one of Rousseau's many performances. The first part of the book is chronological and presents details of Rousseau's life. It is intended to give the reader some sense of the man — his background, his career, and his accomplishments. The second part is concerned with his teaching — his thoughts on such topics as tone production, technique, articulation, and vibrato — and will attempt to give firsthand insights into what it is like to be his student, as expressed by several persons who have studied with Rousseau over the past forty years. I am indebted to his many friends and former students who generously shared their memories with me; I hope they enjoyed recalling an important time in their lives.

Thomas Liley
Director of Scholarly Publications
North American Saxophone Alliance

EUGENE ROUSSEAU:
WITH CASUAL BRILLIANCE

1 Blue Island (1932–1950):
It rang in my ears and left an aural impression I shall never forget

Eugene Ellsworth Rousseau was born on August 23, 1932 in Blue Island, Illinois. Blue Island, as it is now, was a working class community, composed primarily of immigrants who came to the United States for many reasons. Rousseau's forebears had come from France, through Canada to enter the United States through northeastern Wisconsin. His parents eventually settled in the economically promising metropolis of Chicago and its surrounding towns.

Blue Island is located in Cook County, about fifteen miles south of the Loop, the heart of Chicago's downtown. It is even closer to Comiskey Park, which helps to explain Rousseau's lifelong interest in the White Sox and sports in general. The city is so named because it is situated south of a ridge of land that once was an island when the glacial Lake Chicago covered the area thousands of years ago. To nineteenth-century settlers it looked in the distance like an island set against a vast prairie sea; the blue color was the result of atmospheric scattering or, perhaps, blue flowers covering the ridge. The town was established in 1835 as a way station on the historic Vincennes Trail and later became known for breweries built by German immigrants. The early twentieth century brought heavy industry to Blue Island — food processing, oil refining, brick making, and railroads. About four square miles in size, its current population of around 24,000 is not much larger than when Rousseau was born. The city had about 17,000 residents in 1932 and was at the end of a period of tremendous growth which saw a five-fold increase from 1890. The Blue Island in which Rousseau grew up had fifteen churches, six grade schools, four parochial schools, and, according to the City Directory, "one new modern high school."

George Philias Rousseau (Rousseau's grandfather) was born in Lowell, Massachusetts May 22, 1864, after his father Jean emigrated from France through the port of Boston. The family moved to St. Ubald, Quebec and George left home to follow the "timber drives" westward. He ended his travels in Michigan as a carpenter and, later, a carpenter foreman at the mine in Indian River in the Upper

Peninsula. George married Cora Robinson in 1892. Their marriage lasted until her death in 1925; George lived until 1941.

I've been told by distant relatives in Connecticut that my greatgrandfather [Jean] was from Angers.[1] Along with his sons [including George], he came to Quebec province in Canada and then down to northern Michigan. My father was born in Spalding, Michigan, which is a small town in the upper peninsula of Michigan very near the Wisconsin border. He worked on his father's farm until he was about twelve years old. He went through about six years of grade school; that was his education. As a young man, he looked for bigger and better things down in the Chicago area. He got work there and met Laura Schindler. They were married and had three children. They stayed in Blue Island, Illinois, all their lives, although we made frequent trips (at least once a year) back up to northern Michigan and northern Wisconsin. My father had a fairly large family; I think some of the children died when they were quite young due to various illnesses, but I remember Edwin, Alvin (two of my uncles) and Isabelle and Ann, my aunts. They were always very kind and I was always happy to visit them. Some were in Iron River, Michigan, and others were in Wabeno, Wisconsin, and Laona, Wisconsin, not far from the state line of Michigan.

Rousseau's father, Joseph Eugene, was a part of the city's heavy industry, working as a steam shovel operator for the Illinois Brick Company. Born in Spalding, Michigan on November 10, 1895, he married Laura Schindler on December 6, 1917 in Detroit. Her mother, Katherine Schindler, was born in Germany and came to the United States. Laura Schindler was born on November 24, 1894; she died on February 21, 1970. Rousseau's father died five years later on September 2, 1975. Rousseau is the youngest of three children; his brother Earl was born in 1920 and his sister Lucille in 1918.[2] The house where he grew up in Blue Island still stands at 2229 West Market Street in a well-kept neighborhood just south of the Cal-Sag Channel. The Cal-Sag Channel (short for "Calumet-Saganashkee Channel") was completed in the 1920s as a navigation canal that serves as a channel between the Little Calumet River and the Chicago Sanitary and Ship Canal and was completed in the 1920s.

---

[1] Angers is in western France's Pays de la Loire region, about 200 miles southwest of Paris. It has a population of about 270,000 in the metropolitan area. Angers is an ancient city, existing before the Roman Empire, and has churches and abbeys dating back to the eleventh century. Once the capital of the historic province of Anjou, it is interesting to note that Angers is the birthplace of composer Henri Dutilleux in 1916. It is also the birthplace of Henri Rousseau ("*Le Douanier*"), well known for his primitive paintings.

[2] Rousseau family birth and death dates can be found in Appendix F..

I don't know of any musical background in my family. My mother and father both carried tunes well. I remember them singing in church. They both liked music, liked dancing, liked dance music. My father bought some recordings of polkas and waltzes, but I never heard a Beethoven symphony or any classical music as I was growing up.

When Rousseau was five years old, in the summer of 1938, he heard something that would change his life. He heard a neighbor, Lyle Jenner, practicing the saxophone.

The principal reason I began the saxophone was hearing a young neighbor play the instrument and I thought this was such a beautiful sound — the alto saxophone. Lyle Jenner practiced regularly on his back porch. None of us had air conditioning then and so people would open their windows in warm weather; in the case of this young man, he played on the back porch. The sound of that saxophone did something to me. It rang in my ears and left an aural impression I shall never forget. It was the most profound early influence of my life.

Rousseau began his musical studies in the fourth grade at the age of nine. Miss Elda Jansen taught an elementary school band that met before school; she was his first music teacher and started him on the saxophone. He continued to play in Miss Jansen's band through the sixth grade.

When I began to play the saxophone there were no rental programs such as we have today; if you wanted to play an instrument, you had to buy it. My parents bought a saxophone and it was shipped to our home. When it arrived, we opened it up and it was silver. I didn't want a silver instrument. The neighbor boy, Lyle Jenner, had a gold-colored instrument; I cried. My parents exchanged it for a gold-lacquered instrument, a Rudy Wiedoeft model made by the Holton Company. I had no idea in those days who Wiedoeft was but I learned about him later and played his solos. I still have that instrument.[3]

Rousseau also discovered that he had a fine soprano voice and good aural skills. He enjoyed singing and performed as a soprano soloist frequently until his voice changed during the seventh grade.

Band continued through junior high school and Rousseau walked more than a mile to attend twice weekly rehearsals at a different school. Band became an important part of his life.

---

[3] Rousseau also still has the receipt for his first saxophone, purchased in September of 1941 from the Carl Fischer Company in Chicago for $71.50.

> I always looked forward to band; it was quite an experience for me. We had a challenge system — I liked that and I quickly moved up to first chair.

Rousseau began private study upon entering high school.

> I had a very fine teacher in high school — Horace Frederick. He didn't play saxophone or clarinet but he was an excellent trombonist and a fine musician. He knew what the professionals were doing and, if he didn't have the answer to something, he'd find out from one of his musician friends. He led me to some wonderful music, such as the Ibert *Concertino da Camera*, which I played at state contest when I was a junior in high school, and the Vellones *Rapsodie*.

Frederick advised him to begin studying clarinet during his sophomore year in high school.

> Mr. Frederick suggested I learn the clarinet, that it would help my progress on the saxophone. That was the conventional wisdom in those days. Even today, some people still buy into that theory; they don't understand the tremendous differences between the clarinet and the saxophone. I told my parents Mr. Frederick's suggestion and they bought a clarinet for me. I had a few lessons with Mr. Frederick and before too long I was first chair clarinet in the band.

Rousseau was exposed to other important influences during his high school years. He heard saxophone soloist Kenneth Douse[4] with the United States Marine Band, he heard vibrato for the first time from Guy Lombardo's band and he learned to play *All of Me* from Jimmy Dorsey's[5] recording. He later met Dorsey, who posed for a photograph and signed it.

> I heard the Dorsey band when I was in high school. It was in Chicago at the Edgewater Beach Hotel; he sat at the table with us and we chatted. It was a real thrill.

---

[4] Douse, born in England in 1906, studied as a violinist. He began to play the saxophone at the age of seventeen and was largely self-taught. Douse joined the Marine Band in 1926 and was solo saxophonist until 1950, playing solos on hundreds of concerts and radio broadcasts. From 1951 to 1958, he played saxophone and violin in the National Symphony. Douse is perhaps best remembered for his remarkable ability to double- and triple-tongue. He died in 1983.

[5] Born in Pennsylvania in 1904, he and his trombonist brother Tommy formed several bands and became one of the first jazz groups to be broadcast on the radio. Dorsey, who played with such names as Jean Goldkette, Paul Whiteman, and Red Nichols, died in 1957.

Playing in the dance band was another important activity for Rousseau.

It was called a dance band, not a jazz band or a big band. In reality, it actually was a big band with four or five saxophones, a brass section, and a rhythm section. I enjoyed it very much and wanted to go on and play in big bands, to make it a profession.

High school bands of that period frequently performed transcriptions of orchestral literature. Exposure to this music was important to the development of Rousseau's musicianship.

I feel very strongly that transcriptions have great value. Although some people, who are often uninformed, disparage transcriptions, music history is filled with transcriptions by the most famous composers and performers. Playing transcriptions of music by Beethoven, Mozart, Wagner, and Tchaikovsky was my introduction to these great masters. This was not music that I heard at home. My parents weren't opposed to classical music, it was just that they didn't have this kind of background as they were growing up. If it had not been for band, I wouldn't have had this introduction and so it was important for me to be in the high school band.

Despite the proximity of Chicago and its numerous musical performances, Rousseau did not regularly attend concerts until his senior year in high school. Occasionally, a school trip would take him to Chicago for an event.

The first classical saxophonist I ever heard live was Sigurd Rascher.[6] It was at the Midwest Clinic and I was perhaps fourteen years old.

I was a junior or senior in high school, 1949 perhaps, when I went to an all-Gershwin concert at Orchestra Hall, with the Paul Whiteman Orchestra; it was a memorable experience. Al Gallodoro[7] was in that orchestra and he played the opening clarinet solo in *Rhapsody in Blue* and I thoroughly enjoyed it.

---

[6] Born in 1907 in Germany, Rascher was one of the saxophone's pre-eminent soloists. Works were written for him by Ibert, Glazounov, Cowell, Dahl, Martin, Husa, Hindemith, and many others. He performed with numerous orchestras around the world and championed the altissimo register of the instrument. Rascher died in 2001.

[7] Born in Birmingham, Alabama in 1912, Gallodoro was first saxophonist in New Orleans' largest theater at the age of fifteen, playing for such acts as Bob Hope, Edgar Bergen, Joan Davis, and the Ritz Brothers. Going to New York in 1933, he became saxophone soloist with Isham Jones. Gallodoro joined the Paul Whiteman Orchestra in 1936. He became a member of the NBC Symphony in 1942, playing under Arturo Toscanini and Leopold Stokowski. From 1947 to 1967, he was a member of the staff orchestra of WJZ (later WABC) radio. Gallodoro remained an active free-lance musician until his death in 2008.

It was also during high school that Rousseau gained valuable experience performing with two friends, drummer Arthur "Benny" Burmeister and accordionist Paul Jankowski. They formed the "Gene Rousseau Trio" and played on weekends for wedding receptions and in clubs. Before it became a trio, Rousseau quickly learned that all of their music was in concert pitch.

> Paul invited me to join him and Benny to play at a local club one evening. I brought my alto saxophone and started to play. I immediately realized that everything was in C and, of course, the alto saxophone is in the key of E-flat. I had to learn to transpose on the spot.

Rousseau experienced several successes in his high school years, including being named the Illinois State High School Champion Saxophonist in a state-wide competition. He was sponsored by the Blue Island post of the Veterans of Foreign Wars in another state-wide contest. At the age of seventeen, Rousseau was selected by voters to go with his mother to New York City in the summer of 1949. While there, he auditioned for nationally broadcast radio and television programs hosted by Arthur Godfrey and Ted Mack, winning two performances on Ted Mack's *The Original Amateur Hour*.[8] Rousseau appeared first on a radio broadcast on September 8, 1949, and on a television broadcast of September 11.

Another life-changing experience, comparable to hearing the saxophone for the first time at the age of five, occurred during Rousseau's junior year in high school. He was learning Ibert's *Concertino da Camera* and purchased a 78 rpm recording of the work performed by Marcel Mule.[9]

> I was a junior in high school, perhaps 1948 or 1949. When I heard the recording of Marcel Mule performing the *Concertino da Camera*, it did something to me. It became my dream that perhaps someday I would have the privilege of meeting this man and perhaps even studying with him.

> Originally, I wanted to follow in my father's footsteps; he operated a steam shovel. Today we would call it a crane, but in those days the operator had to shovel coal to keep the boiler going. I told him that I

---

[8] *The Original Amateur Hour* was broadcast from 1934 to 1970, moving from radio to the infant medium of television in 1948. The program was aired on both radio and television until 1952. Among those who began their careers on the show are singers Maria Callas, Robert Merrill, and Beverly Sills and entertainers Frank Sinatra and Pat Boone. Interestingly, Ted Mack was an accomplished saxophonist and clarinetist who played with the big bands of Glenn Miller, Benny Goodman, Red Nichols, Jack Teagarden, and Ben Pollack.

[9] Mule's recording, with Philippe Gaubert conducting the Orchestre Société des Concerts du Conservatoire, was the first made of Ibert's famous composition and dates from 1937. It has been re-released on compact disc as part of 'Marcel Mule — 'Le patron' of the Saxophone", Clarinet Classics CC0013.

wanted to do that and I could learn from him. He said, 'No, I want you to go to school. I don't care what you study, I just want you to get an education. That's all that matters.'

When I was a senior in high school, I was asked to give some lessons to clarinet and saxophone students at a local music store, which I did. That was exciting for me and I enjoyed it. They also gave accordion lessons there and one of the teachers, also a high school senior, was Paul Jankowski, who was in the trio with me. Paul was quite accomplished and he, from his high school music teacher, knew about the Chicago Musical College, so he thought that was where he wanted to go to college. I didn't know anything about that so I went to my high school counselor. I told him that I was interested in going to the Chicago Musical College. He didn't know anything about it but he had a book, in which he looked it up and he said to me, 'They are fully accredited. That is very important. If you go there you wouldn't have to worry if you wanted to do a master's degree somewhere else later.'

2 Chicago Musical College (1950–1953):
I was beginning to understand more about the world

The Chicago Musical College has been an important part of the city's cultural atmosphere since its founding in 1867 as the Chicago Academy of Music; it took its present name in 1872. The fourth conservatory in the United States when it was established by Florenz Ziegfeld, Sr. (father of the famous Broadway impresario), it became a charter member of the National Association of Schools of Music in 1924. Another indication of its status was its admission in 1936 to the North Central Association of Colleges and Secondary Schools, the only independent music college in the Midwest to receive full membership. It has been a part of Roosevelt University since 1954, when it moved to the national landmark Auditorium Building at 430 South Michigan Avenue.

When Rousseau began his undergraduate studies there in 1950, the College was housed in an eleven-story building at 64 East Van Buren Street. He enrolled in the Bachelor of Music Education program with a major in clarinet. His goal was to become a band director and, if possible, play professionally in a big band.

> I wanted to be a high school band director when I was in high school. I was not in a good situation but I guess I felt as though I could do better and that's why I pursued that. It seemed to be the way to go for me and I was quite enthused about it. I lived at home and took the Illinois Central train back and forth with Paul Jankowski because he and I had pretty much the same schedule. We continued to play in the same little group on weekends. He's a dear friend, and still living.

This second ambition, to play in a big band, did in fact come to fruition during Rousseau's third year of study. Woody Herman's "Third Herd"[10] came to Chicago while touring with singers Ella Fitzgerald and Frankie Laine and suddenly needed two saxophonists. Rousseau dropped out of school for about ten days in April of 1953 to join the band, traveling to Milwaukee, Minneapolis, Fort Wayne, Indianapolis, and other places. Rousseau realized that, as much as he enjoyed the music, the lifestyle was not one to which he could adapt and he returned to complete his undergraduate studies.

> I wasn't with the Woody Herman band for any real length of time. I think I could have stayed, but it was a sort of a cure, an eye-opener,

---

[10] Woodrow Charles Thomas Hermann was born in 1913 in Milwaukee. He left high school before graduation in order to become a professional musician. In 1939, Woody Herman and his Band That Plays the Blues recorded "Woodchopper's Ball"; it sold five million copies. Members of the Third Herd included Bill Trujillo on tenor saxophone, trombonists Urbie Green and Carl Fontana, pianist Nat Pierce, Red Mitchell on bass, and Art Mardigan on drums.

you could say. The lifestyle wasn't for me. The people in the group were all very nice but the idea of going to bed at 4 in the morning, getting up at 1 o'clock and having a steak dinner or something just didn't suit me. I was just really filling in. Abe Turchen was Woody's manager and I think that if I had stayed in contact with him I could have gone on playing with the band. As it turned out later, it was probably better that I didn't. Abe Turchen was not responsible in caring for the tax commitments, so Woody Herman became deeply in debt, mostly due to mismanagement by Turchen. Herman turned everything over to Turchen and Turchen would always tell him 'everything is taken care of.'[11]

In any event, I think they first called Stan Davis, a prominent Chicago musician, to fill in because they needed two players immediately in Milwaukee and Stan called me. The two we were replacing came back (I don't remember their names — I think one was Sam Staff, the baritone player); there had been some charges filed against them and they had to appear in court. I like jazz and I know some marvelous musicians in jazz but I'm not made to turn days and nights around. This brief experience with the Herman Band had a profound effect on me and was probably the main reason I focused on classical saxophone.

Rousseau entered the Bachelor of Music Education program as a clarinet major.

There was no chance to study saxophone at the Chicago Musical College or at virtually any U.S. university. That was out of the question. My teachers didn't encourage me to pursue the saxophone as a serious instrument. I studied clarinet with Sam Meron, who was a very nice gentleman and very kind. I was with him, I think, for only one year; he introduced me to music like the Brahms E-flat Sonata, for example, and the Weber *Concerto*. I remember playing the Brahms E-flat, never having heard it, never looked at the piano part, and one day I played it with piano and it was a shock because I had no idea what Brahms sounded like. The senior clarinet professor at the CMC was Albert Freedman. Albert Freedman was a teacher in the public schools but taught part-time at the Chicago Musical College. I took lessons from him for perhaps two years and was not required to play a recital.

---

[11] Herman learned in 1947 that he owed $30,000 in back taxes and he entrusted his manager, Abe Turchen, to handle the problem. It has been suggested that, due to Turchen's negligence, by 1985 Herman owed the government $1.5 million. Herman died in 1987.

Being in college was a new experience for Rousseau and for his family. His father had a sixth grade education and his mother had gone to school for eight years. Nonetheless, they were very supportive. Rousseau paid for most of his way through school by working weekends.

> I was really green. By today's standards, if you take a reasonably aware freshman entering college today and compare that with what I knew when I entered, it's unbelievable. For example, when I entered the Chicago Musical College I didn't have a scholarship. Then, as I started to learn a little bit more about how academia worked, I found out that there IS such a thing as a scholarship. In a certain category there was a $250 scholarship, so I applied for it and I got it. I don't know if that was my second year there or my last year but that scholarship covered a lot of expenses. I used to keep the college catalogues, because all the prices were in them and I could not believe how much it cost for a piano lesson with Rudolph Ganz — $35 for an hour lesson in 1950.[12]

Rousseau knew none of the teachers when he entered the Chicago Musical College but he soon met Rudolph Ganz.[13]

> He was a wonderful gentleman. I had him for a class in conducting and still have those notes. One of the things he talked about, I remember, was guest conductors. He said, 'I don't think you understand' and went to the board: "<u>Guess</u>' conductors — we have many of them.' Ganz had a great wit.

> There wasn't a band at the CMC but I played clarinet in the orchestra. There also was a Collegium Musicum and I remember Dr. Siegmund Levarie conducted that. He said to me one day, 'We're short an oboe player' — I wasn't playing oboe yet — 'Would you come in to a rehearsal and transpose it on the clarinet?' I could do this because I had done it in combos and dance bands. It was an interesting experience because the horn player volunteered to do the realization of the figured bass at the keyboard. A couple of us asked him, 'Won't this be a problem?' and I glanced over at his score. On his music, he had

---

[12] In 2010 dollars, this would be the equivalent of more than $300.

[13] Ganz was born in Zurich in 1877. In 1899, he was soloist with the Berlin Philharmonic and in 1900 the Berlin Philharmonic performed his first symphony. Ganz joined the College's faculty in 1900 and, except for a period when he conducted the St. Louis Symphony from 1921 to 1927, remained associated with the school until his death in 1972. His name remains one of the most important in the history of music in Chicago.

studied it and put G minor, C7, all the jazz symbols in his music because he played jazz piano.

Despite missing classes for his short-lived tour with the Herman band, Rousseau graduated in 1953 after only three years of study.

I think I was beginning to understand more about the world and at the same time about myself. I tell my students that one of the great things about getting a college education is that you learn. You learn mostly about yourself: where you are; who you are; how you fit in; what your capabilities are; how you stack up against someone else. As I was finishing my undergraduate work, I realized I had to go on. I had to learn more, do more, and explore more. My parents said, 'We think you should get a master's degree.' So I applied at Northwestern University.

3 Northwestern University (1953–1954): What an experience!

Rousseau had decided as an undergraduate at the Chicago Musical College that graduate study would be necessary in order for him to fulfill his goals. He entered Northwestern University in the fall of 1953 just as their School of Music was entering a new and important phase.

> Northwestern University had and still has an outstanding school of music and it was near my home in Chicago. I started by taking the train up to Northwestern from my home in Blue Island and it was a bit much. It was maybe an hour and 45 minutes one way. I couldn't do it and so I went into the graduate housing at Northwestern.

Because the Chicago Musical College did not have either a concert band or a marching band, Rousseau was eager to make up for this lack of experience. Rousseau auditioned for John Paynter[14] and, in addition to playing in the marching band, was made principal alto saxophone in the concert band. Paynter was not one to belittle any instrument and Rousseau felt that Paynter supported his belief in the saxophone's expressive possibilities.

> For me, as a saxophonist, it was a fantastic experience to be at Northwestern during the first year of John Paynter's tenure, the first year that he was Director of Bands. We played the Hindemith Symphony; the piece was a year and a half, perhaps two years old. What an experience! He helped very much my career with recommendations he gave later; he was very supportive of me. He even encouraged me to apply for the saxophone position at Northwestern because he thought NU should have saxophone in its offerings. He told me to write to the Dean about that, which I did, although I don't exactly remember when. Of course, at that time he didn't even know Fred Hemke,[15] who came to Northwestern in 1963.

---

[14] Paynter, born in 1928, received a Bachelor of Music degree in 1950 and a Master's in Theory and Composition in 1951 from Northwestern. While still a Master's student, he served as Acting Director of Bands during the absence of Glenn Cliffe Bainum and upon graduation was appointed to the full-time faculty as Director of the Marching Band, Assistant Director of Bands, and Instructor of Theory. Two years late, in 1953 when Bainum retired, Paynter became the second Director of Bands in the history of Northwestern University. He was twenty-five years old and he remained Director until his death in 1996.

[15] Born in 1935 in Milwaukee, Wisconsin, Hemke has appeared as a recitalist and soloist with symphony orchestras and wind ensembles in the United States and around the world. He has presented master classes and lectures throughout the United States, Canada, Europe, the Scandinavian countries, and the Far East. In 1956, Hemke became the first American to receive the Premier Prix du Saxophone from the Conservatoire National de Musique, Paris. He is the Louis and Elsie Snydacker Eckstein Professor of Saxophone in the School of Music of Northwestern University.

Rousseau declared neither saxophone nor clarinet as his major instrument when he enrolled at Northwestern. Instead, he felt that it would be to his advantage to learn the oboe and he was accepted without an audition. He was assigned to the studio of Robert Mayer, English horn player in the Chicago Symphony Orchestra.[16] By his own admission, Rousseau at first could barely produce a sound on the oboe but, under Mayer's expert guidance, learned to play the instrument well by the end of the year.

> My emphasis was music education but we had to declare an instrument. I chose oboe because I wanted to learn oboe. This was in line with my goal of becoming a band director. The only oboe instruction I had had was in woodwind techniques, which was virtually nothing. I was to meet the oboe teacher, Mr. Robert Mayer, at his studio at a certain hour. I had not met Mayer before although, interestingly, he was at the commencement at the Chicago Musical College. We were a small class, the graduating class of 1953, and there was a program at Orchestra Hall. Our orchestra played with the addition of a few symphony players; Robert Mayer was one of them. I remember seeing this distinguished gentleman playing oboe. Incidentally, in that graduating class was an honorary doctorate to Alexandre Tcherepnine. I remember that and I have a photo.
>
> When I appeared at the door of Mayer's studio: 'Oh, Mr. Rousseau — where is your oboe?' I said, 'Well, I'd like to speak with you.' 'Please come in.' 'Well, Mr. Mayer, I don't own one. I really don't play oboe but I'd like to learn.' 'Well, let's learn!' Wonderful! Great teacher! I said, 'What about an instrument?' 'I have one I'll let you use.' He went to his closet. Unbelievable! I eventually bought it. I said, 'What about reeds?' 'Oh, that's very simple. I'll give you two reeds; after that you're on your own.'
>
> He was a terrific teacher who could explain everything. I enjoyed very much his lessons and I learned to play oboe pretty well by the end of the year. As a sidelight here, Mayer was a descendant of the French school, which used the so-called short-scrape reed. I think just about everybody today uses a long-scrape reed although I haven't

---

[16] Mayer, born in 1910, was a member of the Sousa Band's final tour before becoming a member of the Chicago Symphony Orchestra in 1930. At twenty years of age, he was the youngest member to have played with the orchestra at that time, remaining there for twenty-five years. In 1939, he helped to found the Chicago Symphony Woodwind Quintet, perhaps the first such ensemble in any major symphony orchestra. The Quintet traveled five weeks a year for more than twenty years, presenting concerts, recitals, and clinics. Mayer was Professor of Oboe and Head of the Woodwind, Brass, and Percussion Department at Northwestern University for fifteen years. He died in 1994.

been current with that for many years. It was very unusual to have those short-scrape reeds but that's the way he did it.

It was during his master's study at Northwestern that Rousseau began his relationship with the Leblanc musical instrument company.

As part of the requirements for the master's degree at Northwestern, one had either to play a recital or do a thesis. As I chose to make oboe my principal instrument, I didn't feel I would be ready to give a full-fledged recital after barely a year of study, so I chose the thesis route. My topic was arrived at after several consultations with Traugott Rohner, who at that time was not only the editor and publisher of *The Instrumentalist* but was a faculty member at Northwestern.[17] I was taking a class from him and he was very creative in his thinking — he wanted to try different things, he wanted to experiment. In consulting with him, we talked about the different materials from which clarinets were made and that became my topic.

I received cooperation from all the major music manufacturers at that time; there was no Yamaha presence in the United States, but Conn, Selmer, and Leblanc were all happy to cooperate with me. They loaned instruments to me of different materials — a laminated wood from Conn, there was plastic, there was hard rubber, wood, metal, and so on — and I did a series of tests. To get the clarinet from Leblanc, I made a trip to Kenosha, Wisconsin, which wasn't very far from Evanston, and there met their young educational director, Don Mc-Cathren. I also met Vito Pascucci. They were very kind and I was fascinated with their new company (they had been established only a few years and this was 1953), and fascinated with the Leblanc saxophone. It was shortly after in 1954 that I went into the military but that connection with Leblanc and the correspondence, all of that remained. When I got out of the military and joined the faculty at Luther College, I purchased Leblanc B-flat and A clarinets and a Leblanc Model 100 alto saxophone, the 'rational' saxophone. That saxophone was and still is a very interesting instrument.

In addition to his work on oboe, Rousseau studied flute with Emil Eck and had a few lessons with bassoonist Wilbur Simpson and clarinetist Jerry Stowell; all

---

[17] Rohner, born in Switzerland in 1906, taught several music education courses at Northwestern from 1933 to 1960. He also taught instrumental music in the Evanston, Illinois, school system from 1931 to 1958. He published the first issue of *The Instrumentalist* in 1946. In addition, Rohner founded the National School Orchestra Association in 1958 and the National Band Association in 1960. Rohner died in 1991.

were members of the Chicago Symphony Orchestra. Cecil Leeson taught saxophone for Northwestern at the time but Rousseau did not study saxophone with him or with any other saxophonist.

I took flute lessons from Emil Eck; he was in the Chicago Symphony and, as I remember, was from Germany; a very nice gentleman. He had a way of expressing that I remember: 'It's too *shteep* [steep]', meaning the angle of the flute. I took bassoon lessons from Wilbur Simpson, who passed away several years ago; he was in the Chicago Symphony. Later I had a lesson from Leonard Sharrow on bassoon; that came before I went to Luther College. I played saxophone in the Wind Ensemble. I thought it would be better to be versatile and that's proved to be true.

While at the Chicago Musical College he had become acquainted with Rafael Kubelik, the Symphony's Music Director. Rousseau felt that it was important for him to gain a more rounded musical background and he attended concerts at Orchestra Hall regularly. His life began to take quite a different direction from what he had imagined a few years earlier as he completed his Master of Music degree in 1954.

4 Military Service (1954–1956):
He heard in the distance the sound of a band

Following his graduation from Northwestern University, Rousseau was drafted into the U.S. Army on November 1, 1954. After basic training in Ft. Chaffee, Arkansas, he was assigned to Ft. Riley, Kansas, to study military intelligence.

> It was a two-year hitch. It was mandatory and so I volunteered for the draft, which was an option at that time. I went in officially on November 1, 1954. I later found out it was possible, if one had a seasonal occupation, to be released up to ninety days early. Having been appointed to the Luther College faculty, I was released on August 15, 1956, which is exactly three years before Norma and I got married.

Incredibly, Rousseau had his musical instruments with him at all times. During basic training he hid his saxophone and clarinet in a crawl space above the ceiling and even took them out occasionally to play briefly.[18] Later, while at Ft. Riley, he played a few dance jobs.

> I'm a risk taker. I would do things that normal people would never do. But it's true that I hid them in the crawl space above. I don't think I'd do that today; I don't think I could and, even if it were possible, I probably wouldn't. But it paid off.

> I had intensive training in military intelligence. I didn't really want to play in a military band. I was looking for something that might be interesting to do. Everyone in the military has a little interview, trying to find what their MOS [Military Occupational Specialty] would be. It so happened that the young man who was interviewing me was a graduate of Northwestern University and so, when I met with him, he saw that I had a master's degree from Northwestern and that got his attention. He said, 'What would you like to do? Do you want to play in a band?' I said, 'Well, playing in a band was all right.' He said, 'You know, there could be some opportunities in military intelligence.' That sounded good to me. I got to the school at Fort Riley; it was a terrific school and I enjoyed it.

---

[18] The author finds this altogether remarkable. About seventeen years later, when I entered the U.S. Navy's Training Center at the Great Lakes Naval Station, everything we brought with us (including clothing, wallets, and any jewelry) was either shipped back to our homes or thrown away upon our arrival.

Upon completion of his training in gathering military intelligence, Rousseau was transferred to Hawaii's Schofield Barracks. Because there was no need for someone with his specific training he was reassigned to the 25th Infantry Division. Of course, he had brought his instruments.

> I was shipped to Hawaii, although I would have preferred Europe. When I got to Hawaii, no one needed a person with an MOS in military intelligence. It wasn't unusual in those days to be trained in one area and then assigned to something else. They asked, 'Why did they ship you here? We could use another infantryman, so report to such and such regiment.' That's when I heard the band.

His first night in Hawaii, he heard in the distance the sound of a band performing an outdoor concert. The sounds evoked a special yearning for Rousseau and he was drawn to the performance. After the concert he introduced himself to the band's leader, Chief Warrant Officer John Hooks, asking him if he needed any more musicians. Hooks acknowledged that he could use some clarinets and invited Rousseau to audition the next morning.

That morning the sergeant of Rousseau's unit told him that he would begin training for the infantry in the afternoon. But first Rousseau auditioned for Hooks and was accepted into the band. Hooks handled the administrative details to facilitate his transfer from the infantry and within a month Rousseau was the band's assistant director. Rousseau played oboe and clarinet as necessary, arranged for and played in the jazz band, and frequently conducted.

> My sergeant didn't know I had my clarinet and saxophone. I walked over to the band unit and Warrant Officer Hooks gave me a condensed score and asked me to play the clarinet line. I said, 'This is in concert pitch. Do you want me to play in concert or should I transpose it?' He told me to transpose it, which I did, and he said, 'We can use you in the band.' I asked him what I should do about the infantry and he said he would take care of everything, which he did. I became assistant band leader and that was a great experience for me. We'd go through these old military band journals. It was my first experience as a conductor.

As his discharge from the army approached, Rousseau sought out positions as a high school band director. This had long been his career goal and he received notices of vacancies from the Northwestern University Placement Service. He applied for several positions.

I applied for several public school positions — good positions, I thought, in good locations. I got the same basic answer from all of them: 'Your credentials look good, you seem to be a good candidate, but we can't consider anyone without a personal interview.' I didn't consider a position in Hawaii. I liked Hawaii but I did miss the seasons, even though I was in Hawaii for a relatively short time. It was beautiful but rather confining.

All of the public school vacancies required a face-to-face interview. The distance from Hawaii to the mainland for interviews, coupled with the expenses involved and his small amount of leave time, made these school positions impossible.

And then, I was approached by Luther College because they had gotten my credentials from Northwestern. I guess they had contacted Northwestern and they saw someone who had a background in woodwind instruments who also was Lutheran. That was very important for them and that was the way I was brought up, in the Lutheran church. After a few telephone calls, including one to a fellow in the 25th Division Band who was a graduate of Luther College to get a reference, they asked a minister in Honolulu to interview me. The interview was successful. That was it and they hired me sight unseen.

Rousseau was offered the position to begin in the fall of 1956. He would spend three years at Luther College and begin to gain the teaching skills for which he has become renowned.

5 Luther College (1956–1959): *I had good colleagues*

Founded in 1861 by Norwegian immigrants, Luther College serves only undergraduate students. For its first seventy-five years, the college admitted men only; it became coeducational in 1936. Located in the small northeastern Iowa town of Decorah, a community of about 8,000, the college is surrounded by wooded hills and limestone bluffs. Nearby are the Laura Ingalls Wilder Museum and the small Czech farming community of Spillville, where composer Antonin Dvořák spent the summer of 1893. The area has a large Czech-American population and it was during his three years at Luther that Rousseau met Norma Rigel, whose ancestors had immigrated to the United States from Czechoslovakia in the nineteenth century.

Luther College's music program already had an excellent reputation, in large part due to the efforts of long-time faculty member Weston Noble[19]. Rousseau was well aware of Luther's music program, thanks to a concert by the Luther College Band that he had heard in the Chicago area while he was a student at the Chicago Musical College. The band was conducted by Noble and the quality of the ensemble and its conductor made a strong impression on Rousseau, who sent a letter of congratulations to Luther College. This letter was later remembered when he was invited to join the faculty.

In 1956, his first year at Luther, Rousseau conducted the Varsity Band (second to Noble's Concert Band) and taught theory and all of the woodwinds. His beginning annual salary was $3600, a little less than $29,000 in 2010 dollars. By his third year, Rousseau was also conductor of the Luther College Community Orchestra.

Luther College's Dorian Festival, begun in 1949, remains an important part of the area's musical atmosphere. Presently, there are five Dorian Festivals (for band, chorus, keyboard, orchestra, and vocal) and two Dorian Music Camps in the summer (for junior high and senior high students). It was as part of the Dorian Festival of 1957 during his first year at Luther that Rousseau, at the invitation of Noble, for the first time presented a full recital program. He played the first half on clarinet and the second half on saxophone.

> I did a recital for the Dorian Festival; I played both clarinet and saxophone. I know that on one occasion I played the Ibert. I don't know if it was the Dorian Festival but I know that at Luther I also played the

---

[19] Noble, born in 1922 near Riceville, Iowa, joined the Luther College music faculty in 1948 to direct the Concert Band and the Nordic Choir. He became an internationally renowned conductor and music educator. Noble was named Outstanding Music Educator of the United States in 1989 and he is the first recipient of the Weston Noble Award for lifetime achievement, presented in 1994 by the American Choral Directors Association. Noble retired in 2005 after a 57-year career at Luther College.

Hindemith clarinet concerto with piano, which isn't played very often. I also played the Hindemith clarinet sonata. With the band, the big number was the *Introduction and Samba* by Whitney. I also did some arrangements for the band. They needed an arrangement of a piece by Barat for a wonderful euphonium soloist which later was, along with many other things, destroyed in a huge fire. I conducted the second band and my third and last year there I conducted the orchestra. In addition, I taught theory and woodwind techniques and all the woodwinds privately.

He quickly established himself as a performer. Rousseau was a soloist and clinician at the Iowa Bandmasters Association in 1958 and at the Minnesota Music Educators Association Convention the next year. He also met a voice student whose name was Norma Rigel.

Luther College had a rather small music department and I had good colleagues. One of the voice teachers told me that she had several students who were participating in *Messiah*, which was an annual presentation there. She said that one of those three or four students had just gotten from her parents a new LP recording of *Messiah*. She knew that I had purchased that first year, 1956, a hi-fi record player which I had in my studio and she asked if the students could come over, perhaps on a Saturday morning, so they could listen to this. I said I would be happy to do that and we set up a time. The young lady who had this set of LPs was named Norma Rigel. She arrived, a very polite young lady, with this wonderful set of recordings and none of her friends showed up. She and I listened to her recording but we also had a rather long conversation. Often, if I talk about meeting Norma, people will say, 'Oh, she was one of your students.' She never was a student of mine. She was an outstanding singer, but never had any classes with me. She completed a Bachelor of Arts at Luther College cum laude and a master's degree at the University of Iowa.

Norma grew up in a close-knit Czech community, the youngest of four children. Her parents were farmers and part of a farming community near Cedar Rapids, Iowa. It's difficult for us today to realize but as she grew up all of the day-to-day business of the farmers was carried on in Czech. Although she is fourth generation Czech, it is difficult for one to imagine how strongly the language was preserved. In fact, when Norma's two older sisters began school they could not speak English. Along with the language, the rich musical traditions — both instrumental and vocal — were observed and a huge part of community life. When I first went to visit Norma's family in the 1950s, there was and still is a street in Cedar Rapids — 16th Avenue — on which the now rather famous National Czech and Slovak Museum is located. President Clinton and President Havel from the Czech Republic both visited there. On that avenue one could see shop after shop with Czech names and it was fascinating to walk along this street back in the 1950s and at the crosswalk press a button to cross the street, the directions for which were only in Czech.

Rousseau became aware that the famous woodwind pedagogue Himie Voxman was only a little more than a hundred miles away in Iowa City at the University of Iowa. Rousseau was familiar with Voxman's name and teaching materials, having used them for years.

> I had known the name of Himie Voxman and had used his books in my teaching for a long time. I thought maybe I should consider pursuing a doctorate.

> I had met Alvin Mistak[20] at the Chicago Musical College. I remember him because he and I both liked chord changes very much. I remember him playing some on the piano. I remember one of the other students dismissing what he was playing as not very important; I thought it was very good and we hit it off. He grew up in Chicago and he and I shared a lot. Like my father, his was a blue collar man and so we knew what that was like. His parents were supportive of him; they wanted him to get an education. I went to Northwestern and I think that was why Paul Jankowski and Alvin Mistak went to Northwestern; we all had our degrees from the Chicago Musical College and our masters' from Northwestern.

> I was at Northwestern for the summer of 1957. I enrolled for some classes because I wanted to take twentieth-century British literature and a course in philosophy. I wanted to explore some of these other areas. Al Mistak and I spent some time together. I don't think that we roomed together that summer but I saw him and that's when I said to him, 'You know, I'm at Luther College, only 150 miles from Iowa

---

[20] Mistak was born in 1930 and received a Ph.D. in music from the University of Iowa in 1969. A fine string bassist, he was for twenty-eight years the highly respected orchestra director and head of music theory and composition studies at Evanston Township High School in Illinois. A talented composer as well — he wrote a saxophone quartet that Rousseau published — he was for more than thirty years a new music reviewer for the magazine *The Instrumentalist*. He died in 2007.

City and Voxman is there. I think we should go there and look it over.' So he came out to Decorah and then the next day we drove down to Iowa City. We met Prof. Voxman and we had a very positive meeting.

In 1959, after three years at Luther College, Rousseau received a leave of absence to begin work on the degree of Doctor of Philosophy in Music Literature and Performance. That same summer in which he left Luther College, Rousseau married Norma Rigel on August 15.[21]

---

[21] They would have two children: Lisa-Marie, born June 18, 1962 in Iowa City as Rousseau was nearing the completion of his doctoral degree and Joseph Eugene, named for his paternal grandfather, born September 24, 1965 in Bloomington, Indiana. There are four grandchildren: Lisa-Marie has twin daughters, Rachel Marie and Claire Elise, born in 1995 and Joseph has two sons, Henry William, born in 2000, and Alec Edward, born in 2003.

6   University of Iowa (1959–1962): Professor Voxman considered the saxophone an instrument worthy of serious musical consideration

Almost everyone who has studied a wind instrument knows the name Himie Voxman. His method books have provided a foundation of teaching materials for more than half a century. Perhaps less well known is his scholarly research. Following World War II, Voxman made several trips to Europe to seek unknown, early examples of clarinet music, finding other woodwind scores as well. It is probable that no one knows as much about woodwind literature as Himie Voxman.

Voxman, born in 1912 in Centerville, Iowa, has been described as "the most significant person in the University [of Iowa]."[22] He arrived in Iowa City in 1929 and received a Bachelor of Science degree with high distinction in Chemical Engineering in 1933, teaching clarinet students to pay for his college expenses. Voxman then entered the master's program in the psychology of music, studying under Carl Seashore, one of the pioneers in developing aptitude tests for music. He became a member of the Iowa University faculty in 1939 and, in 1954, was appointed Director of the School of Music, serving in that capacity until his retirement in 1980. Voxman continues to teach private clarinet students.

The Voxman Music Building was named in his honor in 1995 and he received the Lifetime Achievement Award from the International Clarinet Association in 2000. During his 26-year directorship, the School of Music gained a national reputation and his unwavering attention to the music library has made it an international resource for scholars around the world. His donations of printed music, microfilms, photocopies of manuscripts and early printed editions of woodwind music number in the thousands.[23]

No performance degree in saxophone, clarinet, or any other instrument was available at the University of Iowa when Rousseau was a student; the degree offered was the Doctor of Philosophy in Music Literature and Performance. It was not unusual that saxophone was not offered as a major area of performance. Larry Teal, only a few years earlier in 1953 at the University of Michigan, had become the first full-time saxophone professor in the United States. Rousseau's principal instrument for the degree was clarinet with an academic emphasis in music history and literature.

> I had not been at Luther College very long when the Iowa Band was on tour, a regional type tour. One of their stops was Decorah, Iowa,

---

[22] University of Iowa Director of Bands Myron Welch, *Daily Iowan*, September 27, 2002.

[23] For more information about this remarkable musician, see "Himie Voxman: The Man Behind the Methods" by Andrew Sprung in *The Clarinet*, December 2008.

where Luther College is located, and I was very impressed with the band. They played at the local high school and I met their conductor, Professor Frederick Ebbs. I mentioned that I knew of Professor Voxman, that I was new there — the new kid on the block, so to speak — and that I was interested in exploring the possibility of doing a degree at Iowa.

Shortly after that, I got a very nice letter from Voxman saying that Professor Ebbs had told him of my interest in their school. It's always nice to feel welcome and so that made me feel very good when he wrote to me. Alvin Mistak and I made our trip after that.

Rousseau found the environment quite different from that which he had experienced at Northwestern University. Voxman was much less formal and, over the years, the two became close friends.

Himie Voxman, through the years, has become a wonderful friend. He helped me in so many ways. He has always had a very quiet manner and a love for music combined with a very stable personality — predictable, even, cool, calm, and dedicated. And yet he has always had a tremendous intellectual curiosity and a capacity for scholarship. He was a man who understood how to write well, and who could take a book in German or French and figure out what the meaning was. What I learned from him was that there was always something to learn and that there still is.

The academic environment was very challenging and the performing ensembles were excellent. In addition to Voxman in clarinet and woodwind literature, Rousseau worked with Albert T. Luper[24] in music history. Frederick C. Ebbs[25] was the band director and James Dixon[26] was the director of orchestras.

---

[24] Luper, who lived from 1914 to 1992, wrote with Eugene Helm the highly regarded book *Words and Music* as well as several books on the music of South America.

[25] Ebbs, born in Ohio in 1916, directed the famous Hobart, Indiana, High School Band from 1940 to 1948. He was band director at his alma mater, Baldwin-Wallace College, from 1948 to 1954 and at the University of Iowa from 1954 until 1967, at which time he was named Director of Bands at Indiana University; he remained there until 1982. Ebbs received the Edwin Franko Goldman Award from the American School Band Directors Association in 1969. He died in 1984 and was posthumously inducted into the National Band Association's Hall of Fame of Distinguished Conductors in 1987.

[26] Dixon (1928–2007) was a graduate of the University of Iowa who conducted the U.S. 7th Army Symphony before returning to Iowa in 1954 to conduct the University Symphony Orchestra. He became conductor of the New England Conservatory Symphony Orchestra in 1959, returning once again to Iowa in 1962 as the orchestra's permanent conductor. He was associate conductor of the Minneapolis Symphony Orchestra and guest conductor with the National Orchestra of Greece, the North German Radio Orchestra, the West German Radio Orchestra, the Chicago Symphony Orchestra, and at Tanglewood. He was awarded the Gustav Mahler Medal in 1963. According to Baker's Biographical Dictionary, Dixon followed the interpretive style of Dmitri Mitropoulos, "combining precision of rhythmic flow with expressive shaping of melodic phrases."

One has to remember that my major instrument was clarinet because the saxophone wasn't even a matter to consider. I was not in the band; I played in the orchestra. There were a number of clarinetists, so it was sort of a rotating basis. I got to play in a number of orchestra concerts and that was a wonderful experience, to have the sounds around me of the strings and the orchestral literature, which I hadn't had before except on a very limited basis. Iowa had a good orchestra. The conductor, James Dixon, a protégé of Dmitri Mitropoulos, was outstanding.

There were also occasions when one could just go to orchestra rehearsals. I went to some of his orchestra rehearsals and faculty regularly attended them, just to hear the repertory, to absorb the music. I remember seeing Richard Hervig[27] there and, of course, Voxman and others. There was another side, too. I remember once Mr. Dixon was short of percussionists, so I played the tambourine in *Salome*. It gave still another perspective, being in and hearing the orchestra in a different way.

Although not able to study saxophone, Rousseau was permitted by Voxman to perform saxophone literature as part of his degree recitals. The clarinet literature performed by Rousseau is noteworthy — Debussy's *Rapsodie*, Brahms' two op. 120 clarinet sonatas, Hindemith's *Concerto*, and, with orchestra, Copland's *Concerto*[28]. As a graduate assistant, Rousseau taught all of the saxophone majors.

Professor Voxman considered the saxophone an instrument worthy of serious musical consideration. He allowed me to use the saxophone on the three recitals I performed for my degree. He was supportive of my work in classical saxophone, and yet he couldn't honestly say that there was a future out there. He was encouraging and optimistic, and yet he was realistic.

Rousseau supplemented his graduate assistantship by playing dance jobs.

I don't remember how this connection started, but there was a very good pianist — jazz pianist, jazz and dance, show tunes — named Leo Cortimiglia. I would have welcomed the opportunity to play

---

[27] Hervig, born in 1917 in Story City, Iowa, studied composition at the University of Iowa and joined the faculty in 1955; he became the founding director of the Center for New Music in 1966. Upon his retirement in 1988 he was appointed to a post at the Juilliard School in New York. Hervig died in 2010.

[28] Rousseau, who sent a program of the concerto performance to Copland, still has the letter containing Copland's cordial response.

some weekends because that was a comparatively lucrative way to earn some money. I remember that we spoke on the phone and he wanted to hear me play so he said, 'Let's meet at the River Room.' The River Room was overlooking the Iowa River in the Union Building on campus and there was a piano there. I brought my clarinet and saxophone and he asked me to play this tune and to play that tune and he hired me. It was a terrific group; there was an excellent jazz guitarist named Arnie Erickson, a bass player, Leo on piano, and myself. Leo wanted mostly clarinet, so I played jazz clarinet, basically. Only once in a while would I play saxophone because he preferred the clarinet. Dr. Voxman had absolutely no objection and it was great for me. I improved my improvisational skills, learned some new tunes, and enjoyed these men very much.

His work at Iowa was interrupted by an unparalleled opportunity — the prospect of studying saxophone with Marcel Mule. After a year of study in Iowa City, Rousseau seized the chance.

I had obviously admired Mule since I heard him as a teenager on recordings; the old 78s which I had were pretty well worn out. As part of the degree requirement at Iowa we had to have proficiency in German and in French — reading, not speaking. I had almost no speaking practice in either language but I had a very nice professor named Gillespie — I think she was from Québec province. She was a lovely lady who was teaching us about reading French. I told her I knew of this professor in France and I really wanted to study with him. I asked if I wrote a letter, a brief letter in English, if she would translate it into French so I could send it to him. She did that very willingly; I probably still have a copy of it somewhere.

Just before that, when I was at Iowa the first time during the summer of 1958, they had a Selmer soprano saxophone which I used. I wrote a note to the Selmer Company in Elkhart that I had been playing this soprano and I liked it very much and I hoped that someday I could have my own soprano. I got a letter back from Selmer Elkhart saying that they very much appreciated the letter and that they would send it to the man who was their consultant, Marcel Mule. That got my attention. When I wrote the letter Miss Gillespie translated, I got a very nice letter back from Mr. Mule. As a matter of fact, Mr. Mule never once failed to answer any letter that I ever sent him; I have all those letters.

I remember in Mr. Mule's first letter he wrote that he appreciated that I was interested in the saxophone. I had sent him one of my programs, which included the Bozza *Concertino*. He said someone who can play the Bozza *Concertino* must have a good level of proficiency and, of course, I would be happy to have you as a student. The letter from Selmer heightened my interest. I don't know, then, if Mr. Mule remembered that letter or not because it was after that that I wrote to him. But the fact that they said they would send it to Marcel Mule — wow!

Encouraged by his wife Norma, Rousseau applied for a Fulbright Grant to study saxophone and clarinet at the *Conservatoire National Supérieur de Musique* in Paris. After a year of doctoral work at the University of Iowa, Rousseau was awarded a Fulbright Grant. It would prove to be a life-changing event.

7 Fulbright Study in Paris (1960–1961): *There's nothing to it, you'll just play the first movement of the Ibert*

The Paris Conservatoire is one of the most prestigious music schools in the world and especially so for saxophonists. The school had its beginnings in the *Ecole royale de chant* for singers and actors, established by François-Joseph Gossec in 1784. It was combined in 1793 with a school for musicians of the National Guard and named the *Institut nationale de musique*. It became the *Conservatoire de musique* in 1795 and began with 350 students in October of 1796. Because of various types of government in France during the two centuries of the conservatory's existence, the institution has had several different names and has been the *Conservatoire nationale supérieur de musique* since 1938. It stands at the apex of a system of regional conservatories. The national conservatory's list of renowned teachers — including Arban (cornet), Cherubini (Director), Fauré (Director), Franck (organ), Gounod (composition), Kreutzer (violin), Messiaen (musical aesthetics), and Milhaud (composition) — is exceeded perhaps only by its list of famous students — composers including Berlioz, Debussy, Ravel, and Saint-Saëns and performers such as organist Marie-Claire Alain, trumpeter Maurice André, pianist Alfred Cortot, conductor Neville Marriner, and saxophonist Eugene Rousseau.

The Conservatoire's first Professor of Saxophone was the instrument's creator, Adolphe Sax, who taught there from 1858 to 1870. He was released following the surrender of the French Army at Sedan in September of 1870 during the Franco-Prussian War. This disastrous military defeat cost Sax his most influential ally, Emperor Napoleon III whose Second Empire was ended and the saxophone class was closed, not to reappear until 1942.

When Claude Delvincourt became Director of the Conservatoire in 1941, Marcel Mule "asked for an appointment two months after [Delvincourt] took up the post and he told [Mule] straight away 'I know why you are here, do not worry. It is the first thing I will do.' And he kept to his word, he established the saxophone class."[29] Mule thus became the second Professor of Saxophone in the history of the institution after an interval of seventy-two years.

During Mule's tenure of twenty-six years he established the foundation of systematic saxophone instruction. His pioneering career required him to create a body of pedagogical literature based principally on classic studies for violin, flute, and oboe. In addition, he arranged and transcribed more than a hundred works from the baroque, classical, and romantic periods. All instruction was on the alto saxophone and saxophone quartets were coached not by Mule but in a class for wind chamber music.

---

[29] Claude Delangle, "Interview with the Legendary Marcel Mule on the History of Saxophone Vibrato," translated by Huguette Brassine. *Australian Clarinet and Saxophone*, March 1998: 11.

Mule continued his performances as a soloist and as the leader of his internationally famous saxophone quartet. The culmination of his performing career occurred in 1958 with a twelve-concert tour of the United States as soloist with the Boston Symphony Orchestra. That same year Mule was awarded the *Chevalier de la legion d'honneur*, the highest honor that can be bestowed upon a French citizen. For reasons of health, Mule retired from solo performing in 1960, the year that Rousseau came to Paris. Mule continued to perform in his quartet and he played frequently for his students. He retired from teaching in 1968 to be succeeded by his pupil Daniel Deffayet.

The Fulbright Program for U.S. Students is named for Senator William J. Fulbright who in 1945 introduced a bill in the United States Congress that called for the use of proceeds from the sale of surplus war property to fund the "promotion of international good will through the exchange of students in the fields of education, culture, and science." On August 1, 1946, President Harry S. Truman signed the bill into law and Congress created the Fulbright Program. The primary source of funding is an annual appropriation from Congress to the Department of State.

Since the establishment of the Program, more than 111,000 students from the United States and 183,000 students from 155 other countries have benefited from their Fulbright experience. U.S. Fulbright Student alumni are heads of state, cabinet ministers, ambassadors, members of Congress, judges, heads of corporations, university presidents, journalists, artists, and professors. They include actor John Lithgow, composer Philip Glass, and singer Renee Fleming.

> To have received a Fulbright Grant for study in France was an extraordinary, an exciting prospect for Norma and me. We wanted to go to Europe. We had never been to Europe, although we have European roots, as most of us do. The fact that this gave us a way to go there was great. The Fulbright Commission paid my transportation and I received also a monthly stipend to cover living expenses. We traveled to Europe from New York by ship, which was the way things were in those days. It was the original Queen Elizabeth, not the later QEII. It was a huge ship. I remember I was seasick for several days. This was a long trip and for two or three days I couldn't get my sea legs. It didn't help that we had a storm at sea. Norma was fine and she took care of me. She insisted that I walk and not stay down below, which was the right thing to do and eventually I was OK. We landed in Cherbourg and took a train to Paris. We had a huge steamer trunk with lots of things that we needed for the year, clothing and so on.

> It was through the Leblanc Company that we were able to get an apartment. The Fulbright people would help with housing; they had a list of places where one could rent. It was mostly through the late Vito

Pascucci,[30] who was then the president of Leblanc USA and who was very kind, that we were able to find an apartment. I played a Leblanc saxophone at the time and he wanted to help. He made the contact with Léon Leblanc[31] in Paris and told him that we needed an apartment. We were able through them to rent for a very reasonable fee a very small apartment. It was one room, a tiny kitchen, and bath; I guess we could call it a studio apartment, if we're stretching it a little bit. This room also had a bed — it was not a hide-a-bed — and that was it. We were in a French neighborhood — 7 Rue Manin — and right across from a city park called Buttes Chaumont. It was a nice neighborhood, all in French, so when we went out in the morning to get bread, we had to order in French, and if we wanted milk we had to order in French. It was immersion in the deep end.

The apartment was conveniently located:

One must remember that Paris is not a huge city geographically; as far as the area, it's not enormous. It's spread out now since we were there but the Metro (the Underground, the British would say; the subway here) is a tremendous system and very clear. You got on the Metro, you knew where you wanted to go and everything was by *direction*, which was indicated by the final stop of that particular line. If, for example, the line was *étoile*, one could easily determine the stops along the route and, if necessary, connect to another line (*correspondence*). I practiced every day at the Leblanc factory because where we lived was only a few blocks away. That is where I met Charles Houvenaghel,[32] the man who really introduced me to the acoustic and construction aspects of the saxophone. I had not realized at the time how valuable this would prove to be, nor did I know of Houvenaghel's background. In effect, I had many lessons with him.

---

[30] Born in Kenosha, Wisconsin in 1922, Pascucci went to England as a member of Glenn Miller's Army Air Corps Band in World War II. Miller's untimely death ended their plans to open a chain of music stores after the war but Pascucci met Léon Leblanc in recently liberated Paris. Leblanc asked Pascucci to help him establish his company in the United States. Leblanc USA gained majority interest in the French company in 1989. Pascucci died in 2003.

[31] Leblanc, who lived from 1900 to 2000, established with his father Georges the first full-time acoustical research laboratory for wind instruments. In 1904, Georges had acquired the famous instrument manufacturer Noblet, whose history dates back to 1750. In addition, Léon was awarded the first prize in clarinet by the Paris Conservatoire, the first and only instrument maker to receive such an honor.

[32] Houvenaghel was regarded as the greatest acoustician since Adolphe Sax. With the Leblanc father and son, he pressed the theoretical limits of woodwind design to create the first truly complete clarinet choir. He also created 'le rationnel saxophone' in 1931. The instrument allowed the right hand to lower any pitch by a half-step. Rousseau says it is the only saxophone he knows which is built on the principles of famed flutist and acoustician Theobald Böhm and the only major change since Adophe Sax. This is the instrument Rousseau used on his 1971 recording for Deutsch Grammophon.

Shortly after arriving in Paris, I went to the Conservatory, where I had a certain amount of paperwork, and then saw Mr. Mule. He was very cordial and I remember it was very frustrating for me because I couldn't speak much French at that time. In order to be admitted officially to the Conservatory, I needed a medical statement saying that I was in good health. I had trouble understanding the office personnel and I tried to tell them that I wouldn't have been admitted to the program if this had not been the case. We finally got that straightened out. Mr. Mule was very kind. He told me that I could come to all the classes for his students — it was all done by class — but he wanted to meet with me privately every other week, Saturday morning for three hours and so I went to his home — 43 Rue Bezout.

Saxophone instruction at the Conservatory consisted of twelve hours weekly divided among twelve French students, with five additional openings reserved for foreign students. Lessons were given in front of the class, held twice a week, so that all could benefit. Admission was by competitive audition. Students could not be over twenty-three years of age at the time of entrance and would study for at least two years but no more than five. There was no tuition charge.

Being past the age limit I wasn't a part of the class so I didn't play in front of the others, but I was there and we got to know each other. Everybody was polite. I remember Mr. Mule had one talented student from Switzerland, I don't know if he was sixteen or seventeen years old at the time, named Iwan Roth, who was in the class and still played the metal mouthpiece. Mr. Mule had played the metal mouthpiece somewhere in the 1950s and then he changed back to a rubber mouthpiece. He told me that he thought it had a tone that was more round than the metal mouthpiece. I was playing a Brilhart hard rubber mouthpiece but then bought a Selmer C-star in Paris.

Mr. Mule was still active with his quartet and would often play in the class but no longer made solo appearances. He was a very gentle man; everything was *vous*, very polite, rather than the more familiar *tu*. Once in a while, he would deviate a little bit and talk to the class about something other than music or the saxophone. One time, I know, he said to them, 'You're practicing, all you're thinking is saxophone and some of you don't even know how to write a letter.' He said in a very firm way, 'This is very important, you should know your basic skills.' He would get onto political things too sometimes, just once in a while: 'All that is happening is terrible, I don't understand. This is so unjust, how can people do this?' He was basically a pacifist.

In 1942, which was not a good time politically, he learned German because he thought that maybe France would be occupied forever. There was no guarantee how it was going to end.

Rousseau, who was twenty-eight years old, was past the age limit and therefore could not compete for the prizes awarded at the end of the year. He did not play in the class lessons but was permitted to attend. Rousseau enrolled at the Conservatory in the class for foreign students, which included fellow American Claire Friedman, a young woman from Florida. Although he had been accepted by Mule as a student, it was still necessary to audition for acceptance into the Conservatory.

One had to play an audition; I had no idea. Mr. Mule said, 'There's nothing to it, you'll just play the first movement of the Ibert. Two or three of us will listen to you.' He didn't make much out of it. I arrived at the Conservatory to a room where I was supposed to go and when I got there I quickly realized that many were prepared to audition! It was like a beehive, playing and playing. When it was my turn, someone called my name and I went from the warm-up room where we all were into a recital hall. There was a rather large jury and a woman sitting at the piano. She said, 'I understand you're going to play Ibert.' I said yes. She went through her large brief bag of music, pulled out the Ibert and said, *'Vous êtes pret, monsieur?'* ('Are you ready, sir?'); I said, *'Oui'* ('Yes') and we began. I had never seen this woman before and we played as though we had rehearsed it several times. She knew her part, I knew my part, and she also knew my part. I must say that I also knew her part because I had heard it many times. There were no written comments but I was simply passed. She was Mr. Mule's regular staff pianist, a very nice lady. I remember later that when she played in class, she would have this brief bag full of whatever music they had at the time. It was one of those memorable experiences I shall never forget.

The private lessons covered a huge amount of literature, most suggested by Mule and a few pieces suggested by Rousseau, including music by Bonneau, Bozza, Glazounov, Ibert, Tomasi, and Vellones. Mule frequently demonstrated such matters of phrasing, dynamics, and vibrato. Lessons were conducted in French at Rousseau's request so he could learn the language more readily.

I would have an assignment, usually two pieces, and we would simply start at the beginning of each piece. He taught a lot by playing; he would play a passage — 'this has to be faster, this has to be' whatever it has to be. He would mark my scores. A number of my pieces to this day have his handwriting, where he would write in different things. This was the way he approached it. We didn't really have a technique book, although he had me work out of one of the violin books, Rode or something like that, which he had adapted to saxophone. But mostly he talked about the music — he would play examples, and then I would play. He discussed the style and the tempo. When we did Ibert, for example, he told me about what Jacques had felt about this or that; he had spoken with him. Unfortunately, I did not meet Ibert. I met Mrs. Ibert but I never met Jacques Ibert and I'm sorry that I didn't. Mr. Mule told me that Ibert had written these high notes but then later he put *ad libitum* on those places; he wasn't convinced that this was the best way. Mr. Mule told me that Ibert may have told the publisher that these sections should be *ad libitum*.

He would discuss general musical principles as well. For example, regarding vibrato, he often talked about how you must be certain that you have the center of the tone, that you're at the right spot so the vibrato is not wild. Another principle he often talked about was technique — he said that, like climbing a ladder, be sure your foot is on this rung before you go to the next rung, which is a fine graphic example. I remember one time — I don't remember what I was playing but it was a fast movement — and he told me that I should play it at the tempo. I said, 'I'm sorry, Sir; I'm not ready to play it at that tempo.' He said, 'You can do it! Just play a measure or a short segment at a time.' It was probably the most valuable builder of technique that I learned and I use that today. Even if you can't play the measure, then do half a measure, but at tempo, and then put it together.

He definitely favored using the *bis* B-flat. When I first started, I played some scales and he said, 'It's more practical if you use the *bis* key on that scale.' I was using the side key. I didn't believe him but I respected him and so I practiced it that way. I found out he was right. Of course, in repetition back and forth, one wouldn't want to do that but one would in the basic scales. On open C-sharp, he didn't use the covered C-sharp fingering that most of us use today — and, of course, with the Series III it's not possible — but what he did was add the side C key; open C-sharp with the side C key to bring it up a little bit. It was more for pitch than tone.

Concerning articulation, he always stressed that the notes have to sound. In other words, the tone was the important thing. I don't know if he used this example exactly, but later I heard the expression that a short tone is a long tone played short. He didn't say it that way but that's what he would get at. Someone in the class, I remember, was playing staccato and he got hung up on the tongue movement and the tone wasn't very good. He would say, 'Play that again as if it were all legato. Now get that same tone.' It's pretty fundamental.

He didn't describe the sound but taught principally by example. 'You must play with a round tone. Free reed; the reed must be free.' We all learned later that the embouchure is a combination of dampening the reed and letting the reed vibrate freely; you have to find the spot. He talked about *'langue libre'* [literally, 'free tongue'] very often. One of the things I found was that at a certain passage he would say, *'avec expression'* or *'sans expression.'* What he meant was 'with' or 'without vibrato.' He would very often interchange expression with vibrato.

Mule differed from my former teachers in that anything he would talk about — phrasing, dynamics, vibrato, or whatever the subject — he would then demonstrate. As a result, I had the opportunity to hear him play a great deal. I remember one of his expressions: 'Don't look for the difficult things, look for the simple things.' Whenever he played, it always sounded simple; he made it sound simple. That was the driving force behind him. Another expression he would use was: 'One never arrives.' How true that was, how true that has been, and it is even more true today for me than ever. One never does arrive. Being with Mr. Mule was a great experience. Learning the literature and his approach to the instrument was wonderful. But what impressed me the most was the way he handled people. He was a great gentleman.

Mule did not subscribe to the perceived "conservatory method" in which all students must conform to the same sound and perform the same literature in exactly the same manner. Henri Druart, with whom Rousseau was to study clarinet, took a different approach than Mule.

I had the privilege of being associated with Henri Druart. He was a clarinetist in one of the major orchestras in Paris and was also solo clarinet in the Garde Republicaine. He happened to play a Leblanc clarinet, so that was the connection. I played a Leblanc saxophone at that time and so Mr. Léon Leblanc introduced me to Druart, who was teaching at one of the city conservatories. In Paris, at that time at least, there were several areas throughout the city — I'm not sure they were actually called 'city conservatories' — but they were places where people could enroll to take lessons at little or no charge. It was a governmental initiative. Whichever region it was, Druart was teaching there, in sort of a mixed class (it was a little class; there were maybe six people studying clarinet, typical French class instruction) and so I took lessons from him.

It wasn't the best situation for me for a couple of reasons. First, of course, my primary reason to go to France was to study with Marcel Mule so there was the time factor of keeping up with both instruments. By the way, Mr. Mule knew that I was taking clarinet lessons and he had no problem with that. The other thing is that Mr. Druart was from a certain background and tradition so that, because I was a new student of his, I began with the C major scale. I had already played the Brahms sonatas, the Debussy *Rhapsody*, the Copland *Clarinet Concerto*, and what I wanted to do was get his perspective on musical interpretation. But Mr. Druart, a very nice gentleman, approached things from a different way. After about two months I decided it was best just to spend my energy on saxophone.

I remember, however, one boy who had a marvelous technique and did things I don't think I could ever do. Druart would ask him to play the chromatic scale in major thirds and he'd just whip that off. 'Play the chromatic scale in minor thirds. Do this and that.' I was astounded. One night we were talking — he was a very nice fellow — and I asked him if he had ever played any music of Hindemith, the concerto or the sonata. And he said, 'Who?' I thought maybe it was my pronunciation because I didn't speak French very well at the time, so I spelled it out in block letters. He had no idea who Hindemith was.

My Fulbright grant was in clarinet and saxophone; the Fulbright Commission was willing to pay for my lessons for two teachers and that's the way I started. It was obvious that it was more beneficial for me to spend my time with the saxophone. I told a Fulbright officer that, with what I have to do and the amount of time, it would be better if I just studied with Mule and it was fine with them.

One of the most memorable times at Mule's home occurred during one of our lessons. I still have the conversation tape because I had a little tape recorder. As we were in his apartment, which was on the third or fourth floor and overlooking the main street, we heard sirens. We both looked out the window to see what was happening. It was an open limousine and he said, 'It's President Kennedy.' Kennedy was visiting Paris. Kennedy was very popular and his wife even more so.

> Norma bought from time to time ground meat — hamburger — and the butcher was very nice and he said to her 'Kennedy arrived with his wife, Jacqueline Bouvier.' The students in Paris at that time held a big rally, as they thought Kennedy was something special. They had a chant — Kenne-*un*, through the numbers to Kenne-*dix*. To be in a lesson and look out and see our president was a memorable moment.

Rousseau was accompanied to Paris by his wife Norma, whom he had married in 1959. They lived their year in Paris to the fullest, residing in a French neighborhood, shopping at French markets, and learning to speak the language. In addition, they attended numerous concerts, at least three a week.

> We went to everything — to chamber music concerts, string quartets, piano trio, orchestras, opera, everything. We soaked it up. We both enjoyed France and I think she would have liked to stay another year. I could have had the Fulbright renewed; that wouldn't have been a problem but I wanted to resume my work at Iowa. I really wanted to finish my degree. It's easy to look back and say yes, it would have been nice to stay. Had I stayed another year, I don't think I would have been at Indiana University; the time frame would have been off. We can see that as we look back but we never know that at the time.

After a year in Paris, Rousseau returned to Iowa to complete his doctoral degree in 1962. He and Norma had been profoundly changed by their experiences. They would never forget the culture to which they had been introduced and which had transformed their lives forever.

8 Central Missouri State College (1962–1964):
I didn't have any assistants, so my wife and I worked together on preparing the half time shows

Not all of my recitals at the University of Iowa were degree recitals. I played a recital when I came back from Paris on which I included the Rueff *Concertino* and Constant's *Musique de Concert*. The Rueff and the Constant were pretty new at that time; I don't think anyone had heard them. I don't know if I did the Desenclos *Prelude, Cadence et Finale* then, but I brought the Desenclos back with me. I was teaching the saxophone at Iowa — I was a grad assistant but I was THE saxophone teacher because there was no major teacher of saxophone. There were students at Iowa who were interested in the saxophone — we had a little group that got together and they were very interested in what I had done in France. I remember that when I showed them the Desenclos their eyes widened and they said, 'This is not possible.' It gives an idea of what has happened since 1961!

Shortly after his return to the United States, Rousseau shared his increasing awareness of saxophone literature in an article in *The Instrumentalist*. Following some introductory comments about the instrument's flexibility, Rousseau observes that "Marcel Mule has demonstrated the nature of the true classical saxophone" and that "the saxophone finally appears to be achieving its rightful place among the wind instruments." The list of music is principally for alto saxophone but, after noting the "need for good literature for tenor and baritone saxophones," makes a typically practical suggestion that baritone saxophonists can easily learn to play cello literature by reading it "as if in treble clef and add three sharps." The selected bibliography is graded and includes collections, transcriptions, and original works.[33]

A second article was published in *The Instrumentalist* in 1962, this time concerned with saxophone tone quality. Rousseau cites tonal concept as the most important factor, followed by embouchure and air pressure or support. He suggests a test to check both embouchure and air pressure: "Blow a sustained pitch on the mouthpiece alone at a *fortissimo* level. The approximate concert pitches which should be obtained are A for alto saxophone; G for tenor saxophone; E-flat for baritone saxophone." After discussing reed selection, Rousseau discusses the conical bore of the instrument, concluding that "the saxophone's artistic possibilities, thanks to a handful of dedicated artists, are being realized in this twentieth century."[34]

---

[33] Eugene Rousseau, "Solo Literature for the Saxophone," *Instrumentalist* Vol. XV, No. 8 (April 1961): 72-4.

[34] Eugene Rousseau, "Saxophone Tone Quality," *Instrumentalist* Vol. XVI, No. 10 (June 1962): n.p.

Soon after earning the degree of Doctor of Philosophy in Music Literature and Performance[35] from the University of Iowa, Rousseau accepted a position at Central Missouri State College. Now called the University of Central Missouri, it is located about fifty miles southeast of Kansas City in Warrensburg, a town of about 16,000. The school was founded in 1871 as a teacher's college and that remains its focus. The university has long had a strong music program.

The position was that of Director of Bands and Instructor of woodwinds and theory. The responsibilities as band director included marching band, pep band, and concert band. In addition, Rousseau began a jazz ensemble.

Rousseau's acceptance of the position reveals two important facts. First, it reflects his strong background in bands. Bands are where Rousseau's musical experiences began and they retain an important part of his musical affections. Second, it should be remembered that there were no full-time saxophone positions to be filled. The University of Michigan had hired Larry Teal only nine years before to create the first such position and no other university had followed, although the next year, 1963, Northwestern University would appoint Frederick Hemke.

> The job market is not easy. There's never an abundance of jobs; it doesn't matter when. People will say to me, 'There are so many more positions today than when you were younger.' That's true, but one must think of all the other candidates. It's incredible; the competition is fierce. I was looking, as I was coming near the end of my doctoral degree, for a job. I could have returned to Luther College but I decided not to do that. There certainly were no saxophone positions available anywhere. In looking for a position, what appeared to be the best option was Director of Bands at Central Missouri State. I had some band conducting experience at Luther College for three years and I had been an assistant band leader in the Army and I enjoyed that. Remember the fact that my background was with bands. I have a great feeling for the band movement in America and it holds a place close to my heart.
>
> I applied for the position and I think this sent a red flag up with some people because I was not in the Iowa band. When the Missouri people asked Frederick Ebbs about me, he couldn't say that I was a member of his band but we knew each other and we were on good terms. The Missouri people invited me to be a judge at one of their high school competitions in Warrensburg. I went down — in March, probably

---

[35] Rousseau's dissertation is entitled "Clarinet instructional materials from 1732 to 1825." It has been suggested that Rousseau was the second woodwind performer to receive a doctorate, following John Mohler who was granted a doctoral degree by the University of Michigan in 1960. The University of Iowa did not offer a performance doctorate until 1964.

— and that gave them a chance to look me over. I met some of the faculty at that time and they offered me the position.

Once I accepted their offer, the word got out as to who was coming to be the Director of Bands. I received shortly after that a very nice long letter, which I still have, from Charlie Wells welcoming me to Missouri. He was a businessman with Bohart Music in Kansas City but also played clarinet and saxophone, and was a great supporter of instrumental music education. It was a lovely and welcoming letter. Having gotten that nice letter, we felt welcome. We went into Kansas City and met him and that was the beginning of a lasting association. We became very good friends and he later was godfather to our son. We then met George Wingert, Merrill Jones, and Bob Luyben[36] and got acquainted with other people in the area.

In addition to his conducting, classroom, and studio duties, Rousseau continued his growing activities as a recitalist, performing on saxophone and clarinet and occasionally on oboe.

I didn't have any assistants, so my wife and I worked together on preparing the half-time shows. If they needed a pep band for the basketball game, we had to do that. In addition, I was teaching a theory class and all the woodwind instruments. But I think we got an *esprit de corps* going and by the second year things were really rolling. The woodwinds were 30-minute lessons, so I was doing a lot of quick shifting, whether it was flute to oboe to clarinet or whatever. I enjoyed very much the woodwind techniques class. It was a nice feeling and I thought things were moving in a good direction.

During his first year at Central Missouri, Rousseau was again selected to represent the United States in another country. This time he was part of the U.S. Exposition in Conakry, Guinea, sent jointly by the U.S. Department of Commerce and Leblanc Musical Instruments. Rousseau left from Kansas City in April of 1963 to be in charge of the musical aspects of the exposition. He found a nation that needed years of basic economic progress, many of whose inhabitants could not read or write but possessed a great innate musical ability.

Ostensibly, my assignment included the following: explaining the instruments of the modern band and orchestra; describing the nature of

---

[36] George Wingert and Merrill Jones formed Wingert-Jones Music, one of the foremost music stores in Kansas City, in 1960 and would become Rousseau's first publisher. Luyben Music, also located in Kansas City, began in 1947. Robert Luyben had studied with Daniel Bonade and been a clarinetist with the U.S. Navy Band.

the instrumental music program in the schools and colleges of the U.S.; instructing Guineans in the basic principles of organization, instrumentation, etc.; and organizing a band comprised of native musicians. While none of the above was fulfilled to the extent that I had originally hoped, the experience proved rewarding in a number of ways.[37]

During the summer of 1964, Rousseau, his wife Norma, and their two-year-old daughter Lisa-Marie returned to Iowa City. Himie Voxman and his wife went to Europe for the summer, Rousseau taught Voxman's studio, and he and his family lived in Voxman's home.

It was at the beginning of my second year at Warrensburg. Professor Voxman called and said that he and his wife were going to Europe that next summer and he wondered if I would be willing to come up to Iowa City to teach his students that summer and stay in his home. Of course, we thought that over for about two seconds, because it was a great opportunity.

Before he left, Voxman rather casually mentioned to Rousseau that Indiana University was ready to follow the lead of the University of Michigan and Northwestern University by hiring a saxophone teacher.

When we came up to Iowa City — that's the summer of 1964 — he said, 'By the way, I see Wilfred Bain[38] from time to time and I know they're looking for a saxophone professor at Indiana. Knowing Bain, he's probably trying to get Sigurd Rascher or Marcel Mule but I just thought I'd mention it. You know, it might be worth a try.' I thought about it and Norma said, 'What do you have to lose? It's a three-cent stamp.' There was no email or fax then, so I composed a letter and sent it to Bain in the latter part of June. Immediately after receiving my letter, Dean Bain phoned me: 'I have your letter. We'd like you to come out and talk about this position.' These were the days before affirmative action and equal opportunity and there was no search committee. When Wilfrid Bain decided that he wanted someone, he simply went out and asked the person to accept the position. To get a call from him to be asked for an interview was beyond anything I had ever dreamed of.

---

[37] Eugene Rousseau, "Music in Guinea," *Woodwind World* Vol. VI, No. 1 (September 15, 1964): 6.

[38] Bain (1908–1997) is credited with creating one of the world's great schools of music, serving at Indiana University from 1947 to 1973. He greatly increased enrollment and expanded faculty while emphasizing orchestral performance and opera production.

I got on a plane — I remember it was Lake Central Airlines. I flew from Cedar Rapids to Chicago, changed planes and then a stop at Lafayette. I remember because it was a DC-3 and the pilot came out and said, 'Could three of you men move to the other side of the aircraft so we could keep a better balance?' We flew into Bloomington, Indiana. I took a taxi to the hotel where they had made a reservation for me at the Memorial Union. I had only been to Bloomington, Indiana once; that was in the fall of 1953 as a member of the Northwestern University Marching Band. I got a call from the Assistant Dean, Charles Webb,[39] who welcomed me.

The next morning Dean Bain met me for breakfast. We had a nice chat; I can even remember that he had a bowl of oatmeal! He said, 'Now we'll drive over to the School of Music.' I gathered my saxophone and some music and we came down to his vehicle, which was a Messerschmitt. A Messerschmitt was three-wheeled, really a motorcycle with a bubble. There was room for one passenger behind the driver and I was quite cramped in there. He said, 'Are you comfortable?' and of course I said, 'Yes, sir.' We drove over to the School of Music. He was very clever and he made a very nice impression on me; I could see he was a man with vision and ideas. He said, 'I want you and Dean Webb, who will play piano for you, to do the Heiden Sonata. Why don't you warm up?' While I was warming up in a room, they were in the other room with the intercom on — they were listening to me, of course, which I didn't realize. Then we played; I think we only played the first movement. Dean Bain took me back to the airport and on the way he offered me the position and told me what the salary would be. I told him, 'I would like to accept that but I have an agreement now with Central Missouri State and I have to make sure that everything is in order.'

---

[39] Webb, born in 1933, had recently been named Assistant Dean. He followed Bain as Dean of the School of Music in 1973 until 1997, continuing the School's growth.

9 Indiana University (1964–2000):
No one had to tell me to strive to be better

"The appointment of the saxophonist Eugene Rousseau finally allowed [Dean Wilfred] Bain to say that the School had individual teachers for every band instrument as well every orchestral one."[40] Wilfred Bain had been named Dean of Indiana University's School of Music in 1947 and immediately began to create the largest and, in the opinion of many, the best music school in the world.

The School traces its history back to May 30, 1910 when Charles Diven Campbell was asked by University President William Lowe Bryan to "become Associate Professor of Music, giving certain courses in Music and having next year general charge of the musical interests of the University."[41] Following Campbell's unexpected death at the age of forty-one in 1919, Barzille Winfred Merrill was selected as Head of the Department. His tenure lasted nineteen years and was marked by both expansion and dissension. Robert L. Sanders was named Dean of the School of Music in 1938 and inherited a new music building (now Merrill Hall) and a faculty scarred by years of battles with its leader; Sanders was only thirty-two years of age when he came to Bloomington and his lack of administrative experience was a liability.

Wilfred Bain wasn't much older in 1947 than Sanders had been in 1938 when University President Herman B Wells invited him to Indiana. Born in 1908, Bain had enjoyed tremendous administrative success, principally at North Texas State University (now the University of North Texas) in Denton. Under his leadership the School of Music at North Texas had grown from thirty-five music majors to four hundred and the faculty had grown from five full-time members to twenty full-time and twenty-one graduate assistants. The facilities, which included one practice room when he arrived in 1938, now housed ninety practice rooms with forty more on the way. President Wells planned to make Indiana University one of the greatest universities in the country and Bain saw the opportunity to do on a much larger scale that which he had done at North Texas: to create one of the greatest music schools in the world.

By 1964 Bain had accomplished much of this lofty goal. The thirty-one-year-old Rousseau joined a stellar faculty that included pianists such as Sidney Foster, Menahem Pressler, Gyorgy Sebok, and Abbey Simon; singers such as Ralph Appelman, Margaret Harshaw, and Martha Lipton; and a string faculty that included Josef Gingold, Daniel Guilet, and Janos Starker. Among Rousseau's

---

[40] George M. Logan, *The Indiana University School of Music: A History* (Bloomington, Indiana: Indiana University Press, 2000), 200.

[41] Ibid., 13.

colleagues on the wind faculty were William Bell, Keith Brown, Philip Farkas, James Pellerite, and Leonard Sharrow.

The appointment of a special saxophone teacher completed the roster of individual teachers in the winds and gave truth to the claim that Indiana University had an individual teacher for each instrument of the orchestra and band.[42]

Rousseau was pleased by the academic freedom he found at Indiana. The School of Music did not specify how the saxophone class was to be developed nor did it voice any expectations for him or for the new saxophone curriculum.

> I was in awe. No one had to tell me to strive to be better; I was highly motivated and challenged. The School didn't spell out anything that I was to do and no one ever told me how to teach. I was never told that I could or could not conduct my classes in a certain way. I always felt a great sense of academic freedom.

As the first full-time teacher of saxophone in the history of the School of Music, the administration may have been concerned that it would not initially be possible for there to be a full teaching load with saxophone students alone. Rousseau's original appointment included conducting a jazz ensemble in addition to teaching saxophone.

> When I took the position, it was to teach saxophone and conduct one of the jazz ensembles. When the class list of those who wanted to take saxophone came out, Dean Bain called me. 'Now look,' he said, 'twenty-seven people have signed up for saxophone lessons. If you're going to conduct a jazz ensemble, I'll get someone else to teach some of these students. Or, if you want to teach just saxophone, I will get someone else to do a jazz ensemble.' Of course, you know which route I took. I think that all the students were music performance or music education majors; I don't know if there were any minors in there or secondaries.

The size of that first studio indicated that there was most certainly an interest in the saxophone on the part of the students. But Rousseau also had to create support among his colleagues. He presented a faculty recital in the spring of that first academic year, programming Jacques Ibert's *Concertino da Camera*, the Sonata

---

[42] Wilfrid C. Bain, *Indiana University School of Music, the Bain Regime, 1947-73*. (Bloomington, Indiana: MS, n.d.), 656.

by Paul Creston, the Sonata by Indiana faculty colleague Bernhard Heiden, and Alfred Descenlos' *Prelude, Cadence et Finale*. The pianist was Carl Fuerstner, a talented opera and vocal coach.

> Carl had a studio right next to mine. We talked and he knew so much repertory, so many different instruments. Certainly my colleagues were very pleasant and supportive and I received a very warm reception from them after the recital. But I think those who were most excited about the recital were the students who were studying saxophone. By the way, I was not yet in the studio where I spent so many years. I began on the second floor of the Music Annex in a smaller room. Then I was across the hall into a larger room. When Iannis Xenakis[43] left in 1973, I asked if I could have that studio — MA 004 — on the first floor of the Music Annex.

Recognizing that it was both necessary and desirable to perform in major venues outside of Indiana, Rousseau performed the first saxophone recital at Carnegie Hall in New York City. The recital occurred on January 6, 1965, and Rousseau was assisted by pianist Leonard Klein and violist (and faculty colleague) Allen Winold.[44] In addition to the pair of sonatas by Heiden and Creston and the Desenclos work heard in his Indiana faculty recital, Rousseau presented the *Sonatine* by Claude Pascal, Paul Hindemith's *Trio for Tenor Saxophone, Viola, and Piano, op. 47*,[45] and his own arrangement of Handel's *Adagio and Allegro* from the C minor oboe sonata.

> Leonard Klein was a very competent pianist and good musician who taught theory. He was at Indiana and I had known him at Iowa; he was an Iowa student.

> It's often difficult to be reviewed in New York and I think it's especially difficult today. Sherman Pitluck had been in New York City, but was now managing concerts for IU groups and faculty. He had recommended Mark Bichurin, who was in New York, as an agent to arrange the recital for me, to rent the hall and sell the tickets. I remember that he had represented a couple of very well-known musicians — Rudolf

---

[43] Xenakis (1922–2001) was a prolific composer who connected mathematical concepts with the organization of musical compositions. He was a member of the Indiana University faculty and director of a Center for Mathematical and Automated Music from 1967 to 1973. Xenakis wrote his quartet *XAS* in 1987.

[44] Winold at that time taught music theory as an Assistant Professor at Indiana and later served as Director of Undergraduate Studies and Director of Special Programs. Before coming to Indiana he was a member of the North Carolina Symphony and the Cincinnati Symphony.

45 For the Hindemith work, Rousseau used a Mark VI tenor saxophone borrowed from student Thomas Gorin.

Firkusny and Ruggiero Ricci. He arranged this recital in Carnegie Recital Hall and it was a reasonably good crowd. Two people whom I remember there were Paul Winter[46] and Roger Pemberton[47].

Theodore Strongin, music critic for *The New York Times*, wrote:

> Eugene Rousseau, a fine musician who specializes in the saxophone, made his New York solo debut recital last night at Carnegie Recital Hall, playing the alto and tenor sizes of his instrument.
>
> Mr. Rousseau has a huge dynamic range, a bagful of articulations and, above all, intelligence and good judgment. He put his considerable technique and command of nuance to sober musical use. He has genuine 'classical' tone — round, almost fat, with plenty of body — as contrasted to the wiry and emphatic sound heard from many jazz musicians.
>
> Outstanding for alto saxophone was a sonata by Bernhard Heiden, a colleague of Mr. Rousseau's on the staff of Indiana University. The sonata is idiomatically written, contrapuntally adept, and has a rich, Hindemith flavor entirely suitable to its musical purposes. This piece works. It would have worked better had Mr. Rousseau's vibrato eased up occasionally. Also on alto, Mr. Rousseau played works by Handel, Desenclos, Paul Creston and a rather academic sonata by Claude Pascal. On tenor, the saxophonist offered the Hindemith *Trio, Op. 47* with the help of Leonard Klein, the evening's excellent pianist, and Allen Winold, violist.[48]

It had long been one of Rousseau's goals to present a Carnegie Hall recital, dating back to his student days at the University of Iowa.

> One summer — I don't remember the year — I was playing first clarinet in the orchestra at Iowa; we were doing *La bohéme*. I was seated right behind the first viola, Bill Preucil [Sr.].[49] We had a very nice

---

[46] Born in 1939, saxophonist Winter is best known for his award-winning multicultural *Paul Winter Consort*.

[47] Pemberton is Distinguished Professor Emeritus at the University of South Carolina, where he taught saxophone and jazz until his retirement in 2000.

[48] Theodore Strongin, recital review, *New York Times* (January 7, 1965): 18.

[49] Preucil has performed in more than thirty countries in Europe, the Middle East, Asia, Australia, and throughout North America. He is former principal violist of the Detroit Symphony Orchestra, a founding member of the Stradivari Quartet, and a Professor Emeritus at the University of Iowa.

time because we had some of the same themes. I would sometimes add vibrato and he would turn and nod his head. We would talk and he told me about his New York recital and that was interesting for me — a New York recital. He explained that anybody could play a recital. It was a matter of renting the hall, having somebody prepare publicity and sell tickets or have tickets available, that sort of thing. It was intriguing and that's how I made up my mind that I was going to do a New York recital. I set it up for January of 1965, not knowing that I wouldn't be in Missouri at that time but I was moving to Indiana.

Following his Carnegie Hall success of 1965, Rousseau and pianist Joseph Rezits presented a recital as part of the Phillips Collection Concert Series in Washington, D.C. on November 11, 1966. The works performed were, again, the sonatas by Heiden and Creston, Maurice Constant's *Musique de Concert*, Alexandre Tcherepnine's *Sonatine Sportive*, and the *Concertstück* of Pierre-Max Dubois. Once more, Rousseau's performance received a favorable review, this time from Paul Hume of *The Washington Post*.

Late yesterday afternoon the Phillips Collection presented an unusual concert of music for saxophone and piano in the playing of two members of the faculty of Indiana University. In the hands of Eugene Rousseau the saxophone becomes a facile and beautifully modulated wind instrument, capable of fine song and great flexibility.

Joseph Rezits is an excellent pianist, and together the men brought sonatas by Bernhard Heiden, Alexandre Tcherepnin, and Paul Creston, as well as music by Marius Constant and Pierre-Max Dubois.

Of the sonatas, I found the most to enjoy in the Tcherepnin, called *Sonatine Sportive*. Here, with neat allusions to boxing, intermission, and racing, the composer, through simple enough but nicely applied devices, suggests a gala afternoon of sport, one that is closely matched by the superb Kandinsky called *Succession*, that hangs in the Phillips outer drawing room. The Heiden *Sonata* is rather uninspired in its fine craft, the Creston is openly vulgar. But the novelty of hearing the little-understood saxophone is more than a pleasant way to spend a concert hour.[50]

While Rousseau had found his colleagues at Indiana to be cordial and supportive, there was no way he could have expected the greeting he received from a member of the piano faculty.

---

[50] Paul Hume, recital review, *Washington Post* (November 7, 1966): 16.

I was checking my mail at the faculty mail boxes when I heard a woman say. 'You are Mr. Rousseau and you play the saxophone.' I said that was indeed the case and she introduced herself. 'I am Marion Hall and I would like to read through some saxophone music with you if you are interested. Perhaps you would like to read some of the works by Ibert, Creston, or some others.' I was astonished because we never have a pianist suggest to a saxophonist that they are interested in playing our music.

Marion Hall had served as Marcel Mule's pianist for his recital in Elkhart, Indiana for Selmer as part of his tour with the Boston Symphony. The recital, which took place on February 9, 1958, presented two movements from his transcription of Bach's E major flute sonata, the Concerto by Glazounov, Mule's transcriptions of the Intermezzo from *Goyescas* by Granados and Pierne's *Canzonetta*, the final movement of Bozza's *Concertino*, the *Sonatine Sportive* of Tcherepnine, Pascal's *Sonatine*, the *Concertino da Camera* by Ibert, Bonneau's *Caprice en forme de valse*, and the *Ballade* by Tomasi. Ms. Hall was indeed familiar with saxophone literature; she and Rousseau recorded two albums for Coronet and undertook a European tour in 1967.[51]

In addition to live performances in various concert halls, Rousseau began to record a wide variety of literature. They recorded *Eugene Rousseau Plays the Saxophone* in 1967 and *Virtuoso Saxophone* in 1969. These recordings with Ms. Hall were the first of more than twenty that he has made to date. A list of Rousseau's recordings and their contents is found in Appendix C.

In addition to the recordings, Rousseau and Hall made a momentous European tour in 1967. The tour included the first saxophone recitals presented in Vienna, Berlin, Amsterdam, and London. These performances at such prestigious centers of musical performance were part of Rousseau's long-held goal to further establish the saxophone as a medium of serious musical expression. "I wanted to do these recitals and recordings and Dean Bain was very supportive of his faculty to do things like this."

The performance in London's Wigmore Hall[52] on January 20, 1967 was the first saxophone recital presented in that city. As before, the program included a work which he had newly transcribed. The recital was reviewed by *The London Times*.

---

[51] At a meeting with Rousseau and the author in June of 2004, Ms. Hall said, "The most important playing I did was with the saxophone." Ms. Hall was born in 1910.

[52] Originally called Bechstein Hall, it opened in 1901 with a pair of gala concerts by artists such as Ferrucio Busoni, Eugène Ysaÿe, and Vladimir de Pachmann. Other famed performers including Artur Schnabel, Pablo Sarasate, and Camille Saint-Saëns soon appeared. Renamed Wigmore Hall in 1917, it has hosted Elisabeth Schwarzkopf, Sergei Prokofiev, and Jacqueline du Pré and, more recently, András Schiff, Cecilia Bartoli, and Anne Sofie von Otter among others.

That common complaint: 'Nothing but familiar classics' could not be voiced at Wigmore Hall on Friday. For Mr. Eugene Rousseau arrived there from America with a saxophone, an instrument not patented by its inventor until 1846, and (in spite of attracting some eminent nineteenth-century Frenchmen) not really taken seriously as a solo instrument until quite recent times. Hence Mr. Rousseau's programme of Tcherepnin, Paul Creston, Bernhard Heiden, and Alfred Desenclos, with only a sonata by Giovanni Platti, presumably originally for flute, to represent the past.

Ironically, some of the keenest pleasure of the evening came in the purity of the classical work, which Mr. Rousseau played with finely moulded cantabile and flawless agility on a soprano saxophone, its higher pitch often suggesting the welcome tartness of an oboe.

For the other works Mr. Rousseau used an alto instrument, and all his suavity, brilliance, and musical discernment (not for nothing is he a member of the music faculty of Indiana University).[53]

The recital at Vienna's Palais Palffy[54] on February 2, 1967 presented the same works and received an even more enthusiastic response from the press.

Saxophone recitals in Vienna have the value of rarity. Music lovers conscious of traditional European culture, on listening to the saxophone timbre, caressing, exciting, will think of the lascivious twenties, of dance bands and smoky bars, perhaps even of jazz — at best of Kurt Weill — in any event, of popular music. They wrinkle their noses. The saxophone, patented in 1846, was intended originally for military bands, has been, since the turn of the century, quite acceptable; however, in the concert halls tolerated only temporarily. Nevertheless, Berlioz greeted it enthusiastically. Bizet and Massenet smuggled alto saxophones into the orchestra. Ravel used it in his *Bolero* and even serious composers like Verdi and Hindemith have introduced it occasionally. Not to mention the less serious ones like Strauss, Vaughan Williams, and Britten. And yet, the saxophone does not seem to get rid of its bad, or at least 'mixed', reputation.

---

[53] Richard Maylan, recital review, *The London Times* (January 23, 1967): 17.

[54] Palffy Palace, built in 1357 and also known as the Austria House, is located in the heart of Vienna. It was here that the six-year-old Mozart and his sister, Nannerl, gave a concert in 1762.

Then the Americans came upon the scene. Without prejudice, not loaded down by a false tradition and always ready to help and assist the weaker ones, they go to bat, with enthusiasm and great ability, for the black sheep among the instruments. The composers compose, the soloists interpret and tour. The fight against the unjust neglect of the saxophone has begun.

Eugene Rousseau, as the program notes assure us, is 'one of the most notable concert saxophonists of the USA'. Mark the plural. Is there *one* notable European concert saxophonist? Well, Rousseau really masters his instrument with perfect technique, great musicality and stupendous and alarming breath control. If anyone should be able to establish the saxophone in the concert hall he would be the one. Rousseau and the outstanding pianist Marion Hall certainly have won the battle for the saxophone in Vienna.[55]

Rousseau returned to Europe in 1968, this time with pianist Carl Fuerstner. Another first was added on January 27 at the Salle Gaveau[56] when, according to Marcel Mule, they presented the first saxophone recital in Paris. Included in the audience were Norma Rousseau, Léon Leblanc, clarinetist Henri Druart, and three of the composers represented on the program: Marius Constant, Alfred Desenclos, and Claude Pascal.

The alto saxophone's warm and colorful tone lends itself to certain symphonic works. But can this instrument be heard without weariness in recital? One could doubt it while coming to attend this evening. But the American Eugene Rousseau (who was the pupil of Marcel Mule at the Paris Conservatory) held the attention of his audience with the lone support of a pianist at his side.

It is true that, under the circumstances, the program was short and composed of varied works appealing to the diverse possibilities of the saxophone. Nothing could be more in contrast to the work of Claude Pascal or Alfred Desenclos than the *Musique de Concert* of Marius Constant or the *Concertstück* of Pierre-Max Dubois (very agreeable with its melodic lines which test the voicing of the instrument), or the brilliant *Sonata* of Paul Creston. But, it is also that Eugene Rousseau is a musician, and the *Sonata* of Handel which he transcribed for the

---

[55] Andrea Seebohm, recital review, *Vienna Express* (February 2, 1967): 21.

[56] The thousand-seat concert hall opened in 1907 as part of the home of Gaveau pianos.

saxophone permitted him to display not only his virtuosity but for his art of singing the phrases with great expression. The pianist, Carl Fuerstner, supported the saxophone lines with the solid architecture of his playing.[57]

Rousseau had made great progress toward establishing the saxophone as a classical voice in Europe and in the United States but there still seemed, at this early stage in his tenure at Indiana University, to be some question as to how best his talents could be utilized.

I don't remember the year that I was conducting the wind ensemble, perhaps 1966 or 1967. Dean Bain had called me into his office and said, 'I have a question for you. How many people are there, normally, in a wind ensemble?' I said, 'The Eastman Wind Ensemble — is that it?' 'Yes, yes, that's what I'm talking about.' 'I don't know exactly; it probably varies, I'd say maybe 40 or 42, somewhere in that area.' He nodded his head and handed me a program which read 'Indiana University Wind Ensemble.' He said, 'There are 88 people in that. I want to have two wind ensembles here and I would like you to conduct one.' I thought that was wonderful. The problem was that I was also teaching a full load but I was happy to do that. We were very adventuresome in our programs, I'll say that — Schoenberg Variations, Hindemith Symphony, *La fiesta mexicana* by H. Owen Reed. I didn't realize at the time that he was very unhappy with the Band Department and as that year progressed he told me that he would like me to be Director of Bands. I mentioned it to Jim Neilson,[58] who said, 'If you stop playing now you're not going to begin playing again in 25 years but if you keep playing, you could still conduct in 25 years if you wanted to.' That was a nice way to put it.

Rousseau's concerts as conductor of Indiana University's Concert Band and Wind Ensemble included many of the most important compositions for winds. In addition to the works mentioned above, his programs also included such works as Milhaud's *Suite Française*, the *Trauersinfonie* of Wagner, *Dionysiaques* by Schmitt, and Creston's *Celebration Overture*.

Recordings and performances throughout the United States and Europe were undoubtedly causing people to be more aware of the potentialities of the

---

[57] Recital review, *Journal Musical Français* (January 1968): 12.

[58] Born in Scotland in 1902, Neilson's family moved to Chicago when he was seven years old. Neilson was educated at the Chicago Musical College and the Juilliard Institute of Music. He was Director of Bands at Oklahoma City University from 1936 to 1964 and Educational Director for Leblanc from 1962 until his death in 1985.

saxophone. An opportunity arose at the end of 1968 which offered new possibilities for the advancement of the instrument.

> It was in December of 1968 that I first met Paul Brodie. The occasion was the annual Midwest International Band and Orchestra Clinic, an event that I attended regularly. Paul Brodie was in attendance to present a clinic session, so it was only natural that we spoke about our common interest in and enthusiasm for the saxophone. The meeting coincided with an article that he had written about the need for a world congress of saxophonists, so our conversation led quickly to this subject.
>
> The idea of convening a world meeting involving saxophonists was daunting. 'Would you help me in this undertaking?,' asked Paul. My immediate response was affirmative, but 'Where? When? Who? How?,' I questioned. As we were in the midst of one of the great clinic venues for instrumental music, perhaps the organizers of the Midwest Clinic would consider adding a day to the 1969 schedule for our first meeting. To our delight they agreed. We then made a list of those who should be invited: Cecil Leeson, Marcel Mule, Sigurd Rascher, and Larry Teal were names that headed the list. 'How do we get these people to agree to attend?' was a question we asked each other almost simultaneously.
>
> Paul made a phone call to Sigurd Rascher, telling him that Marcel Mule was planning to attend this auspicious event. I in turn telephoned Marcel Mule, telling him that Sigurd Rascher had agreed to attend. We then made calls to Larry Teal and Cecil Leeson, informing them that both Rascher and Mule were planning to be present. Using these four names as a basis for our organizing plan, it was a relatively simple matter of getting assurances from scores of other saxophonists who would indeed be present for the first World Saxophone Congress.[59]

The one-day event was a tremendous success, attracting more than five hundred persons and far surpassing expectations. There have been fifteen Congresses to date, convening in the United States, Europe, and Asia. The first Congress inaugurated what has become one of its hallmarks — the first performance of new music. Rousseau invited his Indiana University colleague Bernhard Heiden to write a work especially for the occasion. Heiden responded with his *Solo for Alto*

---

[59] Thomas Liley, *A Brief History of the World Saxophone Congress, 1969-2000*. (WSCXIII: University of Minnesota Press, 2003): n.p.

Saxophone and Piano, which concluded the Congress's performances. Rousseau observes:

> As the day unfolded, it was obvious that there was a tremendous enthusiasm. This was something that had been bottled up for a long time. So many of the people wanted to make the saxophone more recognized for its classical potential and there they were, living proof of the support and enthusiasm.[60]

Another "first" was added to Rousseau's achievements in 1971 with the release of the first album devoted to saxophone concertos by a major recording label. Efforts to interest a major company began during his first European tour in 1967.

> I had played in London in 1967 in a recital at Wigmore Hall and the manager for that concert was Basil Douglas, a well-known and reputable manager in London and Europe. Basil and I had talked about the possibility of recording. He was very honest and told me that this project was not going to be easy to do. He said it was very difficult to get a recording company to make a recording of anyone unless there is great name recognition. Nevertheless, he began contacting companies on my behalf. In 1968 I played in London again and Basil told me he had contacted every major recording company and the only one who seemed interested at all was Deutsche Grammophon, and even they were a 'long shot.' He suggested I send them my previous recordings and a letter about myself. I followed his suggestions and didn't hear anything from Deutsche Grammophon at all and I forgot about the entire project. About a year later I received an express mail letter from Deutsche Grammophon proposing a recording for saxophone and orchestra.
>
> From the beginning there were a number of problems associated with putting this project together. The program that was eventually recorded was not the program I had originally proposed. I did not want to do the Ibert *Concertino da Camera* and the Glazounov *Concerto* because there were already several recordings of these works. I had suggested a number of works, including the *Quattro liriche brevi* by Juan Orrego-Salas, an Indiana University composer. However, the people at Deutsche Grammophon, as well as other recording companies, were looking for name recognition and Ibert and Glazounov were familiar to them; to recording executives, name recognition translates into

---

[60] Joel Gronseth, "The World Saxophone Congress and its Impact on the Profession" (M.M. diss, Bowling Green State University, 1996): 98.

sales. In addition to the Glazounov and Ibert, we recorded Villa-Lobos' *Fantasia* and Dubois' *Concerto*. The Villa-Lobos, I must say, had no marks at all on the music. I don't think that particular set of parts had been played by anyone. As we got into it, we realized that the bass part was written an octave too low and we had to take care of that. I'm sure it was the copyist and that it wasn't Villa-Lobos. That was one of the problems and there were some other things, too.

I remember meeting with the conductor, Paul Kuentz, on a weekend and then the following Monday morning I was introduced to his orchestra, the Paul Kuentz Chamber Orchestra. We started recording immediately, doing one piece each day for four days. The orchestra was mostly geared to playing eighteenth-century music. To say the least, it was an enormous adjustment for them to make.

The recording was done in April of 1971 at Notre Dame du Liban in Paris. Rousseau played a Leblanc alto saxophone and, for the Villa-Lobos, a Selmer Mark VI soprano saxophone. He remembers that the venue was chilly ("The hall where we recorded was very cold, which is what no wind player would want.") and that the orchestra often insisted on its own tempos. "The orchestra had not played some of this type of music; for them it was kind of 'stepping out' to do Ibert, for instance." The album was immediately recognized as an important landmark for the saxophone and received high praise from reviewers in the United States and Europe.

> Eugene Rousseau, who is a newcomer to our files, is a virtuoso of quality, combining beautiful tone with a smooth virtuosity devoid of weakness. His performance of works by Ibert, Glazounov, Villa-Lobos, and Dubois bring the saxophone to new heights of respectability.[61]

The British magazine *Gramophone* also praised the performance and added comments about the music as well.

> This is by no means the first time that the saxophone has been taken seriously by a record company, but it is good to be reminded from time to time not only that the instrument is potentially a beautiful one but [and?] that several excellent composers have appreciated the fact. It is a pity that Berlioz, who much admired what he called its '*sérénité magnifique, pour ainsi dire sacerdotale*,' never made a substantial contribution to its literature, for his example might have encouraged

---

[61] Marcel Doisy, record review, *La Revue des Disques* (May 1972): 16.

more composers to listen attentively to its timbre. For many years the classic instance was in Bizet's *L'Arlésienne*; and indeed it is hard to think of a more apt and sensitive use of the saxophone's nasal, plaintive but curiously dignified tone. Of these four concertante works, two spring from France, the country that has most fully responded to the instrument, and the other two are in various ways inspired by French influences.

Ever since jazz composers' discovery of the saxophone's fluency, agility and tonal blend, as well as its particular tonal qualities, the major contributory influence has of course been American. Ibert's *Concertino da Camera* might almost be subtitled, in a return gesture of homage to Gershwin, *A Parisian in America*. Yet it is immaculately Parisian, with a lively opening movement, a very agreeable, bluesy Larghetto and a cheery finale. Ibert belongs to the generation of that particular kind of *insouciant* Parisian smartness in musical manners which could often be trivial but was at its best a brilliant demonstration of the French capacity to civilize and sophisticate the slenderest artistic gesture. The *boulevardier* manner sits more comfortably on his shoulders than on those of Pierre-Max Dubois, who goes through somewhat similar motions — a jokey Allegro after a cadenza, a Lento and a rather self-consciously cheeky finale — but for whom, as a composer born in 1930, all of it has become rather old hat. His best moment is in his Lento, when the strings take up the languid theme and the saxophone lazily decorates it: the idea is not original but it is attractively done. Yet for all the demonstration of smartness and high spirits, there is a distinct note of the skillful pupil (of Milhaud, in fact) going deftly through the motions of his seniors. Dubois is a *Prix de Rome* winner.

Villa-Lobos also makes busy play with jazz rhythms and even more with jazz textures, with his chorus of slowly moving scrunchy chords over with the saxophone discourses. His *Fantasia* was written in 1948, and efficient and typical as it all is, there is little feeling that the ingenious polyrhythms and luxuriant textures cost him very much in the way of compositional effort. Perhaps surprisingly, the best work of the four is Glazounov's *Concerto*. Written and first performed in Paris in 1936, it is a one-movement work that richly exploits the Slav soul which Glazounov detects beneath the saxophone's motley [?]. He writes some beautiful melodies for it, and scores richly for strings without obscuring the solo tone. Only when he comes to the final section does he seem defeated by the task of writing lively music that avoids the merely conventional without moving into the jazz camp.

Eugene Rousseau plays all four works deftly and elegantly. He has a nimble technique and a very suave tone with a nice reediness at its back. Paul Kuentz supports him with bright, brisk playing, and though (especially in Ibert's work) the recording is a little on the reverberant side for my taste in such crisp music, the sound does ample justice to the saxophone's tone.[62]

American critics agreed, as noted in this review:

Classical saxophone discs are another scarce commodity which not only appear seldom, but disappear quickly from the listings. Here is a beauty on a major label, works by four major composers played with consummate artistry and recorded with superb fidelity. Opening with a splendidly constructed showpiece concerto by the contemporary Pierre-Max Dubois, pupil of Darius Milhaud, one is aware of the exquisite tone and technical skill of Eugene Rousseau. The other three works on this well-chosen program continue the impression of this great artist's skill, with varying styles of music from several nationalities. This is the saxophone disc that should never be deleted; it is the best I have ever heard.[63]

The final sentence seems almost prophetic. The recording was re-issued in June of 1997 as a compact disc by Deutsche Grammophon (453-991-2) and by Musical Heritage Society. In addition, the Lento movement of Dubois' *Concerto* has been included on a compilation recording by Deutsche Grammophon.

All of this activity, of course, took place away from Indiana University. Meanwhile, the saxophone studio in Bloomington matured into a highly regarded setting for the development of undergraduate and graduate performers. Invariably, there would be an overload of students who flocked to Indiana to work with Rousseau.

Rousseau gained his first graduate assistant, Jerry Leudders,[64] in 1965, his second year on the IU faculty, and soon had four graduate assistants. Occasionally, he was told by the School of Music administration that financial difficulties would make it necessary to reduce the number of his assistants. He replied that it would then be necessary, because of this loss, for him to restrict the size of the studio to the minimum that was required. Each time, Rousseau's response caused the administration somehow to locate the funding for all of the graduate assistants.

---

[62] Record review, *Gramophone* (August 1972): 19.

[63] E.E. Shupp, Jr., record review, *New Records* (April 1972): 44.

[64] Luedders came to Indiana University from the University of Michigan, where he was a student of Larry Teal. After Indiana he studied at Harvard University and the Paris Conservatory. He is currently Assistant Provost at California State University, Northridge where he also served as Chair of the Department of Music for more than seventeen years.

Indiana University had long attracted foreign students and now saxophone students from around the world were coming to absorb Rousseau's instruction.

The first real interest I had by a foreign student came from Fumiyoshi Maezawa of Japan, I would guess around 1973. There were a number of others who came over the years, some not necessarily full-time students but as Visiting Scholars — Philip Greene of the Edinburgh Academy of Music in Scotland, Richard Ingham and Alan Currie from England, Johannes Kawrza of the Conservatorium für Musik in Klagenfurt, Austria, and Atsuyasu Kitayama from Shizuoka University in Japan. We also had a number of different people, such as Elburn Cooper from Portland, Oregon, who came just to sit in on lessons. Prof. Yushi Ishiwata from the Kunitachi College of Music in Japan spent a whole year there, sitting in on lessons.

It was also around that time that Rousseau began a lengthy and fruitful relationship with Yamaha. Rousseau's years with the Yamaha Corporation date from 1972, when he was named chief consultant for saxophone research and development. Originally associated with the Leblanc Company since 1956, he was introduced to Yamaha executives by Vito Pascucci, the President of Leblanc in the United States. Although perhaps better known to the general public for its motorcycles, outboard engines, and audio/visual equipment, Yamaha was first a musical instrument maker. Torakusu Yamaha founded the company in 1887 to produce reed organs; since then it has become the world's largest manufacturer of a full line of musical instruments. During the 1970s Yamaha made Vito saxophones for Leblanc and sought to expand their market in the United States with their own models.

Yamaha initially contacted Rousseau through Renold Schilke, the renowned trumpet player and manufacturer and a close friend. Schilke arranged a meeting in Chicago between Japanese Yamaha executives and Rousseau. It was decided that Rousseau would go to Japan so both sides could make certain that the arrangement was right. It was the first of more than seventy trips Rousseau would make to Japan; Rousseau has said that he spent two-and-a-half years in Japan, two weeks at a time.

In a very real sense, Rousseau's preparation for his association with Yamaha began in 1960 during his Fulbright study in Paris. He was permitted by President Léon Leblanc to practice at the Leblanc Company every day and it was there he met acoustician Charles Houvenaghel. Houvenaghel (1880–1966) was the leading acoustical authority in Paris and had been involved with the development of clarinets and saxophones for Leblanc and other instrument makers. He designed the E-flat contralto and the BB-flat contrabass clarinets and *Saxophone le Rationnel* for Leblanc. Called the most important innovation to the saxophone in recent years,[65] Houvenaghel's saxophone, invented in 1931, has a mechanism whereby any finger of the right hand lowers the pitch of the left hand one half-step, considerably easing some technical difficulties. After World War I, Georges Leblanc and his son Léon established the first full-time acoustical research laboratory for wind instruments in their Paris workshop. "They recruited the talents of Charles Houvenaghel, regarded at the time as the greatest acoustician since Adolphe Sax."[66] Rousseau and Houvenaghel quickly established a friendship and met almost every day for months. During these meetings, Houvenaghel taught Rousseau the practical aspects of wind acoustics and construction.

> Mr. Houvenaghel was truly a genius in the area of musical instrument acoustics. He was the leading acoustical authority in Paris at that time. He was in his eighties at the time I met him. He had not only been involved with Leblanc and the development of their clarinets and saxophones, but with other instrument makers as well. Here was a man who was not only a great acoustician but was perhaps lonely as well.

> He was very sympathetic to the fact that I was just learning to speak French. We established a very good friendship and I saw him just about every day for months. During that time he would give me lessons on the practical side of instrument construction and acoustics. He would ask me — in French, of course — 'Eugene, can you explain to me why . . .?' and proceed to ask me a question related to the acoustics of the saxophone. I would have to answer, 'No, Mr. Houvenaghel, I cannot.' He would laugh and say, 'Of course you cannot. So I will tell you.' That was his teaching method.

> We would talk about vent keys, emission of tone, various tapers, and many other interesting and important topics related to instrument construction. This was not really something I was going to do anything with, it was just a passing interest at the time. However, it proved to be the foundation for my work with Yamaha because he really got me interested in the acoustical aspect.

> When I made my first trip to Japan I was absolutely fascinated, if not overwhelmed, by what I found. Yamaha's research capabilities were outstanding. I felt the saxophone needed some upgrading and Yamaha had all of the tools necessary to do the job, as well as the determination and enthusiasm. In the saxophone division there were three

---

[65] Wally Horwood, *Adolphe Sax: His Life and Legacy* (Baldock, England: Egon Publishers, 1983): 187–8.

[66] www.gleblanc.com/history/index.cfm

full-time research and development persons; that is a large number for just the saxophone. There were other resources such as tuners, harmonic analyzers, and just about anything else needed to design a fine instrument.

I want to be clear that the connection with Yamaha was through Vito Pascucci. Mr. Kawakami (there were two; this was the senior, who was perhaps sixty years old when I met him) had mentioned to Pascucci that they needed somebody to help with the saxophone. They had Michel Nouaux[67] working with them on the model 61, which I think was their first saxophone that had come to this country. I saw the letter from Vito Pascucci recommending me very highly as a person who could work with them.

In a way, I had an audition at Yamaha when I first visited in 1972. I went there for two or three days and I was asked to play some music with a pianist. Mr. Kawakami was present, of course, and all his assistants and certain workers. It was like playing a recital for a select group of twenty-five to thirty people. 'Play your saxophone... Now play our saxophone, same music.' Mr. Kawakami came up to me and the person he reminded me of immediately was Vito Pascucci. I could see how he and Kawakami would hit it off. Mr. Kawakami was a very atypical Japanese, outgoing, rather flamboyant and expressive, emotional outwardly. The Japanese are very emotional people but they don't always show it outwardly like Westerners. He said, 'When you play your instrument it is beautiful. When you play our instrument it sounds very cheap. We must make good saxophone.' They were determined to do something.

Rousseau's appointment as Yamaha's chief consultant for saxophone research and development was concerned with mechanical, acoustical, and artistic components.

The first area is the mechanical aspect of building a saxophone, including the keys and their function. The key action has to be free and not sluggish. The pads are also a part of this aspect. The second area is acoustical, which takes into consideration the body taper, tone hole placement and calculations, bocal taper, intonation, response, and tone quality. The third and most important aspect is the artistic. It is

---

[67] Born in 1924, Nouaux won a first prize in Mule's class at the Paris Conservatory in 1944. He was soloist with the Garde Républicaine Band and Professor of Saxophone at conservatories in Montreuli and Bobigny. He served as saxophone advisor to Couesnon and Yamaha and succeeded Mule as artistic advisor to Selmer.

very possible to have an instrument that is theoretically correct on paper and seems to be good mechanically but, when the player picks it up, the instrument doesn't feel right. This is a problem because the player must feel that the instrument will offer a viable means of artistic expression.[68]

We've also dealt with problems which were specific to the different-sized saxophones. For example, most baritone saxophone players know that the fourth line D and the top of the staff G-sharp are very sensitive. One octave tube is asked to cover all that. I suggested a double vent tube for the lower part, which is still on the YBS-62, a wonderful instrument. I think it hits a happy medium and it helps both the D and the G-sharp.

Another problem on soprano saxophone is that it's very difficult when overblowing to get a third space C-sharp and the C-sharp above at a reasonable octave; the disparity is pretty great. Most manufacturers use a double tone hole. Selmer, for example, for years had an open C-sharp that is fully open but when one presses the octave key an outside ring closes and there's just a small opening. On many Yamahas, they've eliminated that. Yamaha is still working to improve that, to bring that octave closer together without having the double tone hole, and I think they've come pretty close.

In addition to Rousseau's travels to Japan, his wife was pursuing a long-held interest in Europe. At Rousseau's request she returned with materials which would have a significant impact on the saxophone repertoire.

Norma is not fluent in Czech, although she sounds almost like a native. In fact, when we go to Prague or any place in the Czech Republic or Slovakia she's often asked, 'When did you immigrate to the United States?' Because of her Czech background, she studied Czech at Indiana University. Her major professor there was Hana Beneš. She was married to Vaclav Beneš, the nephew of President Eduard Beneš.[69] He [Vaclav] had to flee the country and became a professor of political science at Indiana. His wife taught courses in Czech and Norma took these classes back in the 1970s and they be

---

[68] Gail Hall, "Eugene Rousseau: His Life and the Saxophone" (DMA diss., University of Oklahoma, 1996): 59.

[69] Eduard Beneš (1884–1943) was forced to resign as President of Czecho-Slovakia following the infamous Munich Pact of 1938. During World War II he led the government-in-exile in London and was re-elected President after the war. Beneš again lost power when the Communists performed a *coup d'état* in 1948.

came very well acquainted. Hana is a good friend who is now well into her nineties but we still stay in touch. Her husband, Professor Beneš, passed away some years ago.

In taking these Czech classes there was an opportunity for students to study intensive Czech in Prague, which was still under the Communist regime. There was little or no cost involved. It was a competitive situation and she applied and was accepted for the four-week course. I took care of our two young children while she was studying at that time. I asked her if she would do some investigation while she was there, to get some recordings or some woodwind solo or chamber music. She came back with quite a few LP recordings and I methodically listened to every one. I thought there was some very nice music but the music of one composer really got my attention — that was the music of Jindřich Feld. I got his address from Antonio de Almeida,[70] a conductor with whom I had worked. He had been to Prague and knew Feld as a very dynamic person. I sent Feld a couple cassettes of my playing and asked him if he would consider writing a piece for me because I liked his music. I got a letter back saying he liked my playing, he would be pleased to write something, and he hoped we could meet. We did meet when I was teaching in Vienna and we took a side trip to Prague. We went to his apartment and he wanted me to play something; he didn't know this instrument. He asked me, 'How high do you play? How is it for this? What is practical? What is not practical?' He was taking notes; extraordinary. The first piece he wrote for saxophone was the Concerto. It began with a double high C; the imagination! That was the beginning.

Several important honors came to Rousseau during that period. In 1979 he was elected the first President of the North American Saxophone Alliance[71] and, in 1982, President of the Comité International de Saxophone.[72] Perhaps the most consequential recognition was his appointment in 1988 by Indiana University as a Distinguished Professor of Music. It is described by the university as "the most prestigious academic appointment it can offer. The rank of distinguished professor honors outstanding scholarship, artistic or literary distinction, or other

---

[70] de Almeida (1917–1995) enjoyed a distinguished international career as a conductor, including several award-winning recordings. He is acknowledged to be the leading authority on the music of Offenbach and his work on behalf of French music gained him the award of the Legion d'honneur. Born in France, he studied with Paul Hindemith at Yale University.

[71] The North American Saxophone Alliance was created in 1976 as a professional organization "to foster the firm establishment of the saxophone as a medium of serious musical expression."

[72] The Comité is responsible for the continued existence of the World Saxophone Congress.

achievements that have won significant recognition by peer." There have been fourteen distinguished professorships in the history of Indiana University's School of Music.[73]

The prior year I was nominated by a colleague, Juan Orrego-Salas, who put together a proposal that was not accepted, for whatever reason. The following year the administration for the School of Music put my name forward and it was accepted.

With the appointment comes access to a small fund every year to enable research activities or creative activities. I think it was about $3000; it was made available to me each year if I wanted to use it and I've taken full advantage of that over the years. I suppose that I could have exceeded that if I had put in a request, whether it was for secretarial help, duplication of materials, or travel. I still am entitled to $1500 a year as a Distinguished Professor Emeritus.

I've viewed the recognition not so much as a reflection on me but on the saxophone — it came to a teacher of saxophone rather than of clarinet or flute. It meant a great deal in that regard because I've always believed in the saxophone. That gave additional recognition and credibility to the instrument.

Through the years, Rousseau has served as guest professor and led master classes around the world at such renowned institutions as the National Conservatory in Paris, and taught a yearly course at the Mozarteum[74] in Salzburg. He was named the first teacher of saxophone at Vienna's Hochschule für Musik[75] in 1981.

I was asked in 1981 to do a three-week course at what was then the Hochschule für Musik in Vienna. I think the idea was they thought that their clarinet players should know something about saxophone, so I had the clarinet players in my saxophone class. One of them was Wenzel Fuchs, now the first clarinet player in the Berlin Philharmonic. The class sessions were interesting. I talked as I would in a class about basics — the fundamentals of the fingering system, how the

---

[73] Martina Arroyo, David Baker, J. Peter Burkholder, George Gaber, Thomas Mathiesen, Susann McDonald, Timothy Noble, Harvey Phillips, Menahem Pressler, Janos Starker, Giogio Tozzi, Violette Verdy, and Virginia Zeani. Eugene Rousseau is the only woodwind faculty member.

[74] Founded in 1916 by Lilly Lehmann, the international summer academy's lecturers have included Luciano Berio, Herbert von Karajan, George Szell, Christa Ludwig, Yehudi Menuhin, and Friedrich Gulda.

[75] One of the largest arts universities in the world, the Hochschule has a long and distinguished history dating from 1808.

embouchure differs from the clarinet, the use of air, and vibrato. They played for me as they played for each other in front of the class. We discussed musical concepts and orchestral excerpts. We discussed solo literature as well and they played not very complicated pieces with piano. Some of them had their own saxophones and some had borrowed saxophones. I was invited back to do that again in 1982.

Ticino Musica is in Lugano, Switzerland. We stayed in Lugano, where I was teaching, while some others were teaching in another area nearby. I had students from Switzerland and from other countries, including Austria and the United States. It's a gorgeous area and we enjoyed it very much.

In 1991 I was asked to present the first saxophone master classes at the Mozarteum Summer Academy in Salzburg and in 2001 I was named an Honorary Professor at the Instituto G. Braga in Italy. It's a conservatory named after a nineteenth-century cellist Braga. He was quite prominent in that area and they named the conservatory after him. It was a bit different from Lugano and Salzburg because here I was working primarily with students of the teacher at that conservatory. There were others as well, including some visitors from Greece, for example. It was a little bit different because the participants weren't as diverse. They were all saxophonists whereas in Vienna I had mostly clarinet players.

I was just the one year [2001] at that particular place but I've been back to Italy. I did a series of classes in Livorno several years ago, not on saxophone, but on the topic of teaching music. 'How do we teach music?' I had a diverse and very nice group of music teachers with excellent questions. I conducted those in English and, because I don't speak Italian, I had a wonderful interpreter. When I'm in Italy, it's usually a combination of English, French (some of the people speak French), and occasionally I throw in a few words of Italian. The students are wonderful because they want to know English and there's usually somebody who recognizes the word and understands what I'm trying to say.

In 1993 following a pair of remarkable performances in Prague, Rousseau was awarded the rank of Honorary Professor at the Prague Conservatory.[76] The first,

---

[76] The Prague Conservatory first offered classes in 1811. Antonin Dvořák was at one time its director and the Conservatory's students include Josef Suk, Rudolf Friml, Franz Lehar, Jan Kubelik, Václav Talich, Karel Ančerl, and Rafael Kubelik.

with the Prague Symphony, took place in October of 1985 and the second, a recital with pianist Leonard Hokanson, was in 1987.

> The appearance of the American saxophonist Eugene Rousseau in the [Jindřich] Feld *Concerto* [written for Rousseau] belonged in the category of the sensational. Rousseau was as good as his reputation as the world-renowned player on this instrument. Feld composed his *Concerto* with maximum imagination, specifically utilizing the melodic, technical and expressive possibilities of the instrument, leading Rousseau to completely exceptional heights of virtuosity. In the soloist's hands the three saxophones (the first and third movements are composed for the alto saxophone, the second movement for the soprano and tenor saxophones) were changed into seldom-heard refined and elegant sonorities in combination with a perfect technical brilliance. Those extremely difficult passages of the solo were voiced absolutely easily and as a matter of course. Rousseau's performance demonstrates an intrinsically spontaneous musicality which is unlearnable, resulting in a musically natural interpretation. Rousseau negotiated the solo parts with such superiority that in places he almost overtook the leading of the accompanying orchestra. In the challenging orchestral score, the orchestra performed on a good artistic level and their work contributed to this successful performance.[77]

The recital of October 1, 1987 was for a sold-out audience in Prague's House of Artists and presented the music of five Czech composers.

> We should like to recall for our readers our experience of a spectacular concert held in Prague on October 12, 1987. In the Small Hall of the House of Artists, saxophonist Eugene Rousseau and pianist Leonard Hokanson from the United States presented a programme consisting, apart from two pieces, entirely of works for the saxophone by contemporary Czech composers. The compositions were by Paul Creston, Paul Hindemith, Alois Haba, Zdeněk Lukáš, Otmar Mácha, Miloslav Kabeláč, and Jindřich Feld. . . . The musicians played to a packed hall and an audience who appreciated the masterful performance, technically brilliant and musically perfect.

> Both artists are known to concert-goers as musicians ranking among the world's best, who have been guests in Prague on several occasions. However, this concert, sponsored by the Music Information

---

[77] Concert review, *Hudební Rozhledy* (October 1985): 43.

Centre of the Czech Music Fund, was something of an exception in its focus on contemporary Czech composers. It served as proof that an instrument such as the saxophone which is rarely heard in our concert halls is capable of sustaining interest in a full-scale recital, and that we have at our disposal a sufficient range of good quality saxophone literature to warrant such a venture.[78]

In 1995 Rousseau was honored by the American Bandmasters Association. He received the Edwin Franko Goldman Memorial Citation, joining such recipients as Vincent Bach, Philip Farkas, Karel Husa, William Ludwig, Sr., Vito Pascucci, and Himie Voxman.[79] A singular honor was awarded on May 31, 1998, when Rousseau was named a Distinguished Alumnus by the University of Iowa, where he had received his doctoral degree in 1962. Other recipients include author John Irving, singer Al Jarreau, composer T.J. Anderson, and, again, Rousseau's mentor Himie Voxman.

Four additional recordings merit special mention. *Saxophone Colors*, released by Delos in 1986, was the first compact disc devoted exclusively to classical saxophone music. The pianist Hans Graf, a professor at the Hochschule für Musik in Vienna, had been a Visiting Professor of Piano at Indiana University in 1970. At that time, he and Rousseau presented several performances, including a television program. It so happened that they would be in Japan at the same time in 1984 and they agreed to perform a recital together as well as make a recording in Yamaha's studio.

> I walked away with the master tapes, not knowing what I would do with them. Some friends who had recorded for Delos urged me to contact the company. I simply wrote them and said, 'I have some tapes, are you interested?' They responded by saying, 'Yes, yes, we're interested!' and they produced the recording shortly after that.[80]

Again, Rousseau's recording was well received.

> Eugene Rousseau is a true master of the instrument (he also directs Yamaha Corporation's saxophone and mouthpiece research and development). Rousseau has designed a program that includes Bach, Debussy, Villa-Lobos, George Gershwin, and a variety of current-day chamber music written specifically for the saxophone. His saxophones

---

[78] Recital review, *Music News from Prague* (October 1987): 16.

[79] Goldman (1878–1956) was solo cornetist in the Metropolitan Opera Orchestra before forming the Goldman Band in 1911. In 1929 he established the American Bandmasters Association, which now awards the Citation for "Distinguished Contributions in the interest of Bands and Band Music in America."

[80] Hall, p. 48.

have a wide variety of timbres and dynamics which are due to the efforts of a gifted musician, as much as the design and quality of the instruments. Hans Graf's piano accompaniment is excellent throughout. Together they render an exquisite Bach *Sonata in E Major*, along with a haunting treatment of the Gershwin medley from *Porgy and Bess*. The alto saxophone is especially effective in Rousseau's treatment of Debussy's *Rhapsody*. The recording quality gets really good marks, showing colors and timbres suggestive of the clarinet and oboe, and really allowing the instrument to 'sing' in the upper registers. Highly recommended.[81]

A second recording, also from Delos, was released in 1995. Rousseau was joined by the Winds of Indiana, comprised of students and faculty at Indiana University and conducted by his long-time friend Frederick Fennell.[82] *Saxophone Vocalise* was the first compact disc completely of music for saxophone and wind ensemble and was also highly praised.

> Eugene Rousseau has pulled out all the stops on this CD. He shows himself to be the veteran artist that he truly is. The combination of compositions and performers on this CD is excellent. The performance rings true to all the artistic creativity that went into the CD's production. Once again, Eugene Rousseau leads the way blazing new hallmarks for the classical saxophone. Do not miss this CD, it is worth its weight in gold.[83]

I met Frederick Fennell in 1957 when I was teaching at Luther College. Fennell was making tremendous tidal waves with the Eastman Wind Ensemble and the wonderful recordings on Mercury. The Iowa Bandmasters invited him out to meet with us and we put a wind ensemble together and he conducted us. He spent some time with us and it was wonderful. That's where I first met him and, subsequently, I saw him from time to time.

Another memorable meeting was about 1962 or 1963. The Minnesota Orchestra was playing in Kansas City and the conductor was

---

[81] Recording review, *Blue Note Journal* (February 1989): 32.

[82] Fennell (1914–2004) is best known for creating the Eastman Wind Ensemble in 1952; their performances and, even more, their recordings changed the history of wind music. Fennell was also principal conductor of the Tokyo Kosei Wind Orchestra, principal guest conductor of the Dallas Wind Symphony, and Professor Emeritus of the University of Miami School of Music.

[83] Recording review, *Saxophone Journal* (May 1996): 75.

Stanislaw Skrowaczewski but the associate conductor was Frederick Fennell. We went to the concert, saw Fennell beforehand in the hotel, and talked with him. I would see him at the Midwest and he always greeted me. I told him that someday I wanted to do a recording; he said that would be fine.

I actually saw him more times in Japan because he quite often conducted the Kosei Wind Ensemble. I would be there and we would have lunch together or would visit. We talked again about this recording possibility and he was in favor of it. I asked him what instrumentation we would need and he told me. Eventually I was able to set that up with Delos and we recorded it in Bloomington with an ensemble of faculty and students. He was eighty years old. I suggested the pieces — he knew some of them, of course, and some he didn't know — and he asked me if there was anything unusual, such as an extraordinary amount of percussion. I asked him about hotel arrangements. I said we have this hotel, that hotel, the Indiana Memorial Union, and you're welcome to stay with us. He said, 'That's what I'd like to do, to stay with you.' He stayed with us and we have some nice memories and some nice photographs. He seemed to particularly like *Kol Nidrei*; he loved that piece and so do I. It's very expressive and especially when one knows the background, a little bit about Bruch and how he grew up, and what Kol Nidrei is.

The year 1997 proved to be especially fruitful, with recordings made in February with the Budapest Strings and in May with the Haydn Trio of Vienna. *The Undowithoutable Instrument*, borrowing Percy Grainger's memorable phrase to describe the soprano saxophone, joined Rousseau with one of Hungary's most distinguished ensembles in a program of music from the Baroque and Classical eras that demonstrated unknown capabilities of the instrument. Rousseau's association with the esteemed Haydn Trio of Vienna dated back nearly thirty years before their collaboration on compact disc. In various combinations, music of Beethoven, Eychenne, Leon Stein, and Rousseau's colleague Juan Orrego-Salas is presented.

Rousseau made his seventieth visit to Japan in 1998 and in October of 1999 the Yamaha Corporation selected Rousseau to inaugurate their *Living Legends* educational video series. In the video, Rousseau discusses his personal and musical history and provides insights to performing, practicing, and teaching. Live performance footage is included as well as conversations with his colleagues and students.

The end to Rousseau's tenure at Indiana came in 2000, following thirty-six years of service. After due consideration, he announced his retirement in March of 2000 to assume a position at the University of Minnesota. One of the events to mark Rousseau's decades at Indiana was an extraordinary program presented by the Indiana saxophone studio entitled "A Musical Tribute to Dr. Eugene Rousseau." The performance was originally to have been a solo recital by Karl Hartman and as the recital began on the evening of May 4 Rousseau still believed it to be just that. According to Hartman,

> I went out on stage and prepared to start the first piece. Another student pretended to get my attention, saying that he had forgotten to distribute the programs. Dr. Thomas Walsh gave one of the real programs to Dr. Rousseau and Mrs. Rousseau. The cat was out of the bag and we were off.[84]

The recital began with an arrangement by Hartman for seventeen saxophones of the *Vienna Philharmonic Fanfare* of Richard Strauss, followed by eight solo performances by Rousseau's students of works strongly associated with Rousseau. Music presented included the final movements of the sonatas by Creston, Heiden, and Feld; the last movement of the concerto by Creston; Rousseau's arrangement of Massenet's *Meditation* from *Thaïs*; the *Caprice en forme de valse* of Bonneau; Bruch's *Kol Nidrei*; and the *Meditation* written by Walter Kaufmann on the occasion of Rousseau's fiftieth birthday in 1982.

Each of the solo performances was stunning. It seemed that each student was saying to Dr. Rousseau, 'This is for you. Thank you for everything you have taught me and done for me. This is what you helped be able to do.'[85]

Hartman, a baritone saxophone specialist, recalled a comment by Rousseau — "You know, before I retire I'd like to hear the first movement of Ibert's *Concertino da Camera* performed in unison by a dozen baritone saxophones." This seemingly off-hand remark made during a lesson was the impetus for the concert finale. Nine, rather than twelve, baritone saxophonists were joined by two pianists to present the famous work. The performance combined many aspects of Rousseau's life and career — his gentle sense of humor, his ability to imagine the saxophone in new ways, his unbounded faith in the instrument, and his dedication to his students and their success as musicians and as persons. He would retain those qualities as he enjoyed a fresh start at the University of Minnesota's School of Music while continuing his worldwide performing, teaching, and recording activities. A third phase of his career was about to begin.

---

[84] Karl Hartman email message to author, August 3, 2008.

[85] Ibid.

10 University of Minnesota (2000–Present): *Wherever I go, I represent the University of Minnesota and the School of Music at the University of Minnesota*

The School of Music at the University of Minnesota traces its beginnings to June of 1902, when Emil Oberhoffer was named director of the new Department of Music; within a year, Oberhoffer was also named conductor of the Minneapolis Symphony Orchestra (now the Minnesota Orchestra). Carlyle Scott assumed the directorship in 1910 and saw the faculty grow from one to thirty. He was followed in 1942 by Paul Oberg, who created the Department of Music Education and in 1966 by Roy Schuessler. Lloyd Ultan became Director in 1975 after serving for thirteen years as Chair of the Music Department at American University in Washington, DC. Ultan hired the first wind faculty, led the transformation to a School of Music, and successfully championed the cause for a new music building. That facility is Ferguson Hall, opened in 1985 and named for Donald Ferguson, who taught music there from 1913 to 1950. Karen Wolff was Director from 1987 to 1992 and Vern Sutton capped his 37-year career at Minnesota by serving as Director from 1992 to 1999. Jeffrey Kimpton, named Director in 1999, oversaw the centennial celebrations and was succeeded by Noel Zahler in 2004 and, following Interim Director Jerry Luckhardt, by David Myers in 2008.

The University of Minnesota has built several arts-related facilities around Ferguson Hall, including those for theater arts, dance, and visual arts and a concert hall, to create the West Bank Arts Quarter. The School of Music now has more than six hundred students and presents more than five hundred performances each year in one of the nation's major metropolitan areas.

Several students who were or who were to have become members of Rousseau's studio at Indiana followed him to Minnesota. Obviously, the studio he had created over thirty-six years in Bloomington did not exist in Minneapolis but his teaching methods, his expectations, and, perhaps most importantly, his warm personality remained unchanged. He set about to build a world-class saxophone studio once more.

> Although I was eligible to retire, I was in no way anticipating my retirement from Indiana.[86] What happened during the thirty-six years I was at Indiana University was that there were two deans and Dean Wilfred Bain had assumed his position seventeen years earlier. Thus, the two deans were in charge for fifty years from 1947 to 1997. If one were to go to any area of study anywhere in the country, I don't think

---

[86] "The Indiana University retirement plan, which was known as 'the 18-20 plan', was an outstanding plan. It was initiated by President Herman B Wells in lieu of being able to give the faculty more salary raises. What it meant was the university would pay all of the retirement money, so I didn't contribute to the retirement fund — Indiana did."

one would find such a situation; it's very unusual. When Dean Charles Webb announced his retirement, there was a search for his successor. I was, in fact, a member of the Search Committee when Dean Webb was appointed. With his retirement forthcoming, a Search Committee was set up and there were a number of candidates, people who wanted to be considered for this position. It came down to three people, one of whom was David Woods, at that time Dean of the College of Fine Arts at the University of Oklahoma. In looking over the dossiers and in talking to people, I was very impressed with David Woods and even wrote a letter to the entire music school faculty supporting him. When the vote was taken, he was the number one candidate. He was offered the position and he declined it. It really would have been for Oklahoma a tremendous loss for him to leave. As I was told — I don't have this factually — even the governor of the state of Oklahoma got involved in this to try to keep David Woods there. Some of us made calls to those we knew at the University of Oklahoma and learned that they were very saddened to think he would leave. So everything pointed to David Woods as the person. I was very pleased when he came in 1997.

In December 2000, Woods resigned as Dean of the IU School of Music. He is now the Dean of the School of Fine Arts at the University of Connecticut.

Prior to that, the University of Minnesota had announced that they had a part-time position available in saxophone. I phoned Jeff Kimpton, who was the Director and is now President of the Interlochen Arts Academy, and told him that I had some fine candidates for this position. He was pleased about that and said to stay in touch with him. After the word came out that David Woods had resigned, Jeff Kimpton called me and said, 'What's going on down there? This man has not even been there three years.' I said, 'I don't want to go into that right now. I'll just say that I'm very unhappy about this.' Jeff laughingly said, 'Does that mean you're now a candidate for the University of Minnesota position?' I said, 'I am.' 'Are you kidding?' I said, 'No.' Jeff responded, 'As this is not a tenure-track position, if you'll write me a letter, the job is yours.'

Rousseau found certain similarities between Indiana University and the University of Minnesota. Both universities are state-supported Big 10 schools and both are highly regarded research institutions. There were clear differences, however, between their schools of music.

The School of Music at Minnesota is not an independent school, as is the case at Indiana. We are part of the College of Liberal Arts here similar to, say, Iowa; we have a Director of the School of Music but not a Dean. More important is the difference in size. The School of Music at Minnesota is about a third the size of the School of Music at Indiana University. Along with the size, whether large or small, come certain advantages or disadvantages. I've served on committees over the years and here I'm not on any committees, which is fine. Also I like the fact that I have a very nice liaison with a number of colleagues — violin, viola, cello, clarinet, voice. I see these people practically every day and I like that. We're all part of the same mission. We work together and know each other. I didn't have quite the same feeling at Indiana because the woodwind department alone was very large. Physically, I was located on another floor away from people and for days on end, I didn't see any faculty; I'd teach and I'd leave. I very much enjoy the collegiality here.

The dynamic of a large city is good. We have two tremendous orchestras — the Minnesota Orchestra, the St. Paul Chamber Orchestra. There are choral groups — Philip Brunelle conducting VocalEssence and Dale Worland, who just recently retired — that are part of a tremendous choral tradition here. Minneapolis has all sorts of cultural activities, at least three art museums, and visiting artists groups coming through; it's a different dynamic. When you have a larger population and more activities. . . Let me give an example. When I was at Indiana, I invited the Zagreb Saxophone Quartet,[87] one of the world's finest saxophone quartets, and I reserved Auer Hall. I don't remember counting the people but I suppose we might have had twenty-five or thirty people in the audience. When the Quartet came here for the first time in our recital hall, we had standing room only. We had elements from the Croatian community who came simply because it said 'Zagreb'. We had other interested people — amateur saxophonists who came to see what this was about, some band directors who came and brought their students. Because there is a larger populace here, certain things are possible.

Whereas the saxophone studio at Indiana was highly regarded internationally and had been a force in the saxophone world for decades, the studio at Minnesota had been nearly dormant since the departure of Ruben Haugen. One of the most

---

[87] The Zagreb Saxophone Quartet was founded in 1989 by Dragan Sremec, Goran Morčep, Saša Nestorović, and Matjaž Drevenšek, all former members of the class of Josip Nochta at the University of Zagreb Academy of Music. They have performed throughout Europe and North America and have recorded extensively.

revered woodwind teachers in the state, Haugen has taught thousands of students over several decades at the University of Minnesota, St. Olaf College, the MacPhail College of Music, and the University of St. Thomas, where he continues to teach. His students include saxophonist and composer Mark Engebretson and Angela Wyatt, who is a member of Minneapolis-based professional Ancia Saxophone Quartet.[88] "Rousseau's arrival instantly marked the University of Minnesota as a prestigious institution at which to study saxophone."[89]

> The studio as I came in was fine, with very nice students, but none whom I had auditioned. I had a studio and some good kids and we got along well. Of course, we began the audition process and some very talented people have come here. It has been a happy challenge. Now, all the students here have had a hand in bringing the saxophone studio into being. My responsibilities are to teach the saxophone but beyond that I feel like I'm an ambassador because I travel so much. Wherever I go, I represent the University of Minnesota and the School of Music at the University of Minnesota. There is in my formal agreement with the University a certain number of students in my studio each semester, but I have the option to accept a larger number. And, of course, I also coach at least one quartet, as the quartet provides an excellent opportunity for improving all aspects of performance, in addition to the experience of learning how to work together. The administration at the University of Minnesota is very supportive of the School of Music, and the School of Music is very supportive of my work. Jeffrey Kimpton, President of the Interlochen Arts Academy, was Director of the University of Minnesota School of Music when I began teaching there in 2000. Noel Zahler, Head of the School of Music at Carnegie Mellon University, succeeded Kimpton. Jerry Luckhardt was Interim Director for one year before the current Director, David Myers, began his tenure. I am very pleased to say that my working relationship with all four of these men has been a real pleasure.

Rousseau continued his extensive international performances and recordings. He had begun in March 2000 to record a compact disc in Croatia with the Zagreb Saxophone Quartet. The quartet's soprano saxophonist, Dragan Sremec, received a Fulbright Grant to study with Rousseau in 1991, much as Rousseau had studied with Mule thirty years earlier. The disc, *Tsunagari*, was released in 2002.

---

[88] Founded in 1990, the Ancia Saxophone Quartet has performed concerts and educational workshops throughout the United States and in Canada and Europe. Its members are Matthew Sintchak, Joan Hutton, David Milne, and Angela Wyatt.

[89] Anna Marie Wytko email message to author, August 31, 2008.

A more recent recording was made in June 2005 in Budapest with the New Budapest String Quartet[90] and released in 2007. Recognizing the absence of music of the Classic and Romantic periods from the saxophone repertoire, Rousseau chose the Mozart and Brahms clarinet quintets. A similar project, newly released, is a recording of the two opus 120 sonatas of Brahms and his Trio in A minor, op. 114. Rousseau recorded the sonatas with pianist Jaromír Klepáč in Prague on May 30 and 31, 2009, and returned later with cellist Michal Kaňka to complete the compact disc with the trio.

Rousseau was in Belgium for yet another recording in March 2002, his second year at Minnesota, when his plans to again establish a saxophone studio of worldwide influence met with an unexpected and potentially devastating hurdle.

It was in the spring of 2002 and I had just recorded a compact disc with the Belgian Air Force Band. While there in Brussels, going from the studio back to the motel, I was on the train and my saxophone was stolen. In the middle of this recording session I had to get a new instrument from Yamaha, which they kindly loaned to me to finish the recording. It may have been a combination of that — I seemed to take it in stride but Norma thought it had a very stressful effect — and, of course, the recording itself.

On the way back as we were flying to the U.S., I just didn't feel well; Norma was going on to Indianapolis and then to Bloomington and I to Minneapolis. At that point we were still living with our daughter Lisa-Marie and her family before we purchased a home in Minneapolis. My wife said to be sure to go to PromptCare, our health provider, for some medical attention, which I did. I was examined and was told that I probably had some virus or a bacterial infection. In any event, I was given some medication and I returned to my daughter's home.

I remember coming into the house and saying, 'You know, I just don't feel well. I just want to go to bed.' I woke up in the middle of the night and when I stood up I fell down; I couldn't use my right leg. I crawled back to the bed and in the morning, when my daughter got up, I tried to go out to the kitchen and fell down again. I must have fallen down at least a half dozen times. I said, 'I need to go back to PromptCare.' 'No,' she said, 'I'm taking you to Abbott Northwestern Hospital.' I fell down again on the way. She got a wheelchair and wheeled me into the Emergency Room.

---

[90] The New Budapest String Quartet was founded in 1971 by graduates of the Liszt Ferenc Academy in Budapest, where all are now faculty members. They have performed across Europe, the Americas, Asia, Africa, and Australia. Members are violinists Béla Bánfalvi and Ferenc Balogh, violist László Bársony, and cellist Károly Botvay.

I know that the doctor's initial thought was 'stroke' but after preliminary examination he said to me, 'Sir, we do not think you've had a stroke but we're having a neurologist come in.' The neurologist told me that I would be there a while, obviously, and they had to do some tests. I was in the hospital for six nights during which time it was determined that I had Guillain Barré syndrome,[91] which basically is caused when a virus attacks the nervous system. It could affect any area — a leg, arm, or respiratory system. In my case, it was just the right leg. It was very strange to be in a hospital and not be able to use my leg. I remember in the middle of one night I rang for the nurse and she came and said, 'Yes, may I help you?' I said, 'Would you put my right leg back in bed, please?' You know it's there but you can't move it; it's an attention-getter. But by about the fourth day I could start to move it just a little bit and then I tried moving it up and down and I could start to get a little motion. They allowed me to walk, although I had to have either someone with me or a walker. I would go down the hall and back a few times. When I left they said, 'You'll need about six weeks of therapy.' I went to the therapist, where I was told 'Do this. Put your leg here. Bend there. You don't need us. You can do these exercises at home; you'll be fine.' The doctor said it was a miracle that I ever snapped back and was probably due to the fact that I was in pretty good physical condition. I've always walked a lot and they thought that helped. It took some days to get the strength back in my leg so that it could fully function again. One of the neurologists explained the possibility of a recurrence this way — he said it would be as though, if you had a certain point where lightning struck, what would be the chances that lightning would strike again, exactly there? I had been told that a year of therapy would not be out of the question. I've known some people for whom this virus attacked the upper respiratory system and they had to be on ventilators, so I was fortunate. Also, I am so grateful for the care that I got at that hospital. Their doctors were absolutely first-rate and so we make a contribution to Abbott Northwestern Hospital[92] every year.

---

[91] According to the Mayo Clinic, Guillain Barré syndrome (GBS) is an inflammatory disorder in which the body's immune system attacks the nerves outside the brain and spinal cord. Although the cause is unknown, research indicates that it may destroy the protective covering of the peripheral nerves, preventing the nerves from transmitting signals to the muscles. The nerve itself may become affected and die, causing permanent damage and disability. Because it can progress rapidly, early treatment is important. Some now believe that President Franklin D. Roosevelt was affected by GBS rather than poliomyelitis.

[92] Abbott Northwestern Hospital dates from 1882, when Northwestern Hospital was created, and 1902, when Abbott Hospital for Women was established; the two were combined in 1970. The hospital is allied with the Sister Kenny Institute, named for the innovative treatments for poliomyelitis by Sister Elizabeth Kenny.

Rousseau's recovery was complete and he moved ahead vigorously with his plans for World Saxophone Congress XIII, scheduled for July 9–13, 2003 at the University of Minnesota. He selected several of his friends and former students to serve as an Organizing Committee of which he was President.

> I had hoped to have an earlier Congress which turned out to be somewhere else. I made a proposal at the meeting in Tokyo at the 1988 Congress that, if we did the one in 1991 in Italy, I would like also at the same time to vote for one in 1994 at Bloomington. My thought was that would be the twenty-fifth anniversary of the Saxophone Congress, which I co-founded with Paul Brodie in 1969. I don't remember why that didn't work,[93] but as soon as I came to the University of Minnesota, I thought Minneapolis would be ideal — the musicians, the venue, and so on.
>
> I arrived here in the fall, the first semester of 2000–2001. One of the main reasons I came was Jeffrey Kimpton, the Director of the School. Jeff and I had worked together when he was Educational Director for Yamaha, so I was well aware of his energy and vision. When I knew he was the Director here it was an easy decision to come to Minnesota, as I wanted to leave Indiana at that time. When I presented the idea of hosting a World Saxophone Congress to Jeff, there was no hesitation. 'Of course, we'll do it. What do you need?' I said, 'We need a letter. Here's a letter I've composed. You may change it but it should come from you, as you're the Director. When we get the proposal formulated, it must be translated in French so that in Montréal, which is bilingual, it can be presented in both languages.'[94]

Many long-time Congress observers were impressed by the extraordinarily high artistic level of the performances. Among the principal factors were the ensembles which supported the soloists. The Royal Belgian Air Force Band, conducted by Sr. Captain Alain Crepin,[95] and the World Saxophone Congress

---

[93] World Saxophone Congress X took place in Pesaro, Italy in 1992. Because of various difficulties, World Saxophone Congress XI was not held until 1997 in Valencia, Spain.

[94] Montréal was the site of World Saxophone Congress XII in 2000.

[95] Born in 1954 in Mettet, Belgium, Crepin studied saxophone, cello, and piano at the Music Academy of Dinant. He graduated from the Royal Conservatory of Brussels, obtaining the Superior Diplomas in saxophone as a student of François Daneels and in chamber music. Crepin has taught saxophone at the Royal Conservatory since 1981 and has been Music Director of the Royal Belgian Air Force Band since 1984. In 2005 he was appointed artistic director of all the bands in the Belgian Army.

Orchestra, conducted by Glen Cortese,[96] alternated the four evening concerts, presenting a total of twenty-one concertos and other works with soloists and quartet.

It was my idea for the Belgian Air Force Band to come over for the Congress but I never imagined it would happen. There were a couple of factors here. As things progress, we very often cannot provide documentation so I'll speculate about what I think happened, not necessarily in order of sequence.

I was invited to be soloist with the Belgian Air Force Band and we played several concerts, one which was in the Flemish section of Belgium before a packed house. Norma was with me and was given a complimentary ticket. After the concert I met her at a very pleasant reception in the lobby. I asked where she had been seated and she said, 'I was right in the center. It was wonderful and there was a very nice gentleman sitting next to me and we had a nice conversation. I'm sorry I don't remember his name but he was wearing a uniform. He is an officer in the Air Force and he's the gentleman talking to Alain Crepin right now.' It was the commanding general of the Belgian Air Force, who is such a fine gentleman. It's my feeling that was the beginning of a kind of rapport.

I had said to Alain at some point, 'You have such a good group it's a pity we can't bring them over for the Saxophone Congress.' He said, 'Maybe we can.' I sent a formal letter of invitation and the Belgian government accepted it. I'm sure it cost them at least $100,000 to send the band over. They had the music well in advance and were very well prepared for the Congress.

I was so proud of the World Saxophone Congress Orchestra. They were a pick-up orchestra made of musicians from the Twin Cities area having never played together as this group. They played ten different concertos with their first rehearsal Monday morning of that week. I don't think there was one person in the orchestra who had played any one of these pieces before.

Many of Rousseau's friends and former students came to Minneapolis to attend the Congress. Unknown to him, many of those same people had joined together

---

[96] Cortese is currently the Music Director of the Greeley, Colorado, Philharmonic Orchestra and Artistic Director of the Oregon Mozart Players and the New York Chamber Sinfonia. He holds the Doctor of Musical Arts degree from the Manhattan School of Music, where he was on the conducting faculty from 1982 to 2000. In addition, Cortese has won several prestigious composition awards, including the Charles Ives Scholarship from the American Academy of Arts and Letters.

earlier in the year to honor him through the commission of a work for saxophone and orchestra by the well-known composer Libby Larsen,[97] who eagerly accepted the invitation.

> I was delighted and overwhelmed by this gift. The announcement of the commission was made at the Congress, at a so-called 'photo session' with former students which turned out to be something else, although we did take some photos. That was a very memorable moment. The piece, the *Song Concerto*, became a reality a little less than three years later. I'm happy with the piece and I'm happy that I got to meet and to know Libby Larsen, a lovely lady. I've played the piece twice now and I look forward to playing it many more times.

Larsen's *Song Concerto* received its first performance by Rousseau and the University of Iowa Orchestra, conducted by William LaRue Jones, as the opening event of the North American Saxophone Alliance Biennial Convention in Iowa City, February 15, 2006. This premiere was followed closely by the first performance of another work for Rousseau by a major composer. *Lamentations (pour la fin du monde)* by Claude Baker[98] was presented in Ljubljana, Slovenia on July 5, 2006, as part of the Fourteenth World Saxophone Congress; the Slovenian Philharmonic was conducted by David Itkin.

> *Lamentations* is also a lovely work and a very unique orchestration. Claude Baker did a wonderful job of utilizing the possibilities within the orchestra for different colors. I like this work very much. It's unique in my career to have presented premieres of works by two major composers within a period of six months. In fact, to have one commission in one year is significant.

In the fall of 2001, Rousseau inaugurated an annual series of International Saxophone Master Classes at the University of Minnesota. A relatively small number of persons were selected to perform for Rousseau not once but twice during the classes. In addition, saxophonists from around the world are invited to

---

[97] Born in 1950, Larsen is one of America's most prolific and most performed living composers. She has created a catalogue of more than 200 works spanning virtually every genre from intimate vocal and chamber music to massive orchestral and choral scores. Her music has been praised for its dynamic, deeply inspired, and vigorous contemporary American spirit. Constantly sought after for commissions and premieres by major artists, ensembles, and orchestras around the world, Larsen has established a permanent place for her works in the concert repertory.

[98] Baker (b. 1948) received his doctoral degree from the Eastman School of Music, where his principal composition teachers were Samuel Adler and Warren Benson. As a composer, Baker has gained a number of professional honors, including an Academy Award in Music from the American Academy of Arts and Letters; two Kennedy Center Friedheim Awards; the Eastman-Leonard and George Eastman Prizes; and a "Manuel de Falla" Prize (Madrid). Baker is currently a Professor of Composition in the Jacobs School of Music at Indiana University.

perform and speak on a broad variety of saxophone topics. Some participants liken it to an annual miniature World Saxophone Congress.

We try to do a master class here every year. The goal is to bring together people who are interested in the saxophone as a medium of musical expression. Whether they're jazz players or classical players, they have a real deep interest in the instrument and the music. I want to bring them together to present different facets of study. For example, Thomas Liley's comparison of Marcel Mule and Sigurd Rascher, their lives and their performances; to have George Wolfe talk, as he did one year, about certain improvisational approaches; Victor Morosco talked about his experiences from his perspective as a seasoned professional, retired now but one who played so many wonderful performances through the years; the Zagreb Quartet; Claude Delangle; Julia Nolan and David Branter, and so on. The participants get different perspectives. While I was at Indiana we had Iwan Roth, Daniel Deffayet, Joseph Wytko, Larry Teal, and Sigurd Rascher, among others, come in for classes.

I want to have only a few people in the master classes as performers so no one is lost in the crowd. I have about five performers so that each student who is a participant can play twice in front of the group. I think it gives a good opportunity to go away with a feeling that one has learned something or feels motivated to do more. I remember many times when I've been asked to do a master class where the student will play and then say to me afterward, 'I wish I had one more chance; I wish I could play again for you.' He or she cannot because the schedule moves along. Here, that second chance lets whatever was learned the first time sink in a bit more.

Another important aspect of Minneapolis is its proximity to Shell Lake, Wisconsin. The Indianhead Arts Center, now the Shell Lake Arts Center, began in 1968 through the efforts of local band director Darrell Aderman as a camp for young musicians to develop their jazz skills. His partner in this undertaking was Jim Christensen, who did not have the opportunity to work in Shell Lake, as he soon assumed the position of Music Director for Disneyland. The Center's program has expanded to provide workshops for students and adults in the visual arts as well and has attracted students from forty-nine states and fifteen countries. Music workshops include study in vocal and instrumental jazz ensembles, concert band, and orchestra and music education workshops such as Latin percussion techniques, marching band techniques, conducting, and electronic music. Individual instrument workshops are offered for guitar, trumpet, and, of course, saxophone. Rousseau began teaching saxophone in Shell Lake at the Jazz Ensemble and Combo Clinic in 1970.

Tom Slattery is a good musician and was a good band director in Sigourney, Iowa, where he had me as soloist with his band. I liked Tom; he had a lot of energy. He was later connected with Shell Lake, working with their stage band, as they were called in the 1960s. In 1969 Tom phoned me and said, 'I've been invited to go to Shell Lake again next summer but I can't because of a commitment. I recommended you but the director would like to meet with you and talk with you.' The director, Darrell Aderman, called me. Darrell was leaving Shell Lake to drive back to his home. I said, 'We're in Wisconsin. I'm not sure exactly where you're headed but we will be in Wabeno, Wisconsin.' He said, 'That's on our way. I was born in Niagra.' We met in downtown Wabeno and drove to my aunt and uncle's place, where we had a nice discussion. He had his whole family, all four children and his wife. It was the beginning not only of a professional relationship but a friendship. He invited me to be a regular member of the faculty but that was a little touchy for me because my understanding was that I was just replacing Tom for that year. I called Tom and he said, 'Go for it.' He was very nice about it.

Because at that time few method books existed for young or inexperienced students, Rousseau wrote a theory book to meet this need. He later wrote a similar book on improvisation. The Saxophone Workshop was initiated in 1972 and by the second year additional staff was required. Distinguished saxophonists have been in residence as a part of Rousseau's workshops, including Larry Teal (1973), Frederick Hemke (1974), and Paul Brodie (1978). In addition, important guests have included Charles Webb, Dean of Indiana University's School of Music; Heinz Medjimorec, pianist with the Haydn Trio of Vienna; and composer Jindřich Feld. Rousseau also brought to Shell Lake experts in the development and manufacture of mouthpieces, such as Elmer Aiello and Abe Wollam, and master repairmen such as Roy Markle and Dick Rees.

The Saxophone Workshops usually begin with a recital presented by Rousseau on Sunday evening. Class sessions begin the next morning, covering a wide variety of topics and offering individual and group performing opportunities. Solo performers are provided with a professional pianist and receive coaching privately and in front of the class. Student soloists, duets, trios, and quartets perform in a concert Thursday evening which concludes with a large saxophone ensemble. A final session is held Friday morning.

We've returned over the years. We like the area very much, I think partly because my father and his brothers and sisters grew up in the upper peninsula of Michigan and northern Wisconsin. From a boy I always felt comfortable in that part of the country — it's more open with lakes and trees. That was part of the attraction. Another part was the wonderful people — not only the Adermans but the medical doctors in the community, the cranberry growers, the business people, and the neighbors where we stayed. It was a pleasure to go up there for eight or nine weeks in the summer. Then, in 1971, our son, who was allergic and asthmatic and also had a congenital heart defect, had heart surgery at the Mayo Clinic. That was another factor because Shell Lake is not far from Rochester, Minnesota, and if there was ever a problem we could get there fairly quickly. Also, I liked the idea of being able to teach in an environment where we solely concentrated on that goal. We had a director who was very supportive and we had a community that was supportive. It made an ideal situation.

In the years since 1970, when Rousseau first came to Shell Lake, he has worked with the Jazz Ensemble and Combo Clinics, the Woodwind Workshop, the Saxophone Workshop, and as Associate Director. He and Norma remain close personal friends with Darrell and Billie Aderman.

Another thread which runs throughout Rousseau's career is his interest in improving "the tools of the trade." In addition to his twenty years as Chief Consultant for Saxophone Research and Development with the Yamaha Corporation, Rousseau has invested time and energy to improve mouthpieces and reeds and to make available saxophone music and recordings. As part of Rousseau Music Products, he has developed an extensive line of mouthpieces for classical and jazz performers.

The person who influenced me most on mouthpieces was the late Bernard Portnoy.[99] We had worked together at the Cumberland Forest Music Camp in Moorhead, Kentucky, in the summer of 1966. The band director in charge was Robert Hawkins, who had been at the Gunnison Music Camp in Colorado. He and some others wanted to revive that atmosphere and environment and that's where I met Bernard Portnoy. I liked him right away and we hit it off. He was freelancing in New York but had been solo clarinet with the Philadelphia Orchestra (I think he was 21 years old when he took that job) and then with Szell in Cleveland and then went back to New York and was very much in demand as a teacher and a player. When we had a clarinet

---

[99] Portnoy (1914–2006) taught at the Juilliard School of Music and the Curtis Institute of Music; he later joined the Indiana University faculty. He was solo clarinetist with the Philadelphia and Cleveland Orchestras and his mouthpieces remain a popular choice for clarinetists.

opening at Indiana, I thought of Portnoy and he came to Indiana, probably in 1969, maybe earlier. He was already making mouthpieces when I met him in Moorhead. We talked and he told me of his experiences, how he started, and what he did. I was pretty intrigued by this and he encouraged me to do something, so I started working with mouthpieces.

While on sabbatical leave in Shell Lake in 1982, Rousseau established Étoile Music. The new enterprise first published his own arrangements of music by Chopin, Debussy, and Platti and, later, Brahms, Haydn, Massenet, Rachmaninoff, and several collections. He added the Larry Teal Collection (including Teal's *Daily Studies for the Improvement of the Saxophone Technique*, *Melodies for the Young Saxophonist*, and his arrangements of composers such as Saint-Saëns), the Michael G. Cunningham Series of original works and transcriptions, and the Robert Sibbing Series. Étoile was absorbed by MMB Music, Inc. of St. Louis in 1987.

Similar to the publication of music, it's difficult to get a recording produced because there is so little money in this for the producer. There is a great disparity in sales between pop and rock as opposed to classical music. Take that small percentage which is classical and what percent is classical saxophone? It's miniscule. I thought maybe we could do our own recordings.

It happened that after I played a recital in Tokyo, a couple came backstage with their teen-aged son. He must have been fifteen years old, fascinated with saxophone, and so pleased. His father worked for Polaroid in Japan and spoke English; the young man didn't speak much English at all. A year or so later, this teen-aged boy came to Shell Lake and a little bit after that he enrolled at Indiana — that was Hideki Isoda. While he was a good saxophone player, his real forte was in electronics and everything connected with that. I could see that, with his energy and ambition and motivation, together we could do some recording. He came up with the name of 'RIAX' when we started the company in 1997.

Rousseau has issued four compact discs on RIAX. Other saxophonists who have recorded for RIAX include Otis Murphy, Kenneth Tse, and Thomas Walsh. The company also has recordings by several Indiana faculty members and has expanded into video productions, winning numerous awards.

In the same way that Rousseau perceived a need for saxophonists to make recordings, he saw that Bloomington did not have a music store to meet the needs of the students and faculty at Indiana University's huge School of Music. As he had with Hideki Isoda, he met and found possibilities within another young person.

It happened that one of my students, Leichen Bjorkman, introduced me to her husband-to-be, Dean Foster, and I could see he was a natural for this enterprise. He had energy and drive and motivation. I suggested to him the possibility of filling this void because he wanted to do something in business; he really had a business orientation. I told him about a place for rent right across from the School of Music. I came up with the name Pro Winds and together we established this. One of our connections was that, whereas he had the business drive, he didn't know the people in the music industry. I could call Alan Fox at Fox Bassoons or I could call whomever — Conn or Leblanc — to try to get the franchise. I was not involved in the sense that I worked in the store but after two or three years he purchased my share.

Reeds have been yet another concern for Rousseau, as they are for most saxophonists. He has made several attempts to develop a reed which will provide reliable artistic results.

I've started and abandoned the idea at least twice because I felt things were not consistent enough. The first time was with Glotin because I knew Mr. Albert Glotin personally from France; that didn't work as well I had hoped. The second time is a little more complex to explain. Mr. Mule had used reeds called 'My Masterpiece' which were made by Mario Maccaferri[100] in New York. Mr. Maccaferri had passed away but I went out there to meet his widow and go through their factory. It was fascinating and I found out that Mr. Maccaferri had grown bored with making reeds and wanted to do other things, such as make a violin out of synthetic material. He didn't pay that much attention to or do that much promotion with reeds but was visited by another company that was very interested in reeds and took over many of his ideas, machinery, and concepts. That company was Rico. Again, consistency was a problem.

---

[100] Maccaferri (1900–1993) was a most interesting person. Born in Italy, at the age of eleven he became apprenticed to the master luthier Luigi Mozzani. Mozzani regarded Maccaferri as a master luthier, an honor he never gave any of his other apprentices. Maccaferri also became an expert classical guitarist, settling in London in 1929. He used his knowledge of luthiere to create guitars, was introduced to Henri Selmer, and patented the Selmer Maccaferri guitar. He came to the United States to escape World War II and established his "French-American Reed Manufacturing Company." Because the primary source of cane for reeds was interrupted by the war, Maccaferri developed a plastic reed. He also created plastic guitars and ukuleles and at the time of his death was developing a plastic violin.

Rousseau received a singular tribute from his students in 2008. Steven Stusek, who earned undergraduate and doctoral degrees with Rousseau at Indiana and is now a professor at the University of North Carolina-Greensboro, conceived "The Rousseau Celebration." The event, to celebrate Rousseau's seventy-sixth birthday, occurred in Greensboro October 3 through 5. Nearly a hundred of Rousseau's students gathered to hear about his life, view photographs, perform music, share stories, and renew friendships encompassing several decades. Former students, many of them now successful college teachers, presented works associated with Rousseau. Some of the music — such as compositions by Creston, Bonneau, Gershwin, Villa-Lobos, and Ibert — has been recorded by Rousseau. Other pieces were arranged by him, including works by Platti and Handel, and still other pieces which were written for him by Feld, Heiden, and Fox. Kenneth Tse gave the world premiere of *Ductus figuratus* by Kirk O'Riordan, composed especially for the Celebration, and Rousseau performed with the UNCG Jazz Ensemble and with piano, woodwind quintet, and band. In addition to his performances, perhaps most memorable were the master classes by Rousseau and the Saxophone Orchestra which he conducted, reminders of his consummate musicianship and insightful teaching. As he nears his seventh decade of performing and teaching, his enthusiasm for students and his commitment to the saxophone are undimmed.

There is a single theme which winds through Rousseau's life and career — his unwavering belief in the saxophone as a vehicle for musical expression. The path of a youngster beguiled by the sound of a young neighbor practicing on a back porch in Blue Island, Illinois, to a renowned concert artist who has played in major halls throughout the world is a continuous one. There has been one goal — to better establish the saxophone as an instrument worthy of composers' best creations and performers' best efforts. To this end, Rousseau has made numerous recordings (including the first complete album of saxophone concertos, the first classical saxophone compact disc, and the first compact disc devoted exclusively to music for saxophone and wind ensemble), performed uncounted concerts (including the first saxophone recitals in New York City's Carnegie Hall, London, Paris, Vienna, Berlin, Amsterdam, and Hong Kong), presented master classes around the world, and created equipment to enhance saxophone performance (including mouthpieces, reeds, and his service as chief consultant for saxophone research and development with Yamaha). He has accomplished all of this with grace, kindness, and good humor, still continuing on the path he has chosen because *on n'arrive jamais* — "one never arrives."

2229 W. Market Street, Blue Island, Illinois, Rousseau's childhood home, as it is today.

Joseph and Laura Rousseau, 1938.

Rousseau with his Rudy Wiedoeft model saxophone, 1942.

High school senior, 1949.

The Gene Rousseau Trio, 1951.
Rousseau, Arthur (Benny) Burmeister,
Paul Jankowski.

Meeting Jimmy Dorsey, 1952.

25th Division Dance Band, Hawaii, 1956.

Chicago Musical College, 1953.

Paris, 1960. Back row: Vito Pascucci (President of Leblanc USA), Léon Leblanc (President of Leblanc France). Front row: Rousseau, Daniel Bonade, Norma Rousseau.

With Marcel Mule in his apartment, Paris, 1961.

Band Director at Central Missouri State College, 1963.

Eugene Rousseau, one of the world's great saxophonists, is a member of the faculty of the School of Music of Indiana University where he teaches his instrument and serves as Chairman of the Woodwind Department. In addition to his interest in teaching, he has published numerous articles on music and art, editions and arrangements of music, and method books for the saxophone. He also presents numerous clinics and lecture-recitals, and is called upon frequently for solo appearances with orchestra or band. During the summers Mr. Rousseau is a faculty member of the Indianhead Arts Camp, Shell Lake, Wisconsin.

Mr. Rousseau has had performing engagements in most of the world's major cities and in virtually all of the United States—including Alaska and Hawaii. Outside the U.S. he has been engaged in Canada, England, France, Germany, Holland, Austria, New Zealand, Australia, and Africa. His solo appearances also include the National MENC, ASBDA, CBDNA, ABA, Mid-West National Band Clinic, All-South Band Clinic, the Midwestern Music and Art Camp at the University of Kansas, The Midwestern Conference on School Music at the University of Michigan, and numerous other state and regional conventions. His professional experience encompasses all types of engagements, including the Woody Herman "Third Herd" and the Gordon MacRae Show.

In 1968 he made his second concert tour of Europe where he was featured soloist with the BBC Orchestra in London, and was the first saxophonist ever to present a full recital in Paris. He records regularly for the Coronet Recording Company, and recently achieved the distinction of being the first concert saxophonist to record an entire album with orchestra, having collaborated in Paris with the Chamber Orchestra of Paul Kuentz for Deutsche Grammophon.

Rousseau began his study of the saxophone at the age of nine under the tutelage of Elda Jansen Bengston. He later studied with Horace Frederick, and Sam Meron and Albert Freedman at the Chicago Musical College, while completing the B.M.E. degree, and did additional study in jazz with Joe Daley. He holds the M.M. degree from Northwestern University, where he studied oboe with Robert Mayer, and the Ph.D. from the University of Iowa, where he studied clarinet and woodwind literature under Himie Voxman. While at Iowa he was awarded a Fulbright Grant enabling him to study saxophone at the Paris Conservatory with Marcel Mule. In 1963 he was appointed musical representative for the United States Trade Fair in Conakry, Guinea, West Africa.

Publicity photo, 1970s.

Frederick Fennell, Frederick Hemke, Cecil Leeson, Donald Sinta, Rousseau, Warren Benson, Sigurd Rascher; Midwest Clinic, Chicago, probably 1970s.

Shell Lake Saxophone Workshop, ca. 1972.

With Joseph Rezits, Shell Lake, ca. 1973.

With Marcel Mule in Sanary, France, July 1974.

With Larry Teal and Mary Teal; World Saxophone Congress, Bordeaux, 1974.

With Heinz Medjimorec, World Saxophone Congress, Bordeaux, 1974.

With musicologist Willi Apel; Rousseau home in Bloomington, 1975.

Marcel and Polette Mule, 1976.

Buddy DeFranco, Renold Schilke, Rousseau, 1977.

With composers Harvey Sollberger and Toru Takemitsu; Rousseau home in Bloomington, 1987.

Publicity photo, ca. 1989.

Premiere of Juan Orrego-Salas' Partita, Heinz Medjimorec, Walther Schulz, Michael Schnitzer, Michael Bennett (Vice-President of Yamaha), Orrego-Salas, Rousseau; Bloomington, 1990.

With Jindřich Feld, Charles Bridge in Prague, 1990.

With Bernhard and Cola Heiden; Rousseau home in Bloomington, 1996.

Norma and Rousseau with Himie Voxman; University of Iowa Distinguished Alumni Award, 1998.

Publicity photo, ca. 1999.

Saxophone Studio, Indiana University, 2000.

With Ida Gotkovsky in Paris, 2001.

Publicity photo, ca. 2002.

With the Zagreb Saxophone Quartet in Zagreb, 2003.

Larsen commission announcement, Minneapolis World Saxophone Congress, 2003.

With Kenneth Fischer, Eric Nestler, Thomas Liley; Minneapolis World Saxophone Congress, 2003.

Claude Delangle, Odile Delangle, Blandine Delangle, Rousseau, Norma Rousseau; International Saxophone Master Class, Minneapolis, 2005.

With William LaRue Jones and Libby Larsen; North American Saxophone Alliance Biennial Conference, Iowa City, 2006.

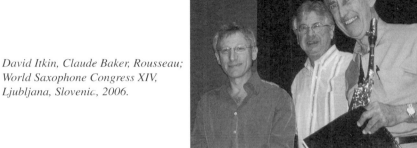

David Itkin, Claude Baker, Rousseau; World Saxophone Congress XIV, Ljubljana, Slovenia, 2006.

With Roger Boutry; World Saxophone Congress XIV, Ljubljana, Slovenia, 2006.

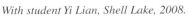

With student Yi Lian, Shell Lake, 2008.

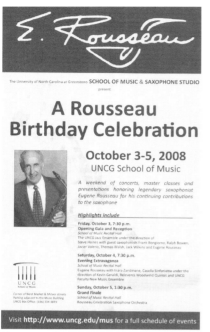

Eugene Rousseau Birthday Celebration, 2008.

University of North Carolina-Greensboro, 2008.

With Thomas Liley, Kenneth Tse; Hong Kong, 2009.

Introduction:
He has been an indelible role model

It is certainly true that Eugene Rousseau has provided audiences with numerous virtuoso performances over the years. His students know that virtuoso teaching is another important part of his career because they have experienced it many times in his studio, workshops, and master classes. His ability to take students from where they are ("We really have no other choice") and guide them to success is remarkable and may prove to be the most enduring part of his legacy — "Teaching is about as close to immortality as most of us get." "Treat each student as an individual" is an important part of his teaching philosophy, as is "We can't teach anybody anything; we can only help them to learn." He maintains that "the best teaching is the least teaching" and that "our basic mission as teachers should be to make ourselves useless, to get out of the way." Rousseau enjoys Arnold Jacobs'[101] observation that "too much analysis leads to paralysis." And he understands that "the only way we can go is forward."

Rousseau was greatly influenced by his study with "le Patron," Marcel Mule. His teaching reflects Mule's kindly yet authoritative manner and, similarly to Mule, his suggestions are firmly grounded in the practical experience born of hundreds of performances around the world. Rousseau's decades of teaching may be distilled to a pair of Mule's favorite quotations — "Don't look for the difficult things; look for the simple things" and "One never arrives."

Rousseau knows the saxophone literature intimately and relates practical hints (such as where best to breathe and which are the appropriate fingerings), historical background (such as the circumstances in which a composition was written), contextual information (where a work fits within a composer's total output), and interpretive suggestions based upon his broad experience in many styles over the years. Although Rousseau has often stated that "imitation is a great teaching tool," one student remembers

> my lessons with ER were different than with previous teachers. Where other teachers demonstrated how something should be played, ER made me think for myself. He would ask me questions about how something should be played and direct me to the correct answer. His was a very scholarly approach to teaching.[102]

---

[101] Jacobs (1915–1998) was an eminent brass teacher and prinicipal tubist with the Chicago Symphony Orchestra for forty-four years.

[102] George Weremchuk email message to author, March 3, 2007.

Students are welcomed to lessons with a handshake or (in later years especially) a handshake and a hug. They are expected to bring a notebook in which Rousseau writes comments about each lesson. Many of his students refer to these notes regularly and have adopted the use of a notebook or journal in their own teaching.

His students also noticed that Rousseau

> always read some kind of a score when teaching, rather than the saxophone part. He was always thinking of the complete picture, even when there was no pianist in the room.[103]

Rousseau believes that a positive, supportive studio atmosphere is vital to students' success. Cut-throat competition and back-biting have no place. From his performances and master classes around the world, he often personally knows prospective students and can sense whether they will fit in. Sometimes current students are asked for their opinions about possible new members of the studio. He knows that he is not the only person in the studio from whom his students will learn.

> He maintained total control over his studio and it ran incredibly well, allowing his students a small 'school' midst a very large department within which to learn and share with each other. I have master's and doctoral degrees from two other schools, yet my deepest friendships within the saxophone community were begun and nurtured at IU and this, I'm sure, is a result of Dr. Rousseau's teaching philosophy.[104]

> I always felt, as I'm sure we all did, that we were part of something really special, an extended family. This is a great, empowering feeling for a student to have — that what you are doing and learning about is important on a large scale.[105]

He is aware that the pursuit of a career in music can be incredibly intense. He has seen students who were unable to endure life in a school of music and his suggestions have proven valuable to members of his studio. One student remembers the first meeting of saxophone students with Rousseau a fall semester thirty years ago.

---

[103] Christopher Kelton email message to author, March 10, 2007.

[104] Michael Hester email message to author, March 11, 2007.

[105] Susan Loy email message to author, February 7, 2007.

The thing that really caught my attention was his advice on how to survive music school. 'There's more to life than just the saxophone. Keep some balance in your life. Read a book every once in a while and not just that awful stuff you have to read for classes. I could tell you to make sure to get enough sleep; you won't, but try to. Get some exercise; you need it. Eat some vegetables; sounds like your mother, right? Everyone needs some quiet time, not sleep but some time to get away from the disco music (!) and collect yourself, maybe think things over a little bit.' He mentioned that one of his students would go to the chapel, not necessarily for a religious service, but just because it was quiet. ER mentioned that he got exercise and quiet time at the same time on his walks to and from school. As I recall, he lived about 2.5 miles from school and covered the distance in half an hour, which is really moving for a walker.[106]

Rousseau has maintained that "the most important characteristic a teacher can possess is kindness" and "encouragement is the most important thing you can say." His students have responded to this environment as lessons in music and in life.

He gave me the great dignity of treating an earnest 17-year-old as a serious student and musician right from the first moment we met. He has been an indelible role model in that and many other ways throughout my professional life.[107]

His manner of criticism was gentlemanly — kindness first, criticism second. He was never condescending, just honest, direct, and tactful. His method of teaching has been the most important role model of my professional life.[108]

It was the most thrilling and exhilarating experience I have ever had. Not having had a teacher for so long, it was a dream come true. He was always encouraging and professional. His professionalism showed in his attire, mannerisms, interaction with students, and high standards in performance and teaching.[109]

---

[106] Christopher Kelton email message to author, March 10, 2007.

[107] Kate Newlin email message to author, February 12, 2007. Ms. Newlin is now a business strategist who works with Fortune 100 companies.

[108] Susan Loy email message to author, February 8, 2007.

[109] Kenneth Tse email message to author, March 25, 2007.

Through his performances and his teaching, Rousseau has always demonstrated his faith in the saxophone as a medium of musical expression. He has presented the saxophone at an extremely high artistic level at all times and the world has taken notice.

> At IU the saxophone was taken seriously. Midst the world-class opera program and musicology professors leading their respective fields, the saxophone was seen as important, truly legitimate, which, as a young and passionate musician, meant the world to me. I remember Dr. Rousseau correcting someone who had identified themselves as being 'just a saxophonist.' 'You are a saxophonist,' he said. 'Never apologize for that.'[110]

In addition to the observations cited above, several other aspects of Rousseau's teaching can be noted. Rousseau knows the value of presenting concrete examples for abstract concepts, giving students something tangible to take with them. He understands the importance of being able to express the same idea in a variety of ways. Rousseau enjoys presenting this example to illustrate how the same thing can be said in two very different ways.

> If you have a flat tire on your car, you can go to a service station and say, 'Hey, Buddy, I got a flat tire on my car. Can you give me a hand?'
>
> Or you can say,
>
> 'Excuse me, my good man. I seem to have encountered a puncture in one of the round rubber wheels on my automotive conveyance. Would it be possible for you to render some assistance?'
>
> You have to use the language which will give the results you want.

At the 1994 Midwest Band and Orchestra Convention in Chicago, Rousseau declared, "I can think of no way to teach any instrument other than through teaching fundamentals." The following pages present some of those fundamentals and the concrete examples he has used to illustrate them.

---

[110] Michael Hester email message to author, March 11, 2007.

11 Tone Production:
I want to play like that, to sound like that

Most saxophonists are initially attracted to the instrument by its sound and that topic is often what Eugene Rousseau addresses first in saxophone workshops, master classes, and his studio. Like Marcel Mule, he speaks of the saxophone in vocal rather than string terms, asking us to make the saxophone sing. His approach to the instrument appeals to listeners who are new to the saxophone as well as those such as the gifted jazz saxophonist Michael Brecker, who said, "I enjoy listening to classical saxophone players. I particularly admire Eugene Rousseau."[111]

Rousseau believes strongly that because the saxophone is a wind instrument it is crucial that a warm stream of air be used — "The air is the soul of the sound."

> The air stream is very similar to exhaling. Think of 'warm air', similar to fogging a mirror. The mouthpiece creates resistance and prevents the dissipation of the air.

The concept of warm air is related to the amount of air employed and to its speed; it should not be confused with support of the air stream. He provides a concrete example to help the student learn to achieve a large, warm stream of air — "A small air stream, which is correct for the clarinet, produces a 'sizzle' sound. To produce a large air stream, fill a circle made with the thumb and finger held a couple of inches from the mouth." Warmer air can also be created by changing the direction of the air stream. Blowing down without changing the position of the head is another of Rousseau's techniques to help the student understand the concept.

The embouchure is the connection between player and instrument.[112] Rousseau has described the embouchure as solid and round, like forming the syllable "o" or "oo." The lower lip is often too smooth or stretched, whereas it should look to be a little bunched in order to form a cushion for the reed and dampen its vibrations. The corners of the mouth must be well-supported and the feeling of roundness should extend back into the mouth; he recommends the player "think of the inside of the mouth as part of the air column" because "the generation of the tone does not start at the tip of the mouthpiece, but back within the player." The amount of mouthpiece in the mouth may only *appear* to be different for each player but a student with a large lower lip in fact may need to take a little more mouthpiece in. Too little mouthpiece and reed in the mouth will cause the sound

---

[111] Interview with John Robert Brown for the Associated Board of the Royal Schools of Music, London. Brecker (1949–2007) was described by the *New York Times* as "the most influential tenor saxophonist since John Coltrane."

[112] "The embouchure is everything between the air and the instrument."

to be muffled; too much mouthpiece and reed causes a lack of control. He has no objection to the use of tape or a dental appliance by those players who have sharp lower teeth as he does. The embouchure is the same for all saxophones, changing only the size and not the shape of the circle. Rousseau warns players not to be afraid to make a slight embouchure change to get the sound they want. This is in keeping with his recent suggestion that a more elliptical pear shape may be a better description than simply round; he cites renowned singer Thomas Hampson[113] as describing tone production in exactly the same way.

One tool for determining the correct amount of pressure around the reed and mouthpiece is the technique of "bumping the octave key." The student plays a left-hand note such as B, A, or G and uses the right hand to flick the octave key. The saxophone should respond immediately, first to the upper octave and then return to the lower. If this does not occur, the air/embouchure balance is not correct and the size of the embouchure needs to be adjusted. The right hand is used to operate the octave key in order to minimize any reaction from the embouchure or air caused by the normal use of the left thumb.

An important method to learn the balance between air and embouchure is the technique of playing the mouthpiece alone. This idea was pioneered by Santy Runyon[114] in the 1930s and later suggested by Donald McCathren.[115] Whereas Runyon and McCathren were concerned exclusively with the embouchure, Rousseau focuses on the air stream and the balance between air and embouchure. He contends that the idea of the mouthpiece pitch puts the tongue and the throat into their proper positions, thus shaping the air stream.

> Produce *concert* A (for some players, B-flat) above the staff on the alto mouthpiece alone at *fortissimo*. If the pitch produced is C or C-sharp, the air pressure is the greatest and the air quantity the least. For tenor, the concert pitch is G. On baritone, the pitch is concert D and, for soprano, C above the staff. Note that the same pitch can be produced on the soprano and the clarinet mouthpieces. The size of the two mouthpieces illustrates the need for more air on soprano. I can play the range of a whole octave on the alto mouthpiece, less on the

---

[113] Born in 1955, Hampson has been described as "America's leading baritone." The winner of numerous awards and honors, he created the Hampsong Foundation in 2003 to promote the art song in America.

[114] Santy Runyon (1907–2003) numbered Paul Desmond, Lee Konitz, and Sonny Stitt among his students. He began making jazz saxophone mouthpieces in 1941. Runyon described how he came to his conclusions regarding mouthpiece pitch in his booklet *Suggestions for Woodwind Players*.

[115] Donald McCathren (1920–2004) was a prominent clarinetist and band director at Duquesne University. He served as Director of Research and Education Services for the Leblanc Company. His booklet *The Saxophone Book* for Leblanc in 1954 recommends playing the mouthpiece alone to determine the correct embouchure pressure. Unfortunately, the suggested pitches to be produced are an octave too low (e.g., A at 440 cps, which is the second space of the treble clef).

other mouthpieces. With such a wide range from which to choose, we must select the correct pitch. Or, stated another way, the embouchure is solid; it's the air stream that is 'loose'.

Rousseau is adamant that the jaw not change position when playing low B-flat or high F-sharp and recommends the practice of slurred descending octaves. Practicing a note *decrescendo*, especially with a tuner, is also an excellent tool for developing the tone. Yet another suggestion is to "verify the tone from time to time with a fermata."[116]

Sometimes a student will have difficulty with the low register. Rousseau suggests:

1) Check the air/embouchure balance (Is the embouchure loose? Is the air stream thin?).
2) Perhaps the bow is too large (This is often the case with Mark VI saxophones).[117]
3) Check the low C-sharp adjustment.
4) The reed is not sealing.
5) The bow seam is leaking. (Early saxophone bows were fitted; today, most are sealed with an adhesive.)
6) The articulated G-sharp key is open and needs to be adjusted.

Problems with palm key notes, such as D through F-sharp above the staff, are addressed through a specific technique. Using the rhythmic pattern of four eighth-notes and a half-note and beginning with high C-sharp, start each note with the air only. Repeat the pattern for high D and continue the pattern chromatically to F-sharp. By eliminating the tongue, the player is forced to use the air correctly. After a short period of reinforcement of learning how to use the air, the tongue can be reintroduced. Rousseau suggests, however, that it is often best to "air articulate" in the high register in any event, especially on soprano saxophone.

Rousseau believes that the playing of octave slurs is one of the best exercises to improve the high register. "A student will automatically find the right [tongue] position with the F octaves. The tongue position controls the speed of the air." An additional exercise is to practice slurs from high B to high C-sharp, to D, and so on. "B is an easy note — bright, clear, and free. Continue that good sound to the higher pitches." In all registers, a decrescendo on the mouthpiece alone is the best long tone exercise — "*That* is the test. One should keep the air going with the

---

[116] "Remember to keep a whole-note sound in sixteenth-note passages."

[117] Rousseau recommends dropping a wine cork in the bell to reduce the displacement of the bow. "The better the wine, the better this works' reminds us of his sense of humor.

same focus as at *forte*. Don't let the air stream thin out by keeping the same basic pitch on the mouthpiece softly as loudly."

Another matter of difficulty, especially on tenor saxophone, is "cracking" on the written G and G-sharp above the staff. Again, Rousseau offers a checklist:

1) This is a result of the lower octave key being too low on the instrument body.
2) It can be corrected by using the "bumping the octave key" technique.
3) Sometimes the player is "too open, too loose . . . going too much for the lower octave."
4) "The air speed does change. The point is that it is much less than people think. It's not 100% the same, but it's darned close."

The construction of the instrument also affects tone quality. There are seven areas to be considered:

1) The length and taper of the tube, including the bocal, mouthpiece, and reed.
2) The thickness of the metal — generally speaking, thinner is better but the optimum thickness is about .085 inch. Incidentally, Rousseau says that Selmer and Yamaha use the same brass alloy (65% copper and 35% zinc) in their saxophones.
3) The location and size of the tone holes, including the pad height and pad material.
4) The number of tone holes, known as "chimneys", which are interruptions to the air column.
5) Dampening factors such as those posts and keys which are hard soldered onto the tube, ribbing which is soft soldered, and leaks.
6) The presence or absence of a rod at the opening of the bell.
7) The use or non-use of annealing during the manufacturing process, in which the metal is heated and then slowly cooled to prevent brittleness.

Reeds and mouthpieces are additional areas of concern. Rousseau observes that almost every classical saxophonist uses medium equipment that is very similar; this is not true of jazz players, who exhibit very personalized forms of expression. Because of the wide tip openings of their mouthpieces most jazz players use 2 or 2 ½ strength reeds. He observes that it is much easier to get a jazz sound on a classical setup than the reverse. The optimum position of the reed is even with the tip of the mouthpiece at eye level.

Rousseau describes dealing with reeds as "a constant process; the 'number one' reed is always changing." He is not committed to one brand of reed but, pragmatically, uses whatever reed produces what he wants.

I used at least one Portnoy reed in the Brahms/Mozart Quintets recording. The reed probably was more than thirty-five years old, but as I rarely discard 'probable' reeds, it was only one of several hundred in various boxes!

Rousseau uses 3½ strength reeds with the NC4 mouthpieces of his design on soprano and alto saxophones. For tenor, he prefers 3 strength reeds. He prefers a medium-soft reed on baritone saxophone with his 5R mouthpiece. "To make good music is challenging enough without making it harder with the equipment."

His students are encouraged to have more than one or two usable reeds on hand. For example, during a lesson he occasionally will set aside a student's "good" reed, requiring the student to perform on another one. "You have to be able to play on a 'E+' reed."

The reed is secured to the mouthpiece by a ligature; Rousseau has selected the BG Tradition model with a single screw on top and many of his students have made the same choice. He feels there is no difference between the lacquered kind and the more expensive gold-plated version.

Once the sensation or "muscle memory" of the air stream is attained, it can be manipulated as necessary to produce pitches in the altissimo register, to adjust intonation, or to do whatever is desired by the player. One especially useful tool is to bend the pitch downward. Finger and play written high E-flat then, while continuing to finger high E-flat, produce high D. Continue to finger high E-flat and progressively play high C-sharp, high C, and so on. Although the jaw can change the pitch really very little, the inside of the mouth can cause a tremendous fluctuation. The inside will open so far that the air stream almost stops. This flexibility exercise is invaluable for learning to control the air. Rousseau has cited Duke Ellington's lead alto saxophonist, Johnny Hodges,[118] as a prime example of using this technique in his performances.

An important component of the saxophone tone is vibrato. "Although the vibrato adds great beauty to the saxophone tone, it is a delicate enrichment and must be used with great care." "While it can enhance the tone it can also be a detriment, so use it carefully." Contrary to the opinions of some teachers, he describes it as "more a change of intensity than of pitch."

Rousseau advocates teaching by imitation: "The vibrato should be introduced by example, with the student listening carefully to a good saxophone tone and then trying to imitate it." Vibrato is produced through the use of "a vah-vah-vah jaw motion while keeping a strong tone. By changing the jaw pressure the vibrations of the reed undulate slightly, causing the pitch to go below, but not above, it's basic level and then return to it. A good vibrato, in addition to a regular change of

---

[118] Hodges, who lived from 1907 to 1970, was an important part of the tonal fabric of Ellington's band. Rousseau has specifically cited Hodges' performance of "I Got It Bad and That Ain't Good" as an example of his use of portamento.

pitch, must have a regular change of air intensity. The intensity change is created by a regular but slight interruption of the air column. This change is made by the jaw movement."

A speed of approximately 320 undulations per minute is recommended. This can be practiced by playing "scales in whole notes at MM 104, producing the vibrato in triplets (3 X 104 = 312). Setting the metronome at 80 and producing the vibrato in groups of four will give 320 undulations per minute (4 X 80 = 320)." If a student's vibrato is very slow, Rousseau recommends producing the vibrato in groups of three at MM 80; the student will soon be able to transfer from groups of three to the desired groups of four at MM 80. It has been occasionally suggested that use of the metronome will cause a student to "play mechanically." Rousseau counters, "If use of the metronome causes a student to play mechanically they were going to play mechanically anyway."

The suggested vibrato speed is to be used as a reference point; any change of speed relates more to the music than to the register being played. On the other hand, the width of the vibrato changes more often in relation to the dynamic level — the softer the music, the narrower the vibrato and the louder the music, the wider the vibrato.

It is crucial that the vibrato be used properly. Rousseau suggests an exercise in which a sustained tone is played four counts without vibrato, four counts with vibrato, and four counts without. The vibrato and non-vibrato notes must be consistent in tone quality; the use of a tuner is advised. If vibrato is used on a relatively short note, it is important that the vibrato end on pitch. Finally, Rousseau recommends, "Don't use vibrato on every note; you'll gain credibility."

In addition to the concepts and strategies above is the example of Rousseau's own performance. His gorgeous, rich tone quality has established a wonderful standard for all of his students while he has helped each to find their own voice. As a student said upon first hearing Rousseau, "I want to play like that, to sound like that."[119]

---

[119] Carolyn Bryan email message to author, March 19, 2007.

12 Tuning and Intonation:
There is an interrelationship between tone and intonation

One of the first impressions the author experienced as a newly arrived doctoral student at Indiana University was how well in tune Rousseau's students played. Tone production and intonation are closely related and, in effect, Rousseau is teaching one when he is teaching the other — the saxophone sounds best when it is played in tune and when it is played with a good characteristic tone the intonation problems are reduced or minimized.

Rousseau provides three not necessarily interchangeable definitions for the topic. "Pitch" is the tuning level, perhaps A=440 cycles per second.[120] "Tuning" is the adjustment one makes to the instrument by moving the mouthpiece to reach that level. "Intonation" refers to the individual adjustments which should be made after the instrument has been made the proper length. Because the saxophone is easier to play in tune than the clarinet, it is also easier to play out of tune. Two pitches should be used to tune the alto saxophone — concert A (which *can* be played sharp) and concert D (which *cannot* be played sharp). Written middle B is slightly flat (by a few cents) on alto, tenor, and baritone. "The instrument is made to play reasonably well in tune when you tune the middle of the horn." Changing the mouthpiece position should be done by sight and distance; one should look to see how far the mouthpiece has been moved, realizing that "the larger the instrument, the larger the amount of tuning adjustment is necessary."

The tuning procedure for quartet uses the same written pitches to keep each saxophone in the same part of the instrument. Have the soprano, alto, and tenor tune to written middle F-sharp and B; tune the tenor to written middle F-sharp and the baritone to written low F-sharp; then have the quartet descend chromatically from their written F-sharps. Note that the soprano often tends to be flat on the F-sharp, while the alto and tenor can be sharp and the baritone can be very sharp. "The fourths, fifths, octaves, and unisons are critical; there is more room to maneuver with thirds and sixths." Another strategy to tune individual instruments is to play a two-octave written D major scale with the piano. This approach provides a different and more realistic context for tuning than playing a single note. Otherwise, it is too easy to fall into the "trap of changing the embouchure and air." Whatever changes are made to the length of the saxophone, realize that adjustments

---

[120] Some very old saxophones are marked "HP" for "High Pitch" and are at A=452. Saxophones marked "LP" for "Low Pitch" are at A=440 which became the standard pitch after an international conference in 1939. In addition, Rousseau believes it is possible that some older instruments were made with the high E and F slightly flat to compensate for the "clarinet approach" of a faster air stream and tighter embouchure.

affect most those pitches closest to the mouthpiece, such as open C-sharp. Rousseau suggests that in rehearsal we can sometimes ask the pianist to play a note so that we can hear it before playing it.

Intonation adjustments are done primarily with the air, not by moving the jaw. Because it is always easier to bring the pitch down than to go up, Rousseau's flexibility exercise is useful. The exercise asks the saxophonist to play from high E-flat down chromatically to C without changing the fingering. To do this, the player must change the air stream rather than move the jaw. The air speed and the size and shape of the area inside the mouth will be dramatically altered as the air is almost stopped and the tongue's position is lowered.[121]

Because the mouthpiece pitch for playing jazz is lower, intonation must be rechecked. This is occurs because jazz playing uses more air than classical playing; therefore, the pitch is lower and the mouthpiece is positioned further on the bocal. In addition, accurate pitch in the high register can be a serious problem with some jazz mouthpieces because of their construction.

Occasionally, a fingering can be changed to improve intonation. The pitches below are written pitches:

High A is sharp — Add either the middle or ring finger of the right hand.

High C-sharp is sharp — Add a right hand *bis* key. Mule always used the right hand and Rousseau sometimes uses the first finger.

Middle D (*piano*) is sharp — Use the LSK2 and the second finger of the left hand. Alternatively, add the low B key (especially on tenor) or use LSK1 instead of the octave key.

Middle C-sharp is flat — Add RSK1 or RSK2.

Side key B-flat is a little lower than *bis* B-flat.

Side key C may be flat on a particular instrument.

Different sizes of saxophones often have specific intonation difficulties:

Tuning the soprano too flat will cause a gurgling sound in the low register.

If the area inside the soprano mouthpiece is too great, turbulence will be created making the high register sharp.

Soprano F-sharp (*forte*) is flat — Use the ring finger of the right hand rather than the middle finger.

Soprano F-sharp (*piano*) is sharp — Use the middle and ring fingers of the right hand with the E-flat key.

Tenor middle B is flat — Add RSK1.

Tenor side D is sharp — Add first finger of the left hand.

Baritone middle E to G-sharp is often sharp.

---

[121] "Bring the cheeks in, flatten the tongue (back and down, almost like choking), and keep the air going (the air speed will slow down)."

Sometimes the instrument itself is in need of adjustment:
If the low C is flat, check the height of the B key.
If a note is sharp in both octaves, line the tone hole.
On many Mark VII saxophones, the low C-sharp key should open further.
If the baritone's bocal is too large, it can cause serious problems in the upper register.
Selmer's middle C may have a hole which is a little too small; use a thin pad to make certain it is as open as possible.
On an associated issue, if E-flat is flat, check the placement of the tone hole to one's pants leg.
The amount of mouthpiece in the mouth also affects pitch; not enough can cause the pitch to be flat.
A reed which is too soft[122] makes the high register flat.

It is important to know general saxophone intonation tendencies as well as the specific intonation tendencies for each of one's instruments. For example, middle D, D-sharp, and E, A above the staff, and high C-sharp are frequently sharp; low C, C-sharp, and D and middle C-sharp are often too low. Middle F and F-sharp are also sharp on baritone. Soprano saxophones have two bore constructions — the one used by Selmer (and Yanigasawa and the Yamaha YSS-62) and the one used by the Yamaha Custom (which is more like the alto and tenor). The different bore constructions create different intonation tendencies and, for example, problems with a duet between Yamaha Custom and Yanigasawa saxophones. Nonetheless, Rousseau believes we have learned so well to adapt that "a perfectly in tune saxophone would frustrate many players" and "a well-constructed saxophone can be played with a tolerance of two to three cycles per second in either direction."

"There is an interrelationship between tone and intonation." A tone which is too low will sound dull in comparison to a tone which is too high.[123] This is the reason that he suggests finding a student's A=440 and mark it on the cork of the bocal; the student needs to know *where* to hear it. In addition, when comparing instruments or mouthpieces, one should be certain that they are being compared at the same pitch level, as it is easy to be fooled by the cork placement when changing equipment. Incidentally, in 1988 for a series of concerts in Austria and Germany where the pitch is higher, Yamaha made an alto especially for Rousseau at A=445. The author has long felt that this remarkable circumstance amply demonstrated the high regard in which Rousseau is held. Perhaps, in one way at least, he had "arrived."

---

[122] "Your reed is tired" — Marcel Mule, as quoted by Rousseau.

[123] "You will get a better one if you play in tune."

13 Technique:
Teach the music and approach technical problems as they occur

Posture and the correct position of the hands over the "keyboard" are Rousseau's first considerations to technical development. When the player is seated, the alto saxophone may be either to the side or in front as is most comfortable to the individual but the instrument must not rest on or against the chair. It is important to sit forward in the chair and to sit up straight. A simple test for a correct seated position is to stand up. If this can be done easily and without shifting the body, the seated position is correct. If standing can not be accomplished without adjusting the body's position, then the position is not appropriate.

The weight of the instrument must rest on the neck strap and not be supported by the right thumb; otherwise, the hands will become tired and tense. The instrument will come to the player without reaching if the neck strap is the correct length. If the player must dip the head the neck strap is too long and if the player must raise the head the neck strap is too short. "Let the saxophone come to you." Rousseau often reminds younger players that the length of the neck strap is different when standing rather than seated. Because players will often stand for a solo in jazz band, he suggests the neck strap be easily adjustable. Rousseau reminds players that the bocal and mouthpiece are also adjustable and should be positioned so that the head is not tilted to one side or the other.

The hands should assume a natural position, with the fingers neither extended nor unnaturally curved. Rousseau suggests the correct hand position is like holding a softball in each hand or, "if you don't like sports, a grapefruit." This position allows the hands to be free from tension and makes use of the most sensitive part of the fingers, which is found just behind the tips — "The fingers should be slightly curved for the maximum sensitivity." Rousseau asks students to imagine touching a hot surface with the fingers and using that same part of the fingers to contact the pearls of the saxophone keys. An exception occurs when moving from low C-sharp to B natural, in which case the left hand little finger should start straight and then be curved.

Because the left hand is asked to do so much, he recommends that special attention be given to its position relative to the first left side key — "Hit it right under the knuckle. It gives access to the main keyboard." The right thumb should not be too far under the thumb hook and the left thumb should be at a 45° angle for the octave key. The left thumb should remain in contact with the octave key at all times, using a rocking motion to operate the key.

The left hand palm keys and right hand side keys are played using a radial motion, much like turning a door knob. Playing low B to low B-flat is best accomplished by keeping the left little finger on the B key and rocking the hand to the B-flat key, using the side of the finger.

Learning how to practice effectively is another component of Rousseau's teaching. He divides practicing into five steps:

1) Daily practice —
   Daily practice helps one to retain what has already been learned and is related to Rousseau's belief in cumulative learning.
2) Goals in practicing —
   Practicing should always have at least one specific goal in mind.
3) Practice plan —
   Rousseau recommends a "balanced diet" that might include vibrato, etudes, solo literature, and ensemble literature. He advocates making a notebook of difficult or troublesome passages for further review.
4) Practice time —
   Practice at the same time each day yields better results. Two good short practice sessions can be more beneficial than one long session when the player is tired.
5) Practice strategies —
   Learn the correct notes with the correct fingerings as soon as possible. "Don't waste time practicing wrong notes."
   "To develop technique, you must know what you're playing; memorization is a strategy. We must associate and transfer what we hear to what we do with the instrument."

Once these habits and concepts are acquired it is possible to develop them in more detail. Rousseau says that "the saxophone technique may be divided into four parts —

1) palm keys
2) table keys
3) right hand
4) left hand."

He recommends that "in developing the technique:
1) Think in terms of the hands.
2) The left hand is asked to do a lot.
3) The ideal hand position requires the least motion; therefore, focus on the first left side key."

Rousseau further suggests that "One can build a whole technique on trills, using the normal fingerings and keeping the fingers in contact with the keys. Do this a few minutes each day."[124] This suggestion is in line with his example that "When playing left hand B to A:

---

[124] Rousseau has spoken of the "economy of the fingers."

1) Never slap the key; push it down.
2) Don't leave the key.
3) The motion must be solid."

Rousseau presents two concepts to be kept in mind regarding finger motion — "The speed of the finger movement is constant; it has to be quick. The fingers must move quickly even if the music doesn't." And, "The frequency of the finger movement is greater in fast passages."

He also reminds us that the saxophonist "must move a great deal of metal; some of the pads are enormous. Compare the size of the pads with those of a flute, a clarinet, or an oboe. It's obvious the saxophone technique requires more energy."[125] In addition, we must be aware that "the action of the instrument is not the same on every key." Still, Rousseau describes the saxophone as "the most logical of all woodwinds."

Rousseau often uses the *bis* B-flat fingering, especially in flat keys. He learned this preference during his study with Mule. Rousseau recommends that young players be taught only two B-flat fingerings, the *bis* (which lowers the B) and the side key (which raises the A). He finds the 1-4 fingering with the first finger of each hand, similar to that often used by young flutists, is flat on saxophone. If a so-called "right hand *bis*" fingering must be used, the 1-5 with the middle finger of the right hand is advised. In addition, Rousseau says it is permissible to slide from the *bis* key, especially on soprano because of the shorter levers. In fact, the *bis* key on Rousseau's alto has been slightly modified to facilitate sliding. However, the slide should not be taught to beginners.

Rousseau also advocates use of the "covered" C-sharp fingering for the pitch in the third space. The fingering takes advantage of the lower octave vent by using the octave key in conjunction with the left hand ring finger; any or all of the fingers of the right hand may also be used. The fingering, which can be used on most saxophones other than the Selmer Series III,[126] is often employed when moving from a note in the second register to C-sharp returning to the second register. It can minimize finger motion, improve intonation of that problematic pitch, and better match the tone quality of the adjacent notes. He finds the "long" C-sharp fingering proposed by some others[127] to be "too sharp for the mainstream."

Another fingering which is useful in certain situations is the "full" A-sharp, which is the G-sharp fingering with LSK1. Although it is slightly flat, this is often outweighed by the facility it offers in rapid passages such as G-sharp/A-sharp/B. The fingering can be used in both registers.

---

[125] "The saxophone differs greatly from the flute, oboe, clarinet, and bassoon because the fingers are **not** the pads."

[126] The covered C-sharp fingering is also useful on Selmer's SuperAction saxophone but without the right hand, which will cause the pitch to be flat.

[127] The fingering was suggested by Sigurd Rascher. Rousseau says that the long C-sharp fingering "may have been and may be all right on older Bueschers," the make preferred by Rascher and many of his followers.

Rousseau's preference is "to teach the music and approach technical problems as they occur." One of his strategies to overcome technical difficulties is to play a note in a passage and then quickly finger but not play the next note. The player can thus focus on the necessary physical motion without concern for anything else. Once the physical motion has been learned, it can be put into a musical context. Another strategy, learned from Mule, is to play as many notes as one can up to tempo, even if it is only two notes. Gradually increase the number of notes which can be performed at tempo until the entire passage is played. Rousseau also advises that scales be practiced by displacing the beat, as well as in groups of five with different articulations. Another tactic which Rousseau does not use himself but he suggests because others have found it useful is to play even notes unevenly, first long-short and then short-long. In addition, the student should make an excerpt list of those passages which present special difficulties and review them regularly until the problems are overcome.

The instrument can create unnecessary difficulties. For example, "Spring tension affects technique. The palm key springs can be too heavy. With the G-sharp key down, check the right hand keys to see if the spring is too light. In addition, those keys held down by springs (C-sharp, G-sharp, and E-flat) are susceptible to sticking."

Rousseau is adamant that technique is "much more than mere finger control. It includes tone and control, articulation, range, vibrato, and twentieth-century techniques such as multiphonics and quarter-tones." And finally, it is interesting to check the tempos of Rousseau's recordings with a metronome. Invariably, his tempos are as indicated by the composer but they never seem hurried or on the verge of losing control. Often his tempos do not seem to be fast until one tries to play the passages at that speed.

14 Articulation:
The tongue is a valve, not a hammer

Rousseau describes articulation (or tonguing) very simply: "While playing the saxophone, if you touch the reed with your tongue you will stop the tone. When you take your tongue away from the reed while blowing, the tone will begin."

He continues to explain that this action should be as natural as possible and "create the least amount of disturbance." "Touch the tip of the reed with that area of the tongue which is most natural (usually just behind the tip)" because "the tongue is a muscle that is not accustomed to doing articulation." And further, "The tongue has two functions: to guide or shape the air stream and to articulate. We have problems when one gets in the way of the other."

Because the purpose of articulation is to "clarify certain notes" the syllable used is important. Rousseau usually uses the syllable tAH but also recommends the syllable dAH; a soft "t" is very much like "d." In either case, it is crucial to note that the consonant of the syllable is smaller than the vowel because "The tone is the vowel; you want the vowel, not the consonant." In fact, Rousseau suggests the player "eliminate the consonant altogether to correct using too much." Going even further, he advises "Don't use the tongue if it doesn't help you"[128] and "When articulating without the tongue, the air must start from the throat." This advice to consider employing an air articulation is particularly useful when playing in the palm keys on the alto saxophone and even more so on the soprano. Using the tongue to articulate in the altissimo register is especially difficult and should be done only when necessary.

Articulation is presented in groups of four with eight possibilities:
Slur in groups of four;
Tongue in groups of four;
Slur two, tongue two;
Tongue two, slur two;
Tongue one, slur two, tongue one;
Slur three, tongue one;
Tongue one, slur three; and
Tongue the first note and slur the remainder in groups of two to create a syncopation. Rousseau also suggests practicing scales in groups of five with different articulations.

Rousseau advocates checking repeated articulations on the mouthpiece alone. There should be no change in pitch if the tongue is used properly. If there is a change in pitch, too much of the tongue is being used and the motion should be minimized in order to maintain the correct tongue position. This strategy of using

---

[128] For example, he says that "an accent is an emphasis which can be created by space" and he suggests that we "don't interpolate an accent on a *fortepiano*; it's usually not good to tongue."

the mouthpiece alone will also help to resolve any confusion that the tongue and the air seem to move in opposite directions. It also helps the player to learn that "the tongue is a valve, not a hammer."

To develop rapidity of articulation, Rousseau has these suggestions:
1) "Strive for lightness first. Make the tongue rebound, like a drumstick bounce, twice and then three times."
2) "Practice continued rapid staccato passages to develop endurance. The tongue is a muscle and must be developed. Use a metronome."
3) "Use these patterns — tongue two/slur two; slur two/tongue two; tongue one/slur two/tongue one; and tongue all four."
4) "In rapid articulations, the 't' functions as both a beginning and an ending. Stop the reed with the tongue only in rapid articulations and even then the last note will end with the air."

Rousseau often quotes the renowned British clarinetist Reginald Kell[129] who said, "A short note is a long note played short." As Rousseau describes it, "Get your basic tone and then give us a piece of that."

Rousseau also suggests that "Some problems can be approached by practicing releases without the consonant, alternated with releases using the consonant." He also advises the use of the fingers to aid in articulation. "Use the left hand first finger if the note is not low. Use the right hand first finger if the note is low. Both are often done without the tongue and encourage the rather long air column to vibrate."

He presents more detailed advice when it is necessary to begin a note in the low register. "Don't use the tongue. Use the right hand first finger — short but direct and incisive." "You can't tongue the same way in all registers. The high register requires a slightly different shape to the air column. Find the tongue position and articulate without changing the basic position."

---

[129] Kell, who lived from 1906 to 1981, inspired a new style of British clarinet playing through his recordings and performances as a member of several prominent orchestras. He resided in the United States from 1948 to 1971.

15 High Tones:
The fingerings are only the means by which to enhance the harmonics

Rousseau's *Saxophone High Tones*, currently in its second edition, has become a standard text in many of the world's most prestigious music schools.[130] As with other aspects of learning, Rousseau believes that an understanding of the fundamental principles is necessary. For example, "From low B-flat to third space C-sharp are fundamentals; from fourth line D up are overtones. The saxophone is an open tube; therefore, it overblows all harmonics."

One of the most remarkable examples of Rousseau's teaching skills is his ability to help a saxophonist to play in the altissimo register for the first time. A student with a controlled basic tone is selected because "One can start teaching vibrato and altissimo as soon as a student has a good solid sound throughout the normal range." Rousseau has the student play the pitches within the staff A, A-sharp with side key, and finally a "sharp" A-sharp with the *bis* key fingering while keeping the RSK1 open. The tone must be strong. Then, using a folded piece of paper or an old reed, Rousseau opens slightly LSK3, also known as the front F key; often the front F key opens too far when the usual fingering is employed.[131] The student, using the same fingerings as earlier, invariably produces successfully the pitches F, F-sharp, and G in the altissimo register — "Don't try to do anything special. Just blow and let the instrument do the work." If the student is not successful, Rousseau advises "Play fortissimo and don't think so high." The next step is to add the octave key. This usually is a little more difficult because the octave key and the slightly opened LSK3 are both functioning as vents and are working against each other.[132]

Having achieved an appropriate air stream (which is accomplished by changing the position of the tongue rather than the throat), Rousseau has the student practice the standard fingerings for high F, F-sharp, and G using the front F key. At this point the fact is introduced that the front F key does not overblow C, as is commonly misunderstood, but rather A. In other words, A overblows to F, A-sharp overblows to F-sharp and the altered A-sharp overblows to G. When playing a passage in the altissimo register, Rousseau strongly recommends that "Any and all fingering combinations should be first practiced repeatedly *without* playing."

---

[130] "It is an indispensable tool for students at the Paris Conservatory . . . a brilliant contribution to the teaching of the saxophone." Claude Delangle, Foreword to *Saxophone High Tones*, second ed., by Eugene Rousseau (St. Louis: MMB Music, 2002), v.

[131] A related strategy is to almost completely cover the F hole with Scotch tape.

[132] "As the LSK3 assumes the true function of a vent key, a conflict between it and the LVT [lower vent tube, i.e., the lower of the two octave vents] is created."

Another tactic offered by Rousseau to help a student produce the F-sharp is first to play high F with the front F key. Add the first two fingers of the right hand to get a little closer to F-sharp. Raise the second finger of the right hand to get still closer and then move to RSK1 for F-sharp. As advised in the other method above, no tongue should be used.

"Most people turn to the fingering chart but first let's understand what's happening. All the high notes are harmonics and the fingerings are only the means by which to enhance the harmonics." Rousseau recommends three approaches to learning how to refocus the air stream to play the above-normal pitches:

1) "Closed tube exercises[133] are a good way to start. Use no tongue; push them with the air. It's very similar to the feeling of the regular fingerings. The air/embouchure balance and the shape inside changes more than the jaw. It's sometimes good to approach them from above.[134] At the top of the overtone series, the tongue is so high that almost no air is coming out."

2) "Overblow sixths from low G-sharp. Use an increasing thickness to vent LSK3. As you do this you can begin to add the octave key. It's much clearer without the octave key."[135]

3) "Overblow sixths from high C-sharp. Try also without the palm key. On baritone, *minor* sixths result but, at the top, the intervals get closer to *major* sixths. Soprano is possible but much more difficult, owing to its short tube. The next fundamental is a fourth. Above that *is* possible — a major third."

Rousseau has made additional comments about each of these procedures. Regarding the closed tube exercises, he reminds us that "The high notes are always easier to play if you get them lower in the series." This observation is often the reason for his recommendations of specific fingerings. In addition, "One of the acoustical peculiarities of the saxophone is that the A overblows a sixth rather than a fifth. The next interval, a fourth, *does* fit in." "As we play overtones on higher notes, the overtones become distorted. For example, the second overtone above second space A is not E but F." Overblowing sixths "aids the development of a facility in playing high tones; is a marvelous way to develop embouchure and air control; and is an enormous help in enhancing tones from high C-sharp to high F-sharp."

Several suggestions are offered to aid in overblowing sixths. "E-flat or E is often the easiest fingering to do first. A possible crutch, to be abandoned as soon

---

[133] Closed tube exercises involve playing the various pitches found in the overtone series. For example, the saxophone's low B-flat contains not only that pitch but also the B-flat an octave higher, the F above that, the B-flat above the staff, the D above the staff, the F above the staff, the A-flat above that, and so on.

[134] In other words, if attempting to play fifth-line F (the third note in the overtone series for low B-flat), play the F with the normal fingering and then shift to the low B-flat fingering while keeping the pitch.

[135] It is a variation of this approach that Rousseau uses to introduce the altissimo register in workshops as described above.

as possible, is to take more mouthpiece inside the mouth.[136] Remember that because the tongue in not in its normal position, push the upper note separately with air but without the tongue."[137]

High G is often the first difficult hurdle to the altissimo register. Rousseau offers four suggestions:
1) "Focus in by making the inside smaller."
2) "Keep the tongue down"
3) "Move the jaw forward slightly."
4) "The embouchure/air balance on the mouthpiece alone will typically equate with A-sharp or B."

"As one plays higher, the air stream becomes increasingly smaller and you use less and less lip." There is a huge change around high D-sharp or E and the embouchure becomes stretched as with the clarinet. In fact, Rousseau has recently suggested that there seem to be two altissimo registers — from high F-sharp to D-sharp and above D-sharp. "By the time we get to high E, the amount of air is miniscule; the mouthpiece pitch is C-sharp."

Rousseau has explicit recommendations for practicing the high tones. In *Saxophone High Tones* he presents several fingerings for soprano, alto, tenor, and baritone saxophones while reminding us that "there is no 'complete' fingering chart for any instrument, and that is especially true for the above-normal range of the saxophone." He suggests that it is important to keep in mind how fingerings relate to each other in terms of tone, response, intonation, and facility. Rousseau advocates the playing of scales full-range, adding a step at the top and then yet another step to make the above-normal tones an extension of the instrument. Another strategy for improving the high register is to work backwards, producing the high tones and then adding the previous note, then the note before that and so on; the problem is often not the high tones themselves but the passage leading to them.

Articulation in the above-normal range of the saxophone is another area to be considered. "The tongue position and throat opening do change as one proceeds into the above-normal saxophone range. Because of this, the tongue is not in a position ordinarily used when tonguing tones in the saxophone's normal range. Therefore, the player who is first attempting the high tones will instinctively use the tonguing technique known to him by the countless hours of conditioning he has experienced. The result is almost invariably that no high tones will respond. . . . Inasmuch as the tongue position is different for producing the high tones, it will also be different for articulating them." To learn this difference, Rousseau recommends

---

[136] "Often the jaw must go forward to free the reed a little more. Do this *very* slightly — otherwise, the notes will be shrill and sharp."

[137] "It may be necessary to air-articulate on slurs. Make it as small a gap as possible."

1) Produce the desired high tone without tonguing it.
2) Repeat the above until the tone is started clearly.
3) Start the tone again by tonguing it.
4) Practice starting the tone, alternating it by tonguing and not tonguing.

The tongue, when used for articulation, must remain as near as possible to the position necessary for high-tone production.

Occasionally special circumstances must be addressed. "Sometimes one must anticipate the change of tongue position and throat opening, for example in the Brahms sonatas or the Finney concerto." In situations where a more brilliant high G is required, "you can get a little more sound by adding keys; for example, low B-flat or the left hand ring finger." Finally, Rousseau reminds us that "high tones are harder when we're tired."

16 The Other Saxophones: *The soprano is not a gold-colored clarinet*

"If you play only one saxophone, you don't play them all." Rousseau believes in the value of versatility, whether it is the ability to speak the language of classical music in addition to the language of jazz, to teach music history and music theory, or to have a working familiarity with soprano, alto, tenor, and baritone saxophones. He encourages his students to perform on more than one member of the saxophone family because "if you play more than one saxophone, you're doubling."

Most important among the differences between the various saxophones is the mouthpiece pitch for each instrument — concert C for soprano, A for alto, G for tenor, and D for baritone. Although soprano and tenor, like alto and baritone, are pitched an octave apart as instruments, the mouthpiece pitch is not. The shape of the embouchure is the same for each saxophone but the size of the shape changes with the size of the instrument — "When changing saxophones, change the size of the circle." The larger saxophones require a larger quantity of air as well — the displacement (i.e., the amount of air inside the instrument) of the tenor is eight times that of the soprano and the displacement of the baritone is eight times that of the soprano. "Each instrument has an optimum amount of air." The soprano, for example, should not use an air stream like the alto or the clarinet — it's in between. An air stream that is too thin on tenor will be, when compared to alto, even more detrimental.

Intonation tendencies also vary. For example, high E and F can be sharp on alto saxophone but are often flat on tenor; low B may be sharp on soprano but flat on baritone. Middle D tends to be sharp on each family member but is markedly so on tenor; sometimes LSK1 can be used instead of the octave key to help with this problem. G above the staff is often quite sharp on baritone and therefore the lower octave should be used to tune concert B-flat. E on alto is high, while on soprano it is low; B on alto will be slightly low, while on soprano it has a tendency to be high. Other tuning situations specific to each of the different saxophones are found in the chapter on tuning.

There are differences between certain registers as well. The soprano, for example, is more resistant than the alto in the lower register. Difficulties with pitches in the soprano's upper register can be similar to the problems encountered in the altissimo register of the alto — in each case, using the air rather than the tongue to articulate is advisable. The baritone's "cracking" between middle D and G-sharp (where the lower octave vent is employed) is characteristic of the instrument. The tenor's high G and G-sharp (the highest notes of the first octave key) are also unstable and as a result have a tendency to crack because the upper vent tube is too low; Rousseau recommends playing the pitches without tonguing in order to "find the target."

There are crucial differences in the altissimo register, which is most difficult on soprano and less so on the larger instruments. The tenor is frequently flat in that register and often should use fingerings that are a half-step higher than the alto; in other words, use the alto's G fingering for the tenor's F-sharp. Unlike the smaller saxophones, the baritone overblows the palm keys a *minor* sixth; as the palm key pitches become higher it gets closer to a major sixth.

Soprano —

The soprano is a saxophone apart, a diagnostic instrument that helps to differentiate between the artists and the blowers, the would-be Rousseaus and the musical clowns.[138]

"The soprano is not a gold-colored clarinet" and therefore requires a different embouchure and air stream than the clarinet. The soprano will feel different because the hands are extremely close to the body but there is no *substantial* difference in the angle between soprano and alto because the angle of the head is different — the critical factor is that the instrument must come to the player comfortably. Be certain that the weight of the instrument is on the neck strap rather than the hands, especially the right thumb. The shorter levers of the soprano compared to the alto will result in much less distance traveled by the keys and will be very obvious to the player. While the Yamaha YSS-62 and Yanagisawa soprano saxophones share similar intonation patterns, Yamaha's Custom soprano has tendencies which are similar to the Custom alto. The highest possible pitch on the soprano mouthpiece is E. "Don't put too much air through the soprano — there's a maximum point." For an instrument with a curved neck, the bell is almost straight down with the right hand very near the body. The straight soprano is at such a different angle (it must either be held out or the player must duck his head) that it may sound very differently to the *performer* but not to the *audience*. Rousseau notes that simply supporting the straight soprano saxophone with the right thumb can create a problem of endurance.

The soprano saxophone seems to present more possibilities for unique trill fingerings.

    High D to E: Trill the LSK3. Trilling the RSK4 may also work.
    C to D-flat: Trill the RSK2 or, possibly, the RSK1 and 2 together.
    A to B: Trill the RSK2.
    A-flat to B-flat: Trill the RSK1.
    Middle D *pianissimo*: Use the RSK3 only.
    Middle C-sharp: It is possible to finger low C-sharp without the first finger of the left hand and with no octave key.

---

[138] Max Holgate, "Some thoughts on the soprano saxophone," Vol. 12, No. 1 *Clarinet and Saxophone* (March 1987): 37-8.

Middle F-sharp: It is possible to use the ring finger (instead of the middle finger) of the right hand.

Tenor —

The tenor saxophone shares many intonation tendencies with the alto. However, both fingerings for high F are flat on tenor; adding the G-sharp key to the front F fingering can help. When playing the tenor from a seated position, don't let the right arm go back. Whether playing seated or standing, the instrument should be kept forward. Unlike the other saxophones, tenors with the RSK4 can play the side keys up to middle F. Rousseau finds that it is easier to get good reeds for tenor and baritone than it is for soprano and alto.

Regarding the construction of the tenor saxophone, Rousseau believes that the low octave vent should be bigger and lower for D. The bocal should probably be redesigned as well.

Baritone —

"You'll never regret getting a baritone with a low A. The high F-sharp is not as important." One should be aware that the low A key will cause the left hand to assume a slightly different position.

Because of the tremendous weight of the baritone saxophone, several approaches have been taken. Rousseau thinks that a floor peg similar to that found on bass clarinet is the best answer. A socket is soldered to the bottom of the instrument and an adjustable rod is screwed into the socket. A harness is also possible as is a tripod, but that seems to be the least satisfactory solution because of the lack of flexibility.

One must remember to play out on the baritone because its sound will not carry as much as the alto. "You will never have too much air with either baritone or flute."

17 Performance:
Remember that there are two levels to every performance

One of Rousseau's great strengths as a teacher is his broad experience as a performer. He has played on five continents in countless varied situations — as a soloist with bands and orchestras, a chamber musician, and a recitalist. He has assisted numerous students of all levels to prepare for their performances.

For a performance with piano, Rousseau prefers the piano lid open. "The instrument is meant to be played with the lid open. If the piano is too loud, the pianist needs to play softer. Having the lid open also affects the saxophone sound because the lid will reflect the sound." The stand should be positioned in the bow of the piano where the saxophonist will have the pianist in their peripheral vision. Make certain that the stand is not too high (approximately waist high at a 45° angle) so the sound is not blocked by the stand and the audience can see the instrument.

All music should be memorized so the score on the stand is simply a reminder. Related to this idea is Rousseau's belief that "memorization is an effective learning tool and some passages require memorization. Some music should be performed from memory, such as Bonneau's *Caprice en forme de valse*, Desenclos' *Prelude, Cadence et Finale*, and the Ibert *Concertino da Camera*."

Rousseau suggests we remember that a performance is like an athletic event. Play the entire program straight through four, five, six times with the pianist to learn what it feels like. One needs to be physically and mentally ready. "Be in good physical condition, which helps improve the mental condition."

Rousseau suggests several relaxation techniques before coming on stage:
1) Bring the instrument to you without playing.
2) Without moving the shoulders, turn the head slowly as far as possible and hold as you count slowly to ten. Do the same in the other direction.
3) With your hands comfortably at your side, slowly rotate them in a radial motion.
4) With your hands still comfortably at your side, move them in a paddling motion.

Rousseau acknowledges that he does get keyed up for a performance and that the adrenaline is flowing. This anticipation is vital to the creation of an emotionally moving performance.

It's important to keep the bocal warm before going on stage. If the program begins, for example, with one or two pieces on soprano and the rest on alto, Rousseau recommends placing the alto bocal in an interior coat pocket so the bocal is at a good temperature when it is placed on the instrument. This aids in tuning and reduces condensation as well.

The performance begins when the performers step onto the stage rather than when the first note is played. The performer must enter with confidence[139] and establish eye contact with the audience.[140] "When you come on stage the audience says 'welcome' and you respond with a slight duck of your head to say 'thank you.' After you've played, the audience says 'thank you' and you say 'you're welcome,' making sure to bring your head down." Know where the piano pitch is; otherwise, a long tuning tells the audience you don't know what you're doing. Finally, "check the pages to make certain they're in the correct order and cue the beginning with a breath or with a motion." Depending upon the composition to be performed, sometimes it is appropriate to "make us want that first note, as in Joan Tower's *Wings*" and sometimes we must "launch the piece, as in Dubois' first concerto."

Never forgetting that the saxophone's sound is produced by the air stream, Rousseau believes that breaths must be marked and practiced — "Breaths should be not *only* where you need them. Take them for musical reasons as well." This suggestion refers not only to taking in air; exhalations can also be noted. "Sometimes it's necessary to exhale before inhaling. Bozza's *Aria* is a good example. Breathe where the piano is duplicating the note to be cut short."

> We all know how to breathe, but often forget when we play. It must be done with greater intensity. Breathe with a sense of urgency, taking a quick, deep breath as though you were surprised. We don't 'fill the lungs' but we do so to a larger degree than usual. We can *approach* capacity with five or six quick breaths in succession; then try to do the same with only one breath.

Rousseau's acknowledged empathy with the audience is found on the concert stage. He advises us to "remember that there are two levels to every performance — what the player perceives and what the audience perceives." It is important that the audience be given the opportunity to understand music with which they are likely to be unfamiliar. To this end, Rousseau observes that "much music is played too fast. Give the audience time to absorb the musical phrases." An example is the second movement of the sonata by Paul Creston: "The rhythmic complexity must be allowed to sound."

But some sounds should not be heard. "Be certain to quietly clear the mouthpiece at every opportunity, as though one were drawing air through a small straw. Condensation is the result of the combination of hot *and* cool air and can add a crackling noise to the tone."

---

[139] "Have enough bricks to build the house."

[140] "You communicate a lot by the way you come out on stage."

Rousseau has offered explicit comments about specific musical situations. Regarding unaccompanied pieces, Rousseau acknowledges that there "are no ensemble problems but you must provide the color, the rhythmic changes, and other factors. Contrast becomes more important and so one must practice dynamics and vibrato. Dynamics, especially *subito*, should be practiced with much and then with less space. Vibrato speed should be checked, as well as the advisability of omitting it in certain spots." He is similarly unambiguous about the performance of cadenzas. "There are only five possibilities to any cadenza — faster, slower, louder, softer, and wait in order to create silence. It's a good idea to practice these possibilities in opposites; for example, *crescendo* becomes *decrescendo* and so forth."

Rousseau is judicious in his use of extended techniques: "Even if we don't want to play the extended techniques [growl tone, flutter tongue, multiphonics, etc.], we must know them."

Inexperienced players will frequently learn their part while neglecting the piano part, the orchestral score, or whatever is the other medium. Rousseau recommends that students become familiar with what else is going on during the performance so that, "rather than counting, you can use your ear to guide entrances." Indeed, Rousseau reminds us that "all music is played by ear, whether we have the score in front of us or not." To this end, he will occasionally introduce ear training into lessons — "Have the student match a pitch on the saxophone without looking."

Rousseau believes in the value of transcriptions, perhaps remembering his early exposure in bands to masterworks. He cites guitarist Andres Segovia[141] and, especially, Ferruccio Busoni, who implied that everything is a transcription even before it is played when he wrote "Every notation is, in itself, the transcription of an abstract idea. The instant the pen seizes it, the idea loses its original form."[142]

The ability to transpose at sight from a C score opens a wealth of flute and oboe literature to soprano and is strongly encouraged.[143] This skill can be valuable in other situations, as related by Rousseau.

> Kari Miller and I played the soprano saxophone sonata by Feld in Helsinki at the Sibelius Conservatory in 1984. It was a manuscript version — it was not yet printed — and I forgot the soprano part in London. Two or three people, including Kari, copied all the solo lines

---

[141] Segovia, who lived from 1893 to 1987, made arrangements and transcriptions (especially the music of J.S. Bach) an important part of his repertoire.

[142] Ferruccio Busoni, "Sketch of a New Esthetic of Music," in *Three Classics in the Aesthetic of Music*, translated by Th. Baker (New York: Dover Publications, New York, 1962): 85. A composer, pianist, and conductor, Busoni (1866–1924) frequently drew inspiration from earlier composers for his own works.

[143] "Regarding ornaments in Baroque and Classical music, if there is a choice use the one which sounds the best."

from the piano part, then cut and pasted a new soprano part for me. I did not look at it before going on stage for the recital. You can imagine my surprise when I saw only concert pitches! Thank heavens I had had much experience in transposing at sight.

Rousseau understands the psychology behind performance, the mental gymnastics that accompany the physical ones necessary to perform well. "We practice in order to get responses and to keep proving to ourselves that we can do something — 'I know that I just played that, but can I do it again?'" As a final point, he states that "in the end, *you* must make your performance convincing."

18 Wit and Wisdom:
He's good, madam, but he's not that good

Eugene Rousseau remains active as a teacher and performer in the year 2011, fifty-five years after he began his career at Luther College. There can be no "concluding chapter" to a life and career that continues to be in full swing, as there are unknown chapters yet to be lived and fulfilled. Rousseau has said that he has numerous projects in mind but wants to perform and record as long as possible, delaying these plans indefinitely.

Among his most recent projects is his edition of the etudes by Wilhelm Ferling. The edition[144] is restricted to the slow (i.e., odd-numbered) etudes in order to present the lyrical style of playing which is at the core of Rousseau's approach to the saxophone. In addition, he feels that other etudes such as those by Guy Lacour address the technical challenges of the instrument better than Ferling's oboe studies.

During the course of his long career, Rousseau has encountered numerous remarkable situations and made many notable observations. The anecdotes that follow serve to illustrate the good humor found at the heart of his personality and the unique perspective which he brings to life, music, and the saxophone.

Rousseau has performed in many of the world's great concert halls and with many renowned pianists, including Hans Graf of Vienna's Hochschule für Musik, Heinz Medjimorec of the Haydn Trio of Vienna, the Englishman John Wilson, Mariko Hattori of Japan, and the American Kari Miller. On another occasion, however, he traveled to a small Indiana town to present a recital. There he was met by two pianists and he assumed that one of the young ladies would play part of the program and the second young lady would play the other works. He was astonished to learn this was not to be the case — they would both play the entire program, one performing the right-hand part while the left-hand part would be done by the second pianist.

While these two pianists were probably not expert musicians, the conductor of an unnamed community orchestra was in fact a professional. Rousseau was brought in by the orchestra as soloist for the concerto by Glazounov and the rehearsals went reasonably well. The performance also progressed smoothly until after the cadenza. When the cello section failed to make its entrance, the conductor rapped his baton on the music stand and barked "Pay attention!" Rousseau had four measures to regain his composure before *his* entrance; he didn't want the conductor to reprimand *him* in front of the audience.

Sometimes it's not the musicians who are responsible for the situation. Rousseau performed many times with Carl Fuerstner, an excellent pianist and

---

[144] *Ferling 24 Melodic Studies from 48 Etudes, op. 31*, ed. by Eugene Rousseau. Minneapolis: Jeanné, Inc. 2010.

Rousseau's colleague at the Indiana University School of Music. Fuerstner was the pianist for Rousseau's first faculty recital at Indiana in 1965 and for his second European tour in 1968. It was during the concerts in Europe that Rousseau and Fuerstner recorded the *Sonatine Sportive* of Alexander Tcherepnine for the British Broadcasting Corporation. The third movement, marked *Course* (or "Race") is a canon in which the saxophone begins and is followed by the piano two measures later, playing the same material. At the movement's conclusion, an officious lady burst from the control room and announced "You'll have to do that last movement again. You weren't together at all!"

The previous year, just before his first recital in London's Wigmore Hall, Rousseau encountered another woman who perhaps did not understand the saxophone. Unable to play in his modest hotel, Rousseau went to another building where practice rooms could be rented. The woman in charge asked if he wanted a room with or without a piano. Rousseau replied, "Without a piano. I'll be playing the saxophone." "Saxophone?! That's a terribly loud instrument, isn't it?" she responded. Rousseau explained that although the saxophone can be played loudly it can also be played quietly. "I'll put you in this room at the end but if any of the pianists complain that you're too loud I'll have to move you." "And I'll be certain to let you know if any of the pianists are too loud," Rousseau replied.

Rousseau loves to play the saxophone and will rarely miss an opportunity to share the instrument with others. As an example, for years one of the highlights of the Midwest Band and Orchestra Clinic, held in Chicago each December, was the performance of the Midwest Christmas Saxophone Quartet. With Rousseau on soprano and either with well-known saxophonists such as Dennis DiBlasio and Dale Underwood or present and former students, the Quartet would play seasonal favorites at various exhibits at the Clinic.

On another occasion, after an especially successful recital, Rousseau received heartfelt congratulations from one of his students. Rousseau replied that he had given an unusual number of performances recently and "performance is the best kind of practice."

One of Rousseau's most unusual performances occurred in an unlikely venue. The setting was a night flight from Atlanta to Indianapolis with only five or six passengers and three or four crew on board. Delta Airlines had an exchange program with Air France at the time and one of the crew members asked Rousseau, in French, what was in his case. Rousseau answered in French that it was a saxophone. She had another crew member join her and they asked him, still in French, if he would play something for them. Rousseau gladly played tunes for them all the way back to Indiana, where he remembers their friendly wave as they shouted, "Au revoir, Eugene!"

Rousseau began early to gather the skills necessary to become a master teacher. While still in grade school, he displayed the curiosity characteristic of youngsters. He had begun to learn the saxophone in fourth grade and, having had some success, was interested in playing another instrument — the trumpet. His teacher, Miss Elda Jansen, knew that this was not a good idea and she also knew how to handle the situation. She gave the young Rousseau a trumpet but no instruction on how to play it. "Here you are," she said. "Come back tomorrow and let's hear what you've done." Rousseau, of course, had no success in figuring out on his own how to produce a sound. He returned the trumpet to Miss Jansen the next day and renewed his focus on the saxophone.

Rousseau's master classes are always filled with such common sense advice. He often shares his wide-ranging performance experiences, seeming to have encountered every conceivable circumstance. Sometimes it's a simple suggestion, such as to move the ligature up on the mouthpiece if a reed begins to warp during a performance. Another example occurred when he played his saxophone for a master class and asked the students their opinions concerning his reed — Did it sound all right? Did it seem to respond well? After everyone agreed that the reed sounded fine, Rousseau removed the reed from the mouthpiece to show them that it was split down the middle into two parts. Rousseau's point was that performers should not be overly concerned about reeds although, as he said, "I don't know that I would use this reed in Carnegie Hall."

Rousseau's students often are quite observant. Early in his years at Indiana he brought to the studio a saxophone he had just gotten from the Leblanc factory. Because it was necessary to leave the factory quickly, there had been no time to lacquer the bocal. After a week of lessons and seeing the unlacquered bocal, his students began to ask how best to remove the lacquer from their bocals. On another occasion, Rousseau lost one of the screws from his ligature and played with only one screw for a few days. Some of his students came to their lessons the next week with a screw removed from their ligatures. In each case they thought they had discovered part of the answer for producing the Rousseau sound.

A lesson with Rousseau will often include the performance of saxophone literature with a pianist. Because student pianists sometimes overuse the sustain pedal, Rousseau keeps a small block of wood handy. This is offered to the pianist to place under the sustain pedal so that the pedal is inoperative and, as Rousseau may tell the pianist, "you can rest your right foot on the pedal if you're more comfortable that way."

Rousseau is aware of the challenges faced by performers while at the same time he realizes that they must be overcome. He will remind students of this fact by recounting one of his lessons with Marcel Mule. Rousseau had been assigned a particular piece containing a passage that was exceptionally complicated. He told Mule that he had found the passage to be especially difficult, at which point Mule looked at the score, picked up his saxophone, played the passage flawlessly, and said "It *is* difficult." Rousseau understood that even the most challenging music must be played well.

Rousseau also shares his intimate knowledge of the saxophone literature and its composers. He regrets not having met Jacques Ibert during his Fulbright study with Mule; Ibert died the next year, in 1962. But he is pleased to have met Marius Constant, Alfred Desenclos, and Claude Pascal after his Paris recital of 1968 which included music by each composer.

Many of the composers are now deceased, including Paul Creston and Rousseau's colleague at Indiana University, Bernhard Heiden. Other composers are still with us and enjoy their personal and professional relationships with him. Karel Husa and Libby Larsen have close ties to Rousseau, as do his Bloomington colleagues Juan Orrego-Salas, Fred Fox, and Claude Baker. Jindřich Feld is an example of a prominent composer who came to the saxophone through Rousseau. Rousseau often spoke with them about their music and their wishes for its performance and many of these conversations can be found in the dissertation by Patrick Jones.[145]

When Rousseau returned to the United States after his year in Paris, he brought with him several pieces of music which were almost unknown in this country. During his first year as a member of the Indiana University faculty he recommended just such a work to a graduate student. Rousseau suggested the student would benefit from studying Guy Lacour's extremely challenging *8 Brilliant Etudes*. According to Rousseau, the student glanced quickly at the set and said, "They don't look to be too long; I'll do two or three of them for next week." Rousseau reports that the student returned the next week "a broken man." In another comment, Rousseau said that he had figured out Lacour's method of composing his etudes — "Whenever Lacour goes to sleep he makes certain that he has manuscript paper and a pencil on his bed stand. Then he wakes up in the middle of the night and exclaims to himself '*That* can't be played!' Lacour writes down the musical passage and, before you know it, he has another etude."

Rousseau greatly enjoys performing chamber music with strings and woodwinds. He recognizes that "if you bring another orchestral instrument to the stage with you, you gain credibility. This is true even if you play music not originally for saxophone, such as the Beethoven op. 11." Rousseau has cited as one of his most memorable performances the concert in which he joined the Haydn Trio of Vienna on the occasion of their twenty-fifth anniversary. The concert took place before an audience that overflowed on to seats placed on the stage — "Never would I have had such an audience for a solo recital."

His repertoire has grown over the years and it has sometimes changed as well. "I play less new music today, although I recently gave the premieres of the concertos by Libby Larsen and Claude Baker. I'm perhaps more likely to play standard literature, such as when I was recently asked specifically to perform the Ibert *Concertino* by an orchestra in Illinois. And I'm playing some music I've missed

---

[145] Patrick Jones, "Interpreting Selected Works for Saxophone-based Performer-Composer Relationships" (DMA diss., University of Minnesota, 2004).

along the way, such as the Tomasi *Concerto* which I did with three different orchestras this past season [2007-2008]."

Rousseau's contacts, of course, include musicians other than composers and these can serve to illustrate the rising status of the saxophone. For example, he has related a comment by famed pianist and Indiana University colleague Menahem Pressler made following a series of auditions by harpists. After hearing several performances, Pressler observed that the literature for saxophone was of much higher quality than the literature written for that highly regarded member of the orchestra, the harp. Pressler would have had no basis for his remark had he not heard performances by Rousseau and his students.

Indiana's School of Music frequently welcomes esteemed guest professors from abroad. The renowned English bassoonist William Waterhouse, who was famous for the unusual sound of his instrument, was such an artist. As part of his time in Bloomington, Waterhouse presented a solo recital. At a reception following the performance, a woman remarked to Rousseau, "He sounds rather like a saxophone, don't you think, Dr. Rousseau?" Rousseau replied, "He's good, madam, but he's not *that* good!"

Other incidents recall the importance of making the most of whatever situation one encounters. Rousseau enjoys remembering when he joined conductor Dr. James Nielsen, who was engaged as clinician for a regional honor band. He was greeted by Nielsen, who had rehearsed the band earlier in the day and told Rousseau that the students were unable to play the music selected for them by their directors — in fact, Nielsen predicted the evening concert would be a disaster. The event, of course, must take place but Nielsen had an idea. At the appointed time, Nielsen came on stage and addressed the audience. He made the usual comments about how happy he was to be there and so forth. He then asked a question of the parents and other family members who had come to hear their youngsters: "I know that all of you have been to band *concerts* but how many of you have attended one of your child's band *rehearsals*?" When only a few persons raised their hands affirmatively Nielsen responded, "That's what I thought and so I have a real treat for you tonight. Rather than another concert, we're going to take you through a rehearsal to show you the learning that takes place every day." Nielsen had turned a potential catastrophe into an enjoyable and memorable occasion, with everybody feeling positively about bands and music.

Rousseau has always been a "morning person." He arises early, dealing with correspondence and practicing before many people have begun the day. When they were younger, he would awaken his children Joseph and Lisa-Marie by playing reveille on the saxophone. His day is invariably full including, when he taught at Indiana, a brisk walk of approximately two miles from his home to his studio. Those of us who have walked with him, whether in Bloomington, Minneapolis, Shell Lake, or elsewhere, know that the pace is fast and the experience invigorating. He has found that his walk is an excellent time to assess the day's objectives and determine how best to meet them. As someone once said, "Walking solves all problems."

Rousseau understands that problems are a part of life. Health concerns and personal relationships can be among the many challenges to be faced and so he has reminded his students, "We all have handicaps: some are external and some are internal. How we deal with them is what determines our character." Similarly, he once advised a student who was about to take his first professional position — "Wherever you are, associate with the best musicians you can find; it'll rub off on you. And associate with the best persons you can find; that will rub off, too."

Many people consider Rousseau to be one of those "best persons you can find." A heartfelt letter from Robert Schott, Chairman of the Department of Music at Pittsburg State University in Kansas, followed a performance and master class there by Rousseau.

> . . . Eugene, as much as I would like to extol the sheer loveliness and artistry of your evening performance and speak of the sensitivity and warmth you brought to everything you played and of the way you reached out to your audience in such a gracious manner, I cannot but help return to thoughts of your gentle manner and the way that you reached out to everyone in such a loving way. As much as you had to offer musically to these aspiring young musicians and possible future teachers, I cannot but help think that the most beautiful thing you gave them and indeed to all of us was a beautiful lesson in selflessness, of reaching out in love and helpfulness to another. . . Thank you for sharing so beautifully your artistry, your gentle manner, and the philosophy of life that shone so brightly in everything you did. We are all the richer for it.[146]

---

[146] Robert Schott letter to Rousseau, April 7, 1986.

Conclusions:
Quietly producing quality wherever he goes, never finding it necessary or expedient to remind people of his achievements

One of Rousseau's students remembers that early in his work with Rousseau he was advised by another member of the studio

> that I must 'watch everything Dr. Rousseau does,' that ER is a very successful man. And it was true, from how he greeted a stranger at the door or answered the phone, to the carefully worded notes written on old programs that he left pinned to his bulletin board, his unfaltering class and dignity and his amazing organization shone through everything he did. [47]

There can be no doubt that Eugene Rousseau has had success at many levels — as a performer, teacher, husband, father, grandfather, and friend to many. Aspiring saxophonists who have come to him have taken away far more than increased musical skills. They have observed how to conduct oneself in a variety of situations, how to treat people with respect, and how to enjoy life. What qualities does he possess that have made that success possible?

His background, growing up in Blue Island, Illinois, was that of a warm, stable home and family with few material comforts. Rousseau recalls going to school with cardboard inserted into his shoes because the soles had worn through and there was no money to repair or replace them. He remembers his father looking for work day after day and, finally, finding a job that brought home $1.50 — for that day. The next morning meant seeking work again. Rousseau understands what it is like to do without and how hard some people will work to achieve something. He also understands that some who have always had financial security may lack the drive to succeed.

Rousseau possesses that desire to succeed, what is sometimes called "fire in the belly." He will do his best to be ready for whatever opportunity presents itself; Rousseau understands that is the true definition of an "opportunist," a term sometimes applied negatively. He tells the story of his performance of a concerto with band. Afterward, the wife of a former saxophone student came backstage to congratulate Rousseau. The student had been a remarkably talented performer. "You know," she said, "my husband can play that concerto, too." "Yes, I know that he can," Rousseau responded. Left unsaid was "but why isn't he?" Rousseau knew from his work with the student that a certain passion had been lacking.

Rousseau often counsels that adaptability and versatility are indispensable to success. He is fluent in the different languages of jazz and classical music, he is

---

[47] Michael Hester email message to author, March 11, 2007.

conversant with other woodwind instruments in addition to the saxophone, and he has experience in such fields as mouthpiece and reed production, instrument design, and music merchandising. He has been a band director, theory instructor, and woodwind teacher. He advises his students that they must be able to do more than play the saxophone brilliantly in order to be employable.

He has cultivated the ability to communicate with others on several levels, including his fluency in German and French. Rousseau thinks it is wrong to assume that all persons will understand the same thing in exactly the same way; therefore, one must be able to speak to different audiences in different ways. He will present the acoustics of the saxophone, for example, at a World Saxophone Congress differently than he might at a workshop for junior high school students. We can recall his story concerning the two ways to ask for help with a flat tire.[148]

Himie Voxman has spoken of Rousseau's intellectual curiosity as a doctoral student at the University of Iowa. That quality both shaped and broadened Rousseau's view of the world and he has spoken approvingly when he has found it in others. He brings a deeper knowledge to the many aspects of music and the saxophone because he believes that an answer to one question often implies additional questions whose answers will present further questions, *ad infinitum*. Rousseau has explained that "The beauty of learning is that it is unlimited; it never has to end."

Perhaps because of his background Rousseau has tremendous empathy for other people. He understands that frustrations can exist, that challenges sometimes can seem overwhelming, and that it is by helping one another that they can be surmounted. He has the ability to make the other person feel valuable and important, that what they have to offer is worthwhile. It is his capacity to see the potentialities in other persons which draws people to him again and again.

Rousseau has acquired the skill of "cumulative learning."[149] He believes that some degree of what is first learned is retained as a base for further learning. He has consciously developed this skill so that, rather than constantly relearning a concept or an intricate musical passage, he can refresh works as necessary while continuing to expand his knowledge and his repertory.

He is not intimidated by his peers. He is unafraid to share the spotlight with other saxophonists of great reputation at his workshops and master classes. Larry Teal of the University of Michigan, the first full-time college saxophone teacher in the country, was a guest at Rousseau's workshop in Shell Lake, Wisconsin, as were Frederick Hemke of Northwestern University and Joseph Wytko of Arizona State University. Rousseau has invited jazz great Phil Woods and Claude Delangle

---

[148] Found on p. 110 in biography.

[149] Cumulative learning is described as using the results of prior learning to facilitate further learning (e.g., building new knowledge structures from experience by combining previously learned structures), according to *On-Line Cumulative Learning of Hierarchical Spars n-grams* by Karl Pfleger, Computer Science Department, Stanford University.

of the Paris National Conservatory to his annual saxophone workshop at the University of Minnesota. He does not need to remind people of his successes or denigrate the accomplishments of others. "His humility is refreshing. He impresses people by quietly producing quality wherever he goes, never finding it necessary or expedient to remind people of his achievements. He has spoken through his instrument, his students, and his teaching. . ."[150]

Much to the probable surprise of many, Rousseau is a self-described risk-taker. He seems to be a person who evaluates possible outcomes before embarking on a project but, once he has satisfied himself as to the likelihood of success, goes forward with great confidence. It may be that it is impossible to accomplish great things without the courage to accept risk. Because those risks have often involved Rousseau's family as well, a successful marriage has been crucial. Further evidence of a solid marital relationship is the ability to maintain two residences — their home in Indiana and a condominium in Minnesota. Rousseau's wife Norma has been an insightful and sympathetic influence for fifty years. Her encouragement and support have made their accomplishments those of a team rather than of an individual.

Speaking personally, I have never met anyone more at peace with himself than Eugene Rousseau. Perhaps this is a separate quality or perhaps this is a result of the confluence of the traits cited above. It helps to explain why so many of his students see themselves as part of a family bound together by their time with Rousseau, that they can remain a member of his extended studio for as long as they wish. That is why large numbers of his former students attend World Saxophone Congresses and North American Saxophone Alliance conferences — they know they will see Rousseau or many of their old friends from his studio. It is why, depending upon the generation, he is a father figure, a grandfather figure, or a trusted friend to whom one can always turn for guidance.

Rousseau's departure from Indiana University for the University of Minnesota in 2000 was as though there had been a shifting of the tectonic plates of the saxophone world. Despite that change, much has remained constant. He continues to teach with kindness and personal authority, he still maintains a worldwide schedule of performances and classes that would exhaust a much younger person, and he remains an inspiration to his recent and long-ago students. He has gained their respect, gratitude, and affection for the enduring example of a life well lived.

---

[150] Harlow Hopkins letter to author, December 2, 1986.

GRAND CONCERT

OF THE

1958

FESTIVAL MASSED BAND

Luther College Music Festival
Arranged by the Dorian Musical Society
Elson Heggen, President

7:45 P. M. - C. K. Preus Auditorium

GROUP ONE
FESTIVAL BAND

DR. ALVIN EDGAR, Conducting

Jubilee March	Kenny
La Forza Del Destino	Verdi-Lake
Pastels	McRae
Fantasie Concertante	Rousseau-Harmon
Dr. Harmon, soloist	
Belle Of The Ball	Anderson
Fairest Of The Fair	Sousa

GROUP TWO

Selected soloists as chosen by Mr. Hendrickson, Mr. Rousseau, Dr. Harmon, Prof. Vossman, and Mr. Scherer from the performances of the day.

GROUP THREE
LUTHER COLLEGE CONCERT BAND

WESTON NOBLE, Conducting

March For Band	Beecham
Fanfare and Allegro	Williams
Valzer Campestre	Mariuzzi-Harding
Introduction and Samba	Whitney
Mr. Eugene Rousseau, Soloist	
Death and Transfiguration	Strauss

Plans are being made for a tour of Norway and other countries of Europe in 1961 for the Luther College Concert Band.

1958 — Luther College Concert Band

EUGENE ROUSSEAU
SAXOPHONIST

Assisting Artists: Leonard Klein, Piano
Allen Winold, Viola

CARNEGIE RECITAL HALL
WEDNESDAY, JANUARY 6th, 1965
At 8:30 P.M.

EUGENE ROUSSEAU

DR. EUGENE ROUSSEAU is Assistant Professor of Music at Indiana University, where he teaches saxophone exclusively. He studied in Paris under Marcel Mule on a Fulbright Grant, and has appeared as guest conductor, lecturer and clinician throughout the Midwest. In April and May of 1963 he was a clinician and musical representative of the U. S. Trade Fair in Conakry, Guinea.

Dr. Rousseau has published numerous articles on the teaching and performing of orchestral wind instruments. He also plays the Leblanc Alto Saxophone.

Program

Adagio and allegro	Handel (arr. E. Rousseau)
Sonate	Bernard Heiden
Allegro	
Vivace	
Adagio-Presto	
Sonatine	Claude Pascal
a l'aise	
lent	
vif	

INTERMISSION

Prélude, cadence, et finale	A. Desenclos
Trio for Tenor Saxophone, Viola, and Piano (op. 47)	Hindemith
Erster Teil: Solo, Arioso, Duett	
Zweiter Teil: Potpourri	
Schnelle - Lebhaft - Schnelle - Prestissimo	
Sonata	Paul Creston
with vigor	
with tranquility	
with gaiety	

Steinway Piano

Tickets: $3.00, $1.80 incl. tax
At CARNEGIE HALL Box Office
Or by mail to Mgt. — BICHURIN CONCERTS CORP.
Carnegie Hall (Room 609), New York, N. Y. 10019

January 6, 1965 — New York Carnegie Hall, Leonard Klein, Allen Winold Debut recital

November 6, 1966 — Washington,
D.C., Phillips Collection, Joseph Rezits

January 20, 1967 — London Wigmore Hall,
Marion Hall
First London saxophone recital

140

January 25, 1967 — Berlin Konzertsaal
Bundesallee, Marion Hall
First Berlin saxophone recital

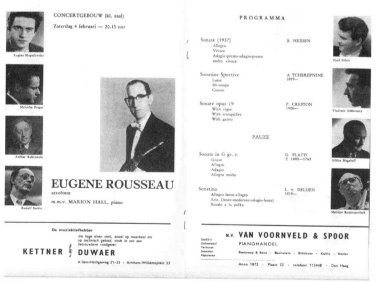

February 4, 1967 — Amsterdam Concertgebouw, Marion Hall
First Amsterdam saxophone recital

January 13, 1968 — BBC Concert Orchestra

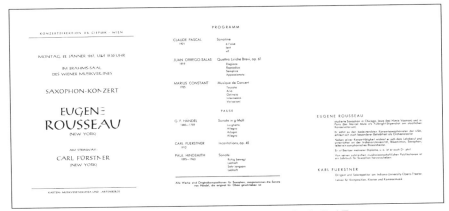

January 22, 1968 (note program error) — Vienna Brahms-Saal, Carl Fuerstner
First Vienna saxophone recital

1968 Paris Recital Flyer

January 27, 1968 — Paris
Salle Gaveau, Carl Fuerstner
First Paris saxophone recital

May 1, 1974 — Washington, D.C., Kennedy Center Festival Orchestra, Lukas Foss

July 9, 1982 — Nuremberg Meistersingerhalle, Munich Radio Orchestra
Feld *Concerto* premiere

April 12 and 14, 1983
Santiago Philharmonic Orchestra

Kari Miller

Kari Miller aloitti pianonsoiton opintonsa viisivuotiaana. Hänen opettajinaan alkuvaiheessa olivat Roland Woolacott, Agnes Rinus ja Ira Swartz. Päästyään yliopppilaaksi hän sai stipendin Philadelphiassa sijaitsevaan Curtisin musiikkiinstituuttiin, jossa hän opiskeli Eleanor Sokoloffin ja Mieczyslaw Horsowskin johdolla.

Hän on voittanut lukuisia palkintoja, mm. vuonna 1983 Johann Sebastian Bachin nimeä kantavassa kansainvälisessä pianokilpailussa Washingtonissa.

Kari Miller on esiintynyt orkesterin solistina Euroopassa sekä lukuisissa konserteissa Yhdysvalloissa. Hänet tunnetaan erinomaisesta yhteistyöstään muiden arvostettujen taiteilijoiden kanssa, ja hän on erittäin kysytty kamarimusiikin esittäjä. Neiti Miller on nykyään kandidaattina Indianan yliopistossa, missä hän opiskelee Michel Blockin johdolla.

EUGENE ROUSSEAU,
altto- ja sopraanosaksofoni
KARI MILLER,
piano

ke 2.10.1985 klo 19.00
Sibelius-Akatemia

 YAMAHA

Musiikki Kaikki

OHJELMA

SONAATTI, op. 29 (1972) — Robert Muczynski (★ 1929)
Andante maestoso
Allegro energico

SONAATTI — Edison Denisov (★ 1929)
Allegro
Lento
Allegro moderato

RAPSODIA — Claude Debussy (1862—1918)
sov. Eugene Rousseau

VÄLIAIKA

SONAATTI — Jindrich Feld (★ 1925)
Moderato — più mosso
Scherzo: Allegro assai
Finale: Allegro con brio —
molto moderato

SONAATTI E-duuri, S. 1035 — Johann Sebastian Bach (1685—1750)
Adagio ma non tanto
Allegro
Siciliano
Allegro assai

Eugene Rousseau

Eugene Rousseaulla, yhdellä maailman suurista saksofonisteista, on laaja kokemus monenlaisesta musiikista ja eri tyylisuunnista. Chicagon seudulta kotoisin oleva saksofonisti suoritti erittäin onnistuneen debyyttin New Yorkin Carnegie Hallissa vuonna 1965. Paitsi joka puolella Yhdysvaltoja, hän on esiintynyt Kanadassa, Englannissa, Ranskassa, Saksan Liittotasavallassa, Hollannissa, Ruotsissa, Norjassa, Tanskassa, Suomessa, Itävallassa, Tshekkoslovakiassa, Afrikassa, Etelä-Amerikassa ja Japanissa.

Hänellä on laaja tuntemus puupuhaltimista, joita hän on käyttänyt koko uransa ajan sekä opettajana että taiteilijana. Hän on suorittanut filosofian tohtorin tutkinnon Iowan yliopistossa ja ollut musiikin professorina Indianan yliopistossa Bloomingtonissa vuodesta 1964 lähtien.

Rousseau on toiminut neuvonantajana Montrealin yliopistossa ja on nykyään Santiagon filharmonisen orkesterin taiteellinen neuvonantaja. Kaudella 1982—83 hän piti järjestyksessä toisen saksofoninsoiton erikoiskurssin Wienin Musiikkikorkeakoulussa. Vuosina 1981—82 hän toimi ensimmäisenä saksofoninsoiton opettajana tässä arvostetussa opistossa. Tänä syksynä hän pitää saksofoninsoiton kurssin myös Prahan konservatoriossa.

Rousseau on levyttänyt useita saksofonille sävellettyjä soolo- ja kamariteoksia. Hänen julkaisuja teoksiaan ovat mm. 2-osainen "Method for Saxophone" (Kjos), sekä myös ranskaksi ja saksaksi julkaistu altissimo-rekisteritekniikkaa käsittelevä "Saxophone High Tones" (Etoile). Hiljattain on ilmestynyt hänen opettajastaan kirjoittamansa elämänkerta "Marcel Mule: His Life and the Saxophone" (Etoile).

Runsaan vuosikymmenen ajan Eugene Rousseau on omistanut suuren osan luovaa kykyään saksofonien ja niiden suukappaleiden kehittämiseen. Vuodesta 1972 lähtien hän on toiminut Yamaha-saksofonien tutkimus- ja kehittämistyön pääneuvonantajana, ja on tänä aikana käynyt Japanissa yli 20 kertaa.

Vuodesta 1978 vuoteen 1980 hän oli Pohjois-Amerikan Saksofoniliiton puheenjohtaja. Tällä hetkellä hän toimii Kansainvälisen Saksofonikomitean puheenjohtajana. Tämä komitea, jossa on edustaja useista eri maista, piti kahdeksannen maailmanlaajuisen saksofonikongressin Marylandin Yliopistossa tämän vuoden kesäkuussa.

The Instrumentalist -lehti julkaisi syyskuun 1983 numerossaan laajan artikkelin Eugene Rousseauta haastatteluineen ja kansikuvineen.

February 10, 1985 — Helsinki Sibelius Academy

WIENER KONZERTHAUSGESELLSCHAFT
MOZART-SAAL

Dienstag, 8. Mai 1990, 19.30 Uhr
Zyklus Vb/HAYDN-TRIO
4. Konzert im Abonnement

WOLFGANG AMADEUS MOZART (1756—1791)
Klaviertrio C-Dur KV 548
(1788)
 Allegro
 Andante cantabile
 Allegro

JUAN ORREGO-SALAS (*1919)
Partita für Altsaxophon und Klaviertrio op. 100
(1987, österreichische Erstaufführung)
 Allegro deciso e cantabile
 Allegretto
 Adagio pensieroso
 Allegro deciso

☐

CLAUDE DEBUSSY (1862—1918)
Rhapsodie für Altsaxophon
(1905)

MAURICE RAVEL (1875—1937)
Klaviertrio a-moll
(1914)
 Modéré
 Pantoum. Assez vif
 Passacaille. Très large
 Final. Animé

HAYDN-TRIO
MICHAEL SCHNITZLER, Violine
WALTHER SCHULZ, Violoncello
HEINZ MEDJIMOREC, Klavier

EUGENE ROUSSEAU, Altsaxophon

May 8, 1990 — Vienna
Konzerthausgesellschaft, Vienna Trio

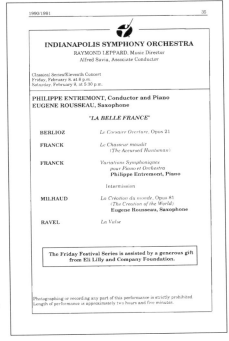

February 8 and 9, 1991 — Indianapolis
Symphony Orchestra, Richard Entremonte
Milhaud *La Création du monde*

APPENDIX A

PUBLISHED WORKS BY EUGENE ROUSSEAU

MUSIC

Brahms, Johannes — Clarinet Sonata in F minor, op. 120, no. 1, arr. for alto saxophone and piano, 1981. Lauren Keiser Music.
Brahms, Johannes — Clarinet Sonata in E-flat major, op. 120, no. 2, arr. for alto saxophone and piano, 1986. Lauren Keiser Music.
Chopin, Frèdèric — Largo from Cello Sonata in G minor, op. 63, arr. for alto saxophone and piano, 1969. Lauren Keiser Music.
Debussy, Claude — Rapsodie, arr. for alto saxophone and piano, 1975, revised 2002. Lauren Keiser Music.
Handel, Georg Frideric — Adagio and Allegro from Oboe Sonata in C minor, arr. for alto saxophone and piano, 1967. Wingert-Jones.
Haydn, Franz Joseph — Andante from Oboe Concerto in C major, arr. for soprano saxophone and piano, 1980. Lauren Keiser Music.
Platti, Giovanni — Sonata in G major, arr. for soprano saxophone and piano, 1969. Lauren Keiser Music.
Rachmaninoff, Sergei — Vocalise, op. 34, no. 14, arr. for alto saxophone (with optional change to soprano saxophone) and piano, 1980. Lauren Keiser Music.
Solo Album for Alto Saxophone, 1980. Lauren Keiser Music.
Solo Album for Tenor Saxophone, 1980. Lauren Keiser Music.
Quartet Album for Saxophones, 1980. Lauren Keiser Music.

PEDAGOGY

Beginning Method for Saxophone, 1965. Leblanc.
Ferling 24 Melodic Studies from 48 Etudes, op. 31, 2010. Jeanné.
Method for Saxophone, Volumes I and II, 1973. Kjos.
Practical Hints on Playing Alto Saxophone, 1983. Alfred Publications.
Practical Hints on Playing Tenor Saxophone, 1983. Alfred Publications.
Practical Hints on Playing Baritone Saxophone, 1983. Alfred Publications.

BOOKS

The Leblanc (Paris) System Saxophones, n.d. G. Leblanc Corporation.
Saxophone High Tones, first ed. 1978, second ed. 2002. Lauren Keiser Music.
Marcel Mule: His Life and the Saxophone, 1982. Etoile.

ARTICLES

"Materials for Making Clarinets." *Instrumentalist* (April 1956).
"The Clarinet Embouchure." *Leblanc Bandsman* (April 1958).
"Essential Points in Teaching Saxophone." *Leblanc Bandsman* (May 1959).
"Solo Literature for the Saxophone." *Instrumentalist*, Vol. XV, No. 8 (April 1961): 72–74.
"Comments on Orchestral Winds in Paris." *Instrumentalist*, Vol. XV, No. 9 (May 1961).

"Saxophone Literature." *Instrumentalist* (May 1961).
"Saxophone Tone Quality." *Instrumentalist*, Vol. XVI, No. 10 (June 1962).
"Rousseau Aids U.S. Effort in Africa." Interview by *World of Music* (Fall 1963).
"Music in Guinea." *Woodwind World*, Vol. VI, No. 1 (September 15, 1964): 6.
"Bases for the Appearance of Musical Instruments in Visual Works of Art." *Missouri Journal of Research in Music Education*, Vol. I, No. 3 (1964): 25–33.
"Beginning Method for Saxophone." Leblanc Publications (1965).
"The Early History of the Clarinet (Part I)." *Woodwind World* (September 15, 1965).
"The Early History of the Clarinet (Part II)." *Woodwind World* (October 1965).
"On the Interpretation of Jacques Ibert's *Concertino da Camera*." *Woodwind World* (November 1965).
"A Selected and Annotated List of Saxophone Literature." *Missouri School Music Magazine*, Vol. 21, No. 5 (May 1967).
"Some Thoughts About the Saxophone Mouthpiece." *Saxophone Journal*, Vol. 11, No. 1 (Spring 1986): 33–38.
"The Saxophone Quartet: Some Observations." *Saxophone Journal*, Vol. 11, No. 2 (Summer 1986): 26–29.

APPENDIX B

WORKS WRITTEN FOR OR DEDICATED TO EUGENE ROUSSEAU

Baker, Claude — *Lamentations (pour la fin du monde)* for alto/soprano saxophones (one player) and orchestra, 2006. Unpublished.
 Premiered July 5, 2006 at World Saxophone Congress XIV in Ljubljana, Slovenia

Cailliet, Lucien — *Eighth Solo* for solo alto saxophone and piano, 1973. Southern Music Company.

Canfield, David DeBoor — *Concerto after Gliere* for alto saxophone and orchestra, 2007. Enharmonic Press.
 Premiered July 8, 2009 by Kenneth Tse at World Saxophone Congress XV in Bangkok

Carmichael, Hoagy, arr. by David Baker — *Medley* (*Skylark; Georgia on my mind; The nearness of you*) for alto saxophone and jazz ensemble.

Ellington, Duke, arr. by David Baker — *Satin Doll*.

Feld, Jindřich — Concerto for alto/soprano/tenor saxophones (one player) and orchestra, 1980. MMB.
 Premiered July 9, 1982 at World Saxophone Congress VII, Nuremberg, Germany

Feld, Jindřich — Concerto for alto/soprano/tenor saxophones (one player) and wind orchestra version, 1984. MMB.

Feld, Jindřich — Quintet for alto/soprano saxophones (one player) and string quartet, 2000. Billaudot.
 Premiered February 21, 2000 at Martinů Hall in Prague

Feld, Jindřich — Sonata for alto saxophone and piano. Leduc.
 Premiered February 1, 1991 in Tokyo

Feld, Jindřich — Sonata for soprano saxophone and piano. Leduc.
 Premiered February 1984 in London

Fox, Frederick — *Hear Again in Memory* for solo saxophone, 1989. Dorn.

Fox, Frederick — *Visitation* for two saxophones, 1981. Unpublished.

Freund, Don — *Sky Scrapings* for alto saxophone and piano, 1977. Unpublished.

Gallaher, Christopher — Sonatina for alto saxophone and piano, 1969. Studio Publications.

Gershwin, George, arr. by Brent Wallarab — *Porgy and Bess Medley* (*Summertime; It ain't necessarily so; Bess you is my woman now*) for alto/soprano saxophones (one player) and jazz ensemble.

Gotkovsky, Ida — *Trio lyrique* for alto saxophone, violin, and piano, 2003. Billaudot.

Green, Johnny, arr. by Rich Shanklin — *Body and Soul.*

Heiden, Bernhard — *Fantasia Concertante* for alto saxophone and nineteen instruments and percussion, 1987. MMB.
  Premiered April 5, 1988 in Bloomington, Indiana

Heiden, Bernhard — *Four Movements* for saxophone quartet and tympani, 1976. MMB.
  Premiered January 26, 1977 in Bloomington, Indiana

Heiden, Bernhard — *Intrada* for woodwind quintet and saxophone, 1970. Southern Music.
  Premiered March 9, 1970 at Music Educators National Conference in Chicago

Heiden, Bernhard — *Solo* for alto saxophone and piano, 1969. Associated Music Publishers.
  Premiered December 16, 1969 at World Saxophone Congress I in Chicago

Kern, Jerome, arr. by Al Cobine — *Medley (All the things you are; Pick yourself up; Yesterdays)* for alto/soprano saxophones (one player) and jazz ensemble.

Kern, Jerome, arr. by Al Cobine — *Medley (All the things you are; Pick yourself up; Yesterdays)* for alto/soprano saxophones (one player) and orchestra version.

Larsen, Libby — *Song Concerto* for alto/soprano saxophones (one player) and chamber orchestra, 2005.
  Premiered February 15, 2006 at North American Biennial Conference in Iowa City, Iowa

Monk, Thelonius, arr. by David Baker — *'Round Midnight* for baritone saxophone and jazz ensemble.

O'Riordan, Kirk — *Ductus figuratus* for alto saxophone and chamber ensemble, 2008.
  Premiered October 4, 2008 by Kenneth Tse in Greensboro, North Carolina

Orrego-Salas, Juan — *Quattro liriche brevi* for alto saxophone and piano or orchestra, 1967. Peer International.
  Premiered January 19, 1968 in Wigmore Hall, London

Orrego-Salas, Juan — *Partita* for violin, cello, piano, and alto saxophone, 1988. MMB.
  Premiered May 8, 1990 in Vienna

Shanklin, Rich — *Chief's Blues* for soprano saxophone and jazz ensemble. Barnhouse.

Spera, Dominic — *Blues for Mr. Mellow* for alto saxophone and jazz ensemble. Barnhouse.

APPENDIX C

RECORDINGS BY EUGENE ROUSSEAU

Eugene Rousseau Plays the Saxophone
Coronet 1292 (1967)
Marion Hall, piano
Ibert: Concertino da Camera
Maurice: Tableaux de Provence (II, III)
Granados/Teal: Intermezzo from *Goyescas*
Delden: Sonatina
Desenclos: Prelude, Cadence et Finale
Handel/Rousseau: Adagio and Allegro (from C minor Oboe Sonata)

Virtuoso Saxophone
Coronet 1601 (1969)
Marion Hall, piano
Bonneau: Caprice en forme de valse
Chopin/Rousseau: Largo from Cello Sonata
Platti/Rousseau: Sonata in G major
Dubois: À l'Espagnole
Ruggiero: Trois Pièces pour deux saxophones
Hindemith: Sonata

Duos for Saxophone and Piano
Coronet 1703 (1971)
Joseph Rezits, piano
Handel/Rousseau: Sonata in C major for viola da gamba and cembalo
Cilea/Rousseau: Sonata in D major for cello and piano
Jolivet: Fantaisie-Impromptu
Orrego-Salas: Quattro Liriche Brevi, op. 61

Saxophone in Chamber Music
Coronet 1709 (1971)
American Woodwind Quintet; Berkshire Quartet; with James Pellerite, Bernard Portnoy, Louis Davidson, and Murray Grodner; Harry Farbman, conducting
Ibert: Concertino da Camera
Bentzon: Racconto
Heiden: Intrada

Concertos for Saxophone
Deutsche Grammophon 2530 209 (1972); re-released as CD 453 991-2;
Also Musical Heritage Society MHS 5148352
Recorded April 1971
Paul Kuentz with the Paul Kuentz Chamber Orchestra
Dubois: Concerto
Villa-Lobos: Fantasia, op. 630
Ibert: Concertino da Camera
Glazunov: Concerto in E-flat major, op. 109

Music for 2 Saxophones
    Crystal S156 (1980)
    Dennis Bamber, saxophone; Wallace Hornibrook, piano
    Loeillet/Hornibrook: Trio
    Smith: Mood Music 2
    Cunningham: Piano Trio
    Lamb: Barefoot Dances

Yamaha Suite
    Golden Crest Records #4224LP (1982)
    Eugene Rousseau Saxophone Quartet (with Dennis Bamber, Steven Goacher, and Jean Lansing); Bobby Shew, trumpet, Milt Hinton, bass, and George Gaber, percussion
    Carisi: Quartet No. 1
    Heiden: Four Movements
    Linn: Quartet
    Paich: Toccata in F

Saxophone Colors
    Delos 1007 (1986)
    Recorded May 27, 1984
    Hans Graf, piano
    Bach/Rousseau: Sonata in E major, BWV 1035
    Debussy/Rousseau: Rhapsody
    Villa-Lobos: Fantasia, op. 630
    Gershwin/Hermann: Medley from *Porgy and Bess*
    Heiden: Solo
    Feld: Elegy
    Orrego-Salas: Quattro Liriche Brevi, op. 61

Meditation from Thaïs
    ALM 7021 (1991)
    Recorded January 29 and 30, 1990
    Mariko Hattori, piano
    Rachmaninoff/Rousseau: Vocalise, op. 34, no. 14
    Kreisler/Rousseau: Liebesleid
    Debussy/Rousseau: Beau Soir
    Ravel/Rousseau: Pièce en forme de Habanera
    Dubois: from Pièces Caractéristiques en forme de Suite, op. 77 (À l'Espagnole, À la Parisienne)
    Puccini/Hermann: *Tosca* Fantasy
    Massenet/Rousseau: Meditation from *Thaïs*
    Haydn/Rousseau: Andante from Oboe Concerto in C major
    Gershwin/Hermann: *Porgy and Bess* Medley
    Kaufmann: Meditation
    Fauré/Rousseau: Après un Rêve
    Kreisler/Rousseau: Schön Rosmarin

Mr. Mellow
    Liscio LAS-01188 (1990)
    E.R. Big Band, David Baker, conductor
    Hagen: Harlem Nocturne
    Arr. Baker: Hoagy Carmichael Medley
    Arr. Cobine: Jerome Kern Medley
    Monk: 'Round Midnight
    Spera: Blues for Mr. Mellow
    Legrand: Summer of '42
    Green: Body and Soul
    Desmond: Take Five
    Flosason: In Memoriam
    Gershwin: Porgy and Bess
    MacDonald-Hanley: Back Home Again in Indiana
    Carmichael: Stardust

Celebration!
    McGill 750042 (1991)
    With the Gerald Danovitch Saxophone Quartet
    Mozart/Sibbing: Serenade, K. 406
    Rachmaninoff/Perrault: Vocalise, op. 34, no. 14
    Hindemith: Konzertstück for two alto saxophones

Saxophone Vocalise
    Delos 3188 (1995)
    Recorded September 12, 13, and 14, 1994
    Frederick Fennell with the Winds of Indiana
    Gershwin/Hermann: *Porgy and Bess* Medley
    Heiden: Diversion
    Bruch/Kimura: Kol Nidrei, op. 47
    Puccini/Hermann: *Tosca* Fantasy
    Heiden: Fantasia Concertante
    Massenet/Curnow: Meditation from *Thaïs*
    Muczynski: Concerto

Saxophone Masterpieces
    RIAX RICA-1001 (1997)
    Recorded October 1992
    Jaromir Klepáč, piano
    Creston: Sonata, op. 19
    Muczynski: Sonata, op. 29
    Heiden: Sonata
    Kabeláč: Suite
    Heiden: Fantasia Concertante

The Undowithoutable Instrument
    RIAX RICA-1002 (1997)
    Recorded February 1997
    The Budapest Strings
    Marcello: Concerto in D minor
    Cimarosa: Concerto
    Attributed to Haydn: Concerto in C major
    Mozart: Concerto in C major, K. 314

Eugene Rousseau and the Haydn Trio of Vienna
    Michael Schnitzler, violin, Walther Schulz, cello, and Heinz Medjimorec, piano
    RIAX RICA-1003 (1998)
    Recorded May 1997
    Eychenne: Cantilène et danse
    Beethoven: Trio, op. 11
    Stein: Trio Concertante
    Orrego-Salas: Partita, op. 100

Eugene Rousseau performs music of Jindřich Feld
    RIAX RICA-1004 (1999)
    Jaromir Klepáč, piano; Janáček Philharmonic Orchestra, Otakar Trhlik, conductor
    Concerto for Alto, Soprano, and Tenor Saxophones
    Sonata for Alto Saxophone and Piano
    Sonata for Soprano Saxophone and Piano
    Elegy for Soprano Saxophone and Piano

Bernhard Heiden Chamber Music
    Cadenza CAD 800 920 (1999)
    Recorded April, 1998
    Cordula Hacke, piano; Thomas Robertello, flute, Nicholas Daniel, oboe, James Campbell, clarinet, Kim Walker, bassoon, and Amy Smith, horn
    Solo for Alto Saxophone and Piano
    Intrada for Woodwind Quintet and Alto Saxophone

Tsunagari
    Liscio
    Recorded October 2000 and May 2001
    Zagreb Saxophone Quartet
    Kechley: Tsunagari
    Baker: Faces of the Blues
    Fox: S.A.X.

The Royal Band of the Belgian Air Force
 Jeanné JDR2271 (2005)
 Recorded 2002
 Alan Crepin, conductor
 Bencriscutto: Serenade
 Bilik: Concertino
 Wiedoeft: Saxema
 Hagen: Harlem Nocturne

The New Budapest Quartet and Eugene Rousseau, saxophone
 Jeanné JDR2272 (2006)
 Recorded June 2005
 Brahms: Quintet, op. 115
 Mozart: Quintet in A, K. 581

Brahms
 Jeanné JDR2273 (2010)
 Recorded June and October 2009
 Jaromír Klepáč, piano; Michal Kaňka, cello
 Trio in A Minor, op. 114
 Sonata in F Minor, op. 120, no. 1
 Sonata in E-flat Major, op. 120, no. 2

Eugene Rousseau and Friends
 Jeanné JDR2274 (2010)
 Bach: Famous Air
 Feld: Quintet
 Dubois: Les Trois Mousquetaires
 Hindemith: Konzertstück
 Milhaud: Le création du monde

Saxophone Concertos
 Jeanné JDR2275 (2010)
 Recorded March 2010
 David Itkin with the University of North Texas Orchestra
 Larsen: Song Concerto
 Baker: Lamentations (pour la fin du monde)
 Tomasi: Concerto

VIDEO PRODUCTIONS

Eugene Rousseau: Steps to Excellence
 Yamaha International Corporation (1985)
 Produced and directed by James Herendeen; 100 minutes

Eugene Rousseau: Living Legend
 Yamaha Corporation of America (2000)

APPENDIX D

PROGRAMS BY EUGENE ROUSSEAU

This list is obviously incomplete, as there are many performances for which programs no longer apparently exist. As an example, one can cite Rousseau's Faculty Annual Report of 1966–1967 to Indiana University. The Report lists a dozen solo appearances for which programs were not found, including five appearances for the American School Band Directors Association and at various music camps during the month of August 1966 alone. In addition, occasionally a specific date is lacking. Information is taken from the programs, sometimes resulting in contradictory listings; e.g. *Medley from Porgy and Bess* and *Porgy and Bess Medley*.

1953
February 8
St. Paul's Church Annex, Blue Island, Illinois
Students of Paul Jankowski and Eugene Rousseau

1958
March 4
Luther College Varsity Band; Eugene Rousseau, conductor
Summer
Luther College Music Festival
Luther College Concert Band; Weston Noble, conductor
Whitney *Introduction and Samba*

November 11
Luther College Varsity Band; Eugene Rousseau, conductor

November 21
University of Iowa Ph.D. recital; Margaret Harvey, piano
Clarinet — Brahms, Schumann, Milhaud
Saxophone — Bozza *Concertino*

1959
February 28
Luther College Community Orchestra; Eugene Rousseau, conductor

March 20
Evanston, Illinois Township High School Concert Band; Robert Werner, conductor
Whitney *Introduction and Samba*

May
Luther College Varsity Band; Eugene Rousseau, conductor

May 11
Luther College Community Orchestra; Eugene Rousseau, conductor

August 7
University of Iowa Ph.D. recital
Clarinet — Hindemith, dello Joio
Saxophone — Heiden *Sonata*

December 27
Rochester, Minnesota: American School Band Directors Association Convention
Luther College Concert Band; Weston Noble, conductor
Whitney *Introduction and Samba*

1960
January 19 and 22
Iowa Band Clinic

February 7
Pipestone, Minnesota High School Concert Band; Allen Opland, conductor
Clarinet — Reed *Serenade*
Saxophone — Whitney *Introduction and Samba*

April
Wisconsin State Solo-Ensemble Festival
Flute juror

May 8
University of Iowa; James Stoltie recital
Absil *Pièces en Quatuor*

May 31
University of Iowa Chamber Orchestra;
Edwin London, conductor
Clarinet — Copland *Concerto*

1961

October 21
University of Iowa; Malcolm Westly,
piano
Heiden *Sonata*

1962

January 5
University of Iowa; James Kohn, piano
Pascal *Sonatine*
Rueff *Concertino*
Dubois *Divertissement*
Constant *Musique de concert*

February 5
Primghar, Iowa Concert Band; James
Wheeler, conductor
Clarinet — Weber, Dixieland Festival
Saxophone — Rueff *Concertino* (III)

March 4
University of Iowa; James Kohn, piano,
Camilla Doppmann, cello
Clarinet — Seiber, Debussy, Hervig,
Brahms *Trio*

1963

No date
Central Missouri State University Phi
Mu Alpha Sinfonia
Clarinet — Stevens
Saxophone — Heiden *Sonata*

January 20
Independence, Missouri; Hugh Williams,
violin, and Barton Hudson, piano
Clarinet — Milhaud *Suite*

January 27
Wadena, Minnesota High School
Concert Band; James Wheeler,
bandmaster
Clarinet — Weber *Second Concerto* (II,
III)

January 31
Central Missouri State University;
Norma Rousseau, soprano, Barton
Hudson, piano
Clarinet — Hindemith, Brahms,
Debussy, Milhaud, Schubert

February 17
Kansas Wesleyan University; Norma
Rousseau, soprano, Barton Hudson,
piano
Clarinet — Hindemith, Schubert,
Debussy, Brahms, Milhaud

March 19
Jefferson City, Missouri High School
Varsity Band; Don Joseph, conductor
Clarinet — Weber *Second Concerto* (II,
III)
Saxophone — Reed *Ballade*

March 21 and 22
Kansas City, Missouri Public Schools
Juror

October 10
Central Missouri State University;
Wesley True, piano
Vellones *Rapsodie*

December 10
Raytown, Missouri South High School
Band; Carroll Lewis, conductor
Clarinet — Weber *Second Concerto*
Saxophone — Whitney *Introduction and Samba*

December 12
Ruskin, Missouri High School Band;
Kenneth Seward, conductor
Clarinet — Weber *Second Concerto* (II, III)
Whitney *Introduction and Samba*

1964

January 8
Helen G. Steele Music Club; Norma Rousseau, soprano, Wesley True, piano
Clarinet — Jacob *Three Songs for Soprano Voice and Clarinet*
Saxophone — Heiden *Sonata*

January 10
Missouri Music Educator's Convention
Central Missouri Music Educator's All-District Band; Eugene Rousseau, conductor

February 27
Central Missouri State University: Norma Rousseau recital; Wesley True, piano
Clarinet — Jacob *Three Songs for Soprano Voice and Clarinet*

March 9
Southwest Harrison (Bethany, Missouri) High School Concert Band; Robert Dillinger, conductor
Clarinet — Weber *Second Concerto*
Selected solos with Mrs. J.B. Ferguson, piano

November
Luther College Recital

1965

January 6
New York City: Carnegie Recital Hall (first ever); Leonard Klein, piano, Allen Winold, viola
Handel/Rousseau *Adagio and Allegro*
Heiden *Sonata*
Pascal *Sonatine*
Desenclos *Prelude, cadence et finale*
Hindemith *Trio, op. 47*
Creston *Sonata, op. 19*

January 8
University of Missouri: Missouri Music Educators' Convention
Raytown South High School Concert Band; Carroll Lewis, conductor
Handel/Rousseau *Adagio and Allegro*
Lewis *Blues for Concert*

January 9
University of Missouri: National Association of College Wind and Percussion Instructors Clinic

January 30
East Carolina College Symphonic Band; James Neilson, conductor
Whitney *Introduction and Samba*

February 21
Lansing: Greater Michigan Annual All-Stars Concert Band; Harry Begian, conductor
Handel *Adagio and Allegro*
Lewis *Blues for Concert*

March
Indiana University Faculty Recital; Carl Fuerstner, piano

March 18
Indiana University Wind Orchestra; Arthur Corra, conductor
Dahl *Concerto*

April 1
United Township (Moline, Illinois) High School Band — Soloist

Undated
Indiana University Summer Concert Band; Ronald Gregory, conductor
Lewis *Blues for Concert*

1966

February 6
Iowa State University Symphonic Band; Frank Piersol, conductor
Handel/Rousseau *Adagio and Allegro*
Whitney *Introduction and Samba*

February 7
Centerville, Iowa High School Band
Soloist

February 12
Huntington, Pennsylvania: All-State
Band Region 1; James Thurmond,
conductor
Whitney *Introduction and Samba*

February 20
Centerville, Iowa High School Concert
Band; John Holeman, conductor
Whitney *Introduction and Samba*
Handel/Rousseau *Adagio and Allegro*
Reed *Ballade*
Lewis *Blues for Concert*

March 12
Northwestern University: American
Bandmasters Association
VanderCook College of Music Concert
Band; James Neilson, guest conductor
Whitney *Introduction and Samba*

March 25
Wheeling: West Virginia Music
Educators Association; Wesley True,
piano
Concert

March 26
Wheeling: West Virginia Music
Educators Association, Wheeling
Clinic

May 18
Marion, Indiana High School Concert
Band; George Thompson, conductor
Handel/Rousseau *Adagio and Allegro*
Reed *Ballade*

July 13
Indiana University Concert Band;
Eugene Rousseau, conductor

July 22
Indiana University; Carl Fuerstner, piano

October 26
Indiana University Symphonic Wind
Ensemble; Eugene Rousseau, conductor

November 6
Washington, DC: Phillips Collection;
Joseph Rezits, piano
Heiden *Sonata*
Tcherepnine *Sonatine Sportive*
Creston *Sonata, op. 19*
Constant *Musique de Concert*
Dubois *Concertstück*

November 7
Frostburg State College; Joseph Rezits,
piano
Heiden *Sonata*
Tcherepnine *Sonatine Sportive*
Creston *Sonata, op. 19*
Constant *Musique de Concert*
Dubois *Concertstück*

November 10
Concord (West Virginia) College; Joseph
Rezits, piano
Heiden *Sonata*
Tcherepnine *Sonatine Sportive*
Creston *Sonata, op. 19*
Constant *Musique de Concert*
Dubois *Concertstück*

November 26
Indiana University Symphonic Wind
Ensemble; Eugene Rousseau, conductor

December 5
Indiana University Symphonic Wind
Ensemble; Eugene Rousseau, conductor

December 12
Indiana University; Joseph Rezits, piano
Heiden *Sonata*
Tcherepnine *Sonatine Sportive*
Creston *Sonata, op. 19*
Constant *Musique de Concert*
Dubois *Concertstück*

1967

January 20
London: Wigmore Hall (first ever);
Marion Hall, piano
Heiden *Sonata*
Desenclos *Prelude, cadence et finale*
Tcherepnin *Sonatine sportive*
Platti/Rousseau *Sonata in G*
Creston *Sonata, op. 19*

January 25
Berlin: Konzertsaal Bundesallee (first ever); Marion Hall, piano
Creston *Sonata, op. 19*
Desenclos *Prelude, cadence et finale*
Tcherepnine *Sonatine Sportive*
Platti/Rousseau *Sonata in G*
Krol *Sonate*

January 30
Vienna: Palais Palffy (first ever); Marion Hall, piano
Heiden *Sonata*
Desenclos *Prelude, cadence et finale*
Tcherepnin *Sonatine sportive*
Platti/Rousseau *Sonata in G*
Creston *Sonata*

February 4
Amsterdam: Concertgebouw (first ever); Marion Hall, piano
Heiden *Sonata*
Tcherepnine *Sonatine Sportive*
Creston *Sonata, op. 19*
Platti/Rousseau *Sonata in G*
Delden *Sonatina*

February 19
Indiana University
Desenclos *Prelude, Cadence et Finale*
Platti/Rousseau *Sonata in G*

March 5
Elkhart, Indiana Municipal Band; Arthur Singleton, conductor
Creston *Concerto, op. 26*

March 8
Indiana University Symphonic Wind Ensemble; Eugene Rousseau, conductor

April 11
Indiana University Symphonic Wind Ensemble; Eugene Rousseau, conductor

May 5
Enid: Oklahoma Music Educators Association Clinic

May 13
Wittenberg (Ohio) University Wind Ensemble; Richard Butts, conductor
Creston *Concerto, op. 26*

July 12
Indiana University Concert Band;
Eugene Rousseau, conductor

July 13
Indiana University Symphonic Band;
Eugene Rousseau, conductor

July 19
Indiana University Concert Band;
Eugene Rousseau, conductor

July 25
Indiana University Concert Band;
Eugene Rousseau, conductor

August
Bemidji (Minnesota) Music Camp

August
Morehead (Kentucky) State University Clinic

October 26
Gary, Indiana: American Federation of Teachers
Speaker

November 9
MacMurray College Band; Henry Busche, conductor
Clinic, Soloist

November 19
Coe (Iowa) College Concert Band;
Thomas Slattery, conductor
Whitney *Introduction and Samba*
Lewis *Blues for Concert*

1968

January 5
Park Hill, Missouri High School
Symphonic Band; William Mack,
conductor
Whitney *Introduction and Samba*

January 13
London: BBC Concert Orchestra;
Marcus Dods, conductor
Ibert *Concertino da camera*

January 19
London: Wigmore Hall; Carl Fuerstner,
piano
Pascal *Sonatine*
Orrego-Salas *Quattro Liriche Brevi*
(premiere)
Constant *Musique de Concert*
Handel/Rousseau *Sonata in G minor*
Dubois *Concerstück*
Hindemith *Sonata*

January 22
Vienna: Brahms-Saal; Carl Fuerstner,
piano
Pascal *Sonatine*
Orrego-Salas *Quattro Liriche Brevi*
Constant *Musique de Concert*
Handel/Rousseau *Sonata in G minor*
Fuerstner *Incantations* (to have been
played but remains unwritten)
Hindemith *Sonata*

January 27
Paris: Salle Gaveau (first ever); Carl
Fuerstner, piano
Pascal *Sonatine*
Desenclos *Prélude, cadence et finale*
Constant *Musique de Concert*
Dubois *Concertstück*
Handel/Rousseau *Sonate in G minor*
Fuerstner *Incantations* (to have been
played but remains unwritten)
Creston *Sonata, op. 19*

February 2
Kansas City, Missouri American Legion
Band; Keith House, conductor
Whitney *Introduction and Samba*
Lewis *Blue for Saxophone and Band*

February 6
Springfield, Illinois Symphony
Orchestra; Harry Farbman, conductor
Ibert *Concertino da camera*

February 23
Marion College; Nouvel Ensemble
— Irving Ilmer, violin/viola, and Joseph
Rezits, piano
Loeillet *Sonate a Trois*
Tcherepnine *Sonatine Sportive*
Heiden *Sonata*
Pierné *Sonata da Camera pour
Saxophone, Viole et Piano*

February 29
Collinsville, Illinois High School
Concert Band; Irwin Brick, conductor
Whitney *Introduction and Samba*

March
Pacific University (Oregon); Joseph
Rezits, piano
Heiden *Sonata*
Tcherepnine *Sonatine Sportive*
Creston *Sonata, op. 19*
Constant *Musique de Concert*
Dubois *Concertstück*

March 5
North Manchester (Indiana) Civic and
Manchester College Symphony
Orchestra, David McCormick, conductor
Debussy *Rapsodie*
Badings *Concerto*

March 10
Indiana University Symphonic Band;
Frederick Ebbs, conductor
Hartley *Concerto*

March 15
Seattle: Music Educators National
Conference; Joseph Rezits, piano
Heiden *Sonata*
Tcherepnine *Sonatine Sportive*
Creston *Sonata, op. 19*

March 22
Washington State University; Joseph
Rezits, piano
Heiden *Sonata*
Tcherepnine *Sonatine Sportive*
Creston *Sonata, op. 19*
Constant *Musique de Concert*
Dubois *Concertstück*

April 10
Eastern Washington State College;
Joseph Rezits, piano

April 16
Los Angeles City College; Joseph Rezits,
piano
Heiden *Sonata*
Tcherepnine *Sonatine Sportive*
Creston *Sonata, op. 19*
Dubois *Concertstück*

April 18
Humboldt State College; Joseph Rezits,
piano
Heiden *Sonata*
Tcherepnine *Sonatine Sportive*
Creston *Sonata, op. 19*
Constant *Musique de Concert*
Dubois *Concertstück*
Also in April with Rezits — University
of Montana; Washington State College;
University of California — Los Angeles;
San Fernando Valley State College;
California State University; George Fox
(Oregon) College

April 28
Stillwater (Minnesota) High School
Band

May 16
McAllen (Texas) High School Varsity
Band, L.M. Snavely, conductor
Whitney *Introduction and Samba*
Gershwin/Hermann *Porgy and Bess
Medley*

June 30
University of Kansas: Midwestern Music
and Art Camp Concert Band; Russell
Wiley, conductor
Whitney *Introduction and Samba*

July 23
University of Kansas: Midwestern Music
and Art Camp; Richard Reber, piano
Granados/Teal *Intermezzo from
Goyescas*
Tcherepnine *Sonatine Sportive*
Bentzon *Racconto* (with John Boulton,
flute, Austin Ledwith, bassoon, and Stan
Ricker, bass)
Handel/Rousseau *Sonata in G minor*
Chopin/Rousseau *Largo*
Bonneau *Caprice en forme de valse*

August
Cumberland Forest Music Camp

December 7
Wilmington (Ohio) High School
Symphonic Band, Rodger Borror,
conductor
Whitney *Introduction and Samba*
Gershwin/Hermann *Porgy and Bess
Medley*

1969

January 19
Iowa Band Clinic
Clinic

January 30
Jekyll Island, Georgia: All South Band
Clinic
Clinic
Durham (North Carolina) High School
Band, Robert Fleming, conductor
Handel/Rousseau *Adagio and Allegro*
Gershwin/Hermann *Selections from
Porgy and Bess*

February 1
Wartburg (Iowa) College
Clinic

February 4
Mid-Prairie (Wellman, Iowa) High
School Band, Robert Gaston, conductor
Handel/Rousseau *Adagio and Allegro*
Gershwin/Hermann *Porgy and Bess Medley*
Lewis *Blues for a Concert*

February 6
Marceline (Missouri) High School Band
Clinic

March
Lindsborg (Kansas) College
Clinic

March
Everett (Denver, Colorado) Junior High
School
Clinic

March 19
Boulder (Colorado) High School
Symphonic Band, Edward Kehn,
conductor
Handel/Rousseau *Adagio and Allegro*
Whitney *Introduction and Samba*
Gershwin/Hermann *Porgy and Bess Medley*
Lewis *Blues for a Concert*

March 22
Montgomery: Alabama Bandmasters
Convention
Clinic

March 23
Des Moines: Iowa Bandmasters
Association Convention
Clinic

June
Canadian Broadcasting Corporation
(Quebec)
Broadcast and recordings

June 29
Confederation des Harmonies-fanfares
du Quebec
Solos

July 19
Daniel Boone Forest Music Camp
Rousseau Concert Band; Eugene
Rousseau, conductor
Puccini/Hermann *Tosca Fantasy*
(premiere — Vincent Abato, soloist)

October 24
Olivet Nazarene College Concert Band;
Harlow Hopkins, conductor
Creston *Concerto, op. 26*

December 6
University of Wisconsin-Eau Claire
Band
Soloist

December 16
Chicago: First World Saxophone
Congress; Bernhard Heiden, piano
Heiden *Solo* (premiere)

1970

January 16
University of Michigan: Midwestern
Conference on School Music
Lecture-demonstration

January 18
Chicago Heights Youth Orchestra;
Robert Slider, conductor
Badings *Concerto*

January 31
Cooper (Minnesota) High School
Symphonic Band; DuWayne Kloos,
conductor
Hagen *Harlem Nocturne* (with Stage
Band)
Whitney *Introduction and Samba* (with
Symphonic Band)
Handel/Rousseau *Adagio and Allegro*

February 7
Coe (Iowa) College Instrumental Festival; Eugene Rousseau, conductor
Puccini/Herman *Tosca Fantasy* (Charles D'Camp, conductor)

February 20–22
Morehead State (Kentucky) University Band Clinic

March 9
Chicago: Music Educators National Conference
Heiden *Sextet [Intrada]* (with Harry Houdeshel, flute, Earl Bates, clarinet, Jerry Sirucek, oboe, Philip Farkas, horn, and Leonard Sharrow, bassoon; premiere)

March 11
Boulder (Colorado) High School Symphonic Band; Edward Kehn, conductor
Reed *Ballade*
Pierné *Canzonetta*
Puccini/Herman *Tosca Fantasy*

March 19
Albion (Michigan) College Chamber Orchestra; Jerry Troxell, conductor Clinic, concert
Ibert *Concertino da camera*

April 9
Warren Central (Indianapolis) Concert Band; James Chandler, conductor
Reed *Ballade*
Whitney *Introduction and Samba*
Gershwin/Hermann *Medley from Porgy and Bess*

April 24
Northwestern High School Symphonic Band; Terrance Mahady, conductor
Whitney *Introduction and Samba*
Puccini/Hermann *Tosca Fantasy*
Northwestern High School Orchestra; Jacqueline Hunt, conductor
Cimarosa *Concerto*

April 26
Fort Wayne, Indiana All-City Band; Frederick Ebbs, conductor
Gershwin/Hermann *Porgy and Bess Medley*

May 8
Memorial Junior High School Concert Band; Paul Jankowski, conductor
Pierné *Canzonetta*
Puccini/Herman *Tosca Fantasy*
Gershwin/Hermann *Porgy and Bess*

July 12
University of Kansas: Midwestern Music and Art Camp Concert Band; Russell Wiley, conductor
Puccini/Hermann *Tosca Fantasy*

July 15
Daniel Boone Forest Music Camp, Morehead State University
Bonneau *Caprice en forme de valse*

July 18
Daniel Boone Forest Music Camp, Morehead State University Rousseau Concert Band; Eugene Rousseau, conductor

July 24
Daniel Boone Forest Music Camp, Morehead State University Rousseau Concert Band; Eugene Rousseau, conductor

July 27
Indiana University Saxophone Seminar

July 29
Indiana University; Charles Webb, piano, Bernard Portnoy, clarinet, Jerry Sirucek, oboe, Artemus Edwards, bassoon
Cimarosa *Concerto*
Hartley *Duo*
Glazounov *Concerto*
Heiden *Solo*
Dubois *Les Trois Mousquetaires*

August 4
Redlands Bowl, California Symphony Orchestra; Harry Farbman, conductor
Ibert *Concertino da camera*

August 19
Vienna: Palais Auersperg; Heinz Medjimorec, piano
Ibert *Concertino da camera*
Desenclos *Prelude, Cadence et Finale*
Maurice *Tableaux de Provence* (II, III)
Bonneau *Caprice en forme de valse*
Dubois *A l'Espagnole*

October 24
Olivet Nazarene (Illinois) College Band; Harlow Hopkins, conductor
Creston *Concerto*

November 10
Indiana University; American Woodwind Quintet
Heiden *Intrada*

November 12
Cornell University; Joseph Rezits, piano
Heiden *Solo*
Orrego-Salas *Quattro Liriche Brevi*
Tcherepnine *Sonatine Sportive*
Constant *Musique de Concert*
Jolivet *Fantaisie-Impromptu*
Husa *Elegie et Rondeau*

November 14
Indianapolis: Indiana Music Educators Association
Clinic

November 29
England: Christine Gough, piano, Raphael Sommer, cello, Christopher Taylor, flute, Sidney Sutcliffe, oboe, Paul Harvey, clarinet, Anthony Brooks, bassoon, Denzil Floyd, horn; all first performances in Great Britain
Debussy *Rapsodie*
Hartley *Duo*
Raphael *Divertimento*
Villa-Lobos *Fantasia*
Heiden *Intrada*

December 18
Chicago: Mid-West Band and Orchestra Clinic, Richmond (Missouri) High School Concert Band; Kenneth Seward, conductor
Benson *Concertino (II)*

1971

January 6
University of New Mexico Wind Ensemble; William Rhoads, conductor
Badings *Concerto*
Whitney *Introduction and Samba*

January 12
University of California at Los Angeles; Joseph Rezits, piano
Selected from:
Cilea/Rousseau *Sonata in D*
Constant *Musique de Concert*
Creston *Sonata, op. 19*
Dubois *Concertstück*
Handel/Rousseau *Sonata in C*
Hartley *Duo*
Heiden *Sonata*
Husa *Elegie et Rondeau*
Jolivet *Fantaisie-Impromptu*
Orrego-Salas *Quattro Litiche Brevi*
Tcherepnine *Sonatine Sportive*

January 14
University of Hawaii; Joseph Rezits, piano
Handel/Rousseau *Sonata in C*
Heiden *Sonata*
Tcherepnine *Sonatine Sportive*
Constant *Musique de Concert*
Jolivet *Fantaisie-Impromptu*
Cilea/Rousseau *Sonata in D*

Alaska Music Trails — These were the final concerts of a 21-year-old series begun in 1950. Managed by Jane Schapiro Livingston, the series brought some 85 artists who performed in 14 cities in the Far North. Typically, the tour would include 14 major concerts and 35 to 45 school concerts in five to six weeks.

February 23
Sitka (Alaska); Carl Fuerstner, piano
Debussy *Rapsodie*
Ibert *Concertino da camera*
Tcherepnine *Sonatine Sportive*
Platti/Rousseau *Sonata in G*
Creston *Sonata, op. 19*

February 25
Juneau (Alaska); Carl Fuerstner, piano
Glazounov *Concerto*
Dubois *Dix figures a danser*
Tcherepnine *Sonatine Sportive*
Cimarosa *Concerto*
Ibert *Concertino da camera*

February 27
Haines (Alaska); Carl Fuerstner, piano
Glazounov *Concerto*
Dubois *Dix figures a danser*
Tcherepnine *Sonatine Sportive*
Cimarosa *Concerto*
Ibert *Concertino da camera*

March 5
Seward (Alaska); Carl Fuerstner, piano
Debussy *Rapsodie*
Ibert *Concertino da camera*
Tcherepnine *Sonatine Sportive*
Platti/Rousseau *Sonata in G*
Creston *Sonata, op. 19*

March 7
Homer (Alaska); Carl Fuerstner, piano
Debussy *Rapsodie*
Ibert *Concertino da camera*
Tcherepnine *Sonatine Sportive*
Platti/Rousseau *Sonata in G*
Creston *Sonata, op. 19*

March 10
Anchorage (Alaska); Carl Fuerstner, piano
Debussy *Rapsodie*
Ibert *Concertino da camera*
Tcherepnine *Sonatine Sportive*
Platti/Rousseau *Sonata in G*
Creston *Sonata, op. 19*

March 13
Whitehorse (Yukon); Carl Fuerstner, piano
Debussy *Rapsodie*
Ibert *Concertino da camera*
Tcherepnine *Sonatine Sportive*
Platti/Rousseau *Sonata in G*
Creston *Sonata, op. 19*

March 16
Grand Prairie (Alaska); Carl Fuerstner, piano
Debussy *Rapsodie*
Ibert *Concertino da camera*
Tcherepnine *Sonatine Sportive*
Cimarosa *Concerto*
Creston *Sonata, op. 19*

March 20
Terrace (British Columbia); Carl Fuerstner, piano
Debussy *Rapsodie*
Ibert *Concertino da camera*
Tcherepnine *Sonatine Sportive*
Platti/Rousseau *Sonata in G*
Creston *Sonata, op. 19*

March 21
Kitimat (Alaska); Carl Fuerstner, piano
Debussy *Rapsodie*
Ibert *Concertino da camera*
Tcherepnine *Sonatine Sportive*
Platti/Rousseau *Sonata in G*
Creston *Sonata, op. 19*

March 23
Prince Rupert (British Columbia); Carl Fuerstner, piano
Debussy *Rapsodie*
Ibert *Concertino da camera*
Tcherepnine *Sonatine Sportive*
Cimarosa *Concerto*
Creston *Sonata, op. 19*

March 27
State University of New York at Buffalo; Frina Boldt, piano
Lecture-Recital

March 28
State University of New York at Buffalo
Concert Band; Frank Cipolla, conductor
Badings *Concerto*

July 14
Evansville, Indiana Tri-State Concert
Band; Harry Hart, conductor
Puccini/Hermann *Tosca Fantasy*
Gershwin/Hermann *Medley [from Porgy and Bess]*

July 16–18
Indiana University Saxophone Seminar

July 18
Indiana University Recital; Joseph
Rezits, piano
Handel/Rousseau *Sonata in C*
Orrego-Salas *Quattro Liriche Brevi*
Cilea/Rousseau *Sonata*
Husa *Elegie et Rondeau*

November 18
Manchester (Indiana) College
Symphonic Band; James Carlson,
conductor
Clinic, Soloist
Hartley *Concerto*

December 12
Richmond, Missouri High School
Concert Band; Kenneth Seward,
conductor
Puccini/Hermann *Tosca Fantasy*
Kreisler *Liebesleid*
Gershwin/Hermann *Porgy and Bess Medley*

December 14
Indiana University; Hans Graf, piano,
Milan Turković, bassoon
Loeillet *Trio Sonata in B minor*

1972

January 15
Bradford, Wisconsin High School
Symphony Band; Stanley DeRusha,
conductor

Badings *Concerto*
Puccini/Hermann *Tosca Fantasy*
Cimarosa/Rousseau *Introduction and Allegro*

February 17
Omro, Wisconsin High School Concert
Band; Jerry Menli, conductor
Puccini/Herman *Tosca Fantasy*
Gershwin/Hermann *Porgy and Bess Medley*
Reed *Ballade*

February 20
Crete-Monee, Illinois High School
Symphonic Winds; Robert Slider,
conductor
Badings *Concerto*
Kreisler *Liebesleid*
Gershwin/Hermann *Porgy and Bess Selections*

February 27
Montrose, Michigan: Greater Michigan
All-Stars
Clinic, Recital
Cimarosa *Concerto* (I, II)
Koechlin Etudes 2 and 3

March 14
Shell Lake, Wisconsin: Quad City All
Star Band
Puccini/Hermann *Tosca Fantasie*
Whitney *Introduction and Samba*
Gershwin/Hermann *Themes from Porgy and Bess*
Lewis *Blues for a Concert*

March 15
Northeastern Illinois University; ER,
Irving Ilmer violin/viola, William Schutt,
piano
Loeillet *Trio Sonata in B minor*
Pierné *Sonata da Camera*

March 22 and 23
University of Michigan-Flint Wind
Ensemble; Raymond Roth, conductor
Clinic, Soloist

March 24
Kansas Music Educators Association
Convention
Clinic
Fort Hays State College Symphonic
Band; Lyle Dilley, conductor
Badings *Concerto*

April 9
Indiana University Symphonic Band;
Karel Husa, guest conductor
Husa *Concerto*

April 16
Indiana University dedication of Musical
Arts Center; Hans Graf, piano
Orrego-Salas *Quattro liriche brevi*

May 10 and 11
Northeast Louisiana University
Symphonic Wind Ensemble; Jack White,
conductor
Clinic
Glazounov *Concerto*
Gershwin/Hermann *Porgy and Bess Medley*

May 25
Southern Illinois University-
Edwardsville Symphonic Band; Dale
Fjerstad, conductor
Creston *Concerto, op. 26*
Hagen/Reed *Harlem Nocturne*

August 7
Brigham Young University; Ronald
Staheli, piano
Dubois *Dix figures a danser*
Platti/Rousseau *Sonata in G*

August 12
Brigham Young University Sounds of
Summer Concert Symphony Orchestra;
Lawrence Sardoni, conductor
Creston *Concerto, op. 26* (III)

August 20
Toronto: World Saxophone Congress III;
Carl Fuerstner, piano
Recital

August 21
Toronto: World Saxophone Congress III;
Carl Fuerstner, piano
Archer *Sonata*

October 13
Louisville, Kentucky Southern Baptist
Theological Seminary, Nouvel Ensemble
— Irving Ilmer violin/viola, Joseph
Rezits, piano
Loeillet *Sonate à Trois*
Hindemith *Trio, op. 47*
Pierné *Sonata da Camera*
Eychenne *Cantilene et Danse*
Stein *Trio Concertante*

October 30
University of Alberta Symphonic Wind
Ensemble; John Iltis, conductor
Badings *Concerto*
Archer *Sonata* (Howard Janzen, piano)

November 5
Washington, DC: Phillips Collection;
Nouvel Ensemble — Irving Ilmer, violin/
viola, Joseph Rezits, piano
Loeillet *Sonate à Trois*
Hindemith *Trio, op. 47*
Pierné *Sonata da Camera*
Eychenne *Cantilene et Danse*

November 28
DePaul University; Nouvel Trio —
Irving Ilmer, violin/viola, Joseph Rezits,
piano
Loeillet *Sonate à Trois*
Pierné *Sonata da Camera*
Stein *Trio Concertante*
Eychenne *Cantilene et Danse*
Hindemith *Trio, op. 47*

1973

No date
British Columbia Music Educators
Association, University of British
Columbia Wind Ensemble; Paul
Douglas, conductor
Badings *Concerto*

February 6
Springfield, Illinois Symphony
Orchestra; Harry Farbman, conductor
Glazounov *Concerto*

April 15
Philharmonic Orchestra of Indianapolis;
Wolfgang Vacano, conductor
Creston *Concerto, op. 26*

April 26
Greenville, South Carolina Symphony
Orchestra; Peter Rickett, conductor
Ibert *Concertino da camera*
Glazounov *Concerto*

May 1
Appleton West, Wisconsin High School
Symphonic Band; I.N. Spangenberg,
conductor
Badings *Concerto*
Cimarosa/Rousseau *Larghetto and Allegro*
Gershwin/Hermann *Porgy and Bess (Highlights)*

May 15
Indianapolis Philharmonic; Wolfgang
Vacano, conductor

June 24–29
Elon College Music Festival
Clinic

September 10
Indiana University for Wilfred Bain's
80th birthday; Charles Webb, piano
Gershwin/Hermann *Highlights from Porgy and Bess*

October 19
Wright State (Ohio) University; Claude
Cymerman, piano
Heiden *Sonata*
Debussy *Rapsodie*
Cimarosa *Concerto*
Glazounov *Concerto*

November 16
Indiana University; Eugene Rousseau,
conductor
Walton *Façade*

December 16
Richmond, Missouri High School
Concert Band; Kenneth Seward,
conductor
Puccini/Hermann *Tosca Fantasy*
Cimarosa/Rousseau *Concerto*
Nestico *Persuasion*

1974

January 12
Central College of Iowa Symphonic
Band; Thomas Cook, conductor
Creston *Concerto, op. 26*
Glazounov *Concerto*

January 17
Saint Mary-of-the-Woods (Indiana)
College; Claude Cymerman, piano
Heiden *Sonata*
Debussy *Rapsodie*
Cimarosa *Concerto*
Glazounov *Concerto*

February 4
London, Ontario: Youth Band of Ontario;
Martin Boundy, conductor
Puccini/Hermann *Tosca Fantasy*
Cimarosa/Rousseau *Larghetto and Allegro*

March 20
University of Wisconsin-Milwaukee
Heiden *Intrada*

March 20
University of Wisconsin-Milwaukee
Clinic

May 1
Washington, DC: Kennedy Center
Festival Orchestra; Lukas Foss,
conductor
Orrego-Salas *Quattro Liriche Brevi*

May 12
Southwest Minnesota State College Concert Band; James Siewert, conductor
Glazounov *Concerto*
Cimarosa/Rousseau *Larghetto and Allegro*

May 15
Evergreen Park, Illinois Symphonic Wind Ensemble; James Gilworth, conductor
Badings *Concerto*
Gershwin/Hermann *Porgy and Bess*
Puccini/Hermann *Tosca Fantasy*
Whitney *Introduction and Samba*

July 6
Bordeaux, France: World Saxophone Congress IV; Heinz Medjimorec, piano
Heiden *Solo*
Dubois *Concerto (1)*
Hartley *Duo*
Husa *Élégie et Rondeau*
Villa-Lobos *Fantasia*

November 6
Madison: Wisconsin Music Educators' Conference
Clinic "The Saxophone in the Stage Band"

November 7
Wisconsin State Music Convention
Clinic

December 20
Chicago: Mid-West Band and Orchestra Clinic
VanderCook College of Music Band; Richard Brittain, conductor
Lieb *Short Ballet*

1975

No date
Augsberg College Select High School Band; James Carlson, conductor
Banton *Alto Mood*
Creston *Concerto, op. 26*

January 16
Unnamed Concert Band, Symphonic Band, Wind Ensemble, Stage Band; F. Gaymon, S. Leander, and D. Gjerdrum, conductors
Reed *Ballade*
Puccini/Hermann *Tosca Fantasy*
Gershwin/Hermann *Porgy and Bess Medley*
Spera *Patty*

February 19
Vienna Radio Orchestra; Antonio de Almeida, conductor
Glazounov *Concerto*

March 3
Luther College Music Festival Concert Band; Frederick Nyline, conductor
Cimarosa *Concerto*
Puccini/Hermann *Tosca Fantasy*

March 5
Ames, Iowa: Coyle Music Center
Clinic

March 6
Ohio University; Marion Hall, piano, Eugene Carinci, saxophone, Norma Rousseau, soprano
Debussy *Rapsodie*
Dubois *Dix figures à danser*
Desportes *Blablablas*
Platti/Rousseau *Sonata in G*
Bach *Seufzer Thränen, Kummer, Noth*
Glazounov *Concerto*

May 8
Philadelphia: Zapf's Music Store
Clinic

May 11
Iowa State University Wind Ensemble; Jimmie Reynolds, conductor
Cimarosa/Rousseau *Larghetto and Allegro*
Gershwin/Rousseau *Porgy and Bess Medley*

July 9
Indiana University; Wilber England, conductor
Gershwin/Hermann *Porgy and Bess Medley*

1975 Fall Concert Tour
Augsberg Concert Band; James Carlson, conductor
Badings *Concerto*

November 11
Minnetonka, Minnesota High School Wind Ensemble and Jazz Ensemble; Daniel Geldert, conductor
Puccini/Hermann *Tosca Fantasy*
Cimarosa/Rousseau *Concerto*
White *February's Child* (Jazz Ensemble)
Gershwin/Hermann *Porgy and Bess Medley* (with Wind Ensemble)

November 13
Augsberg College; Kay Carlson, piano
Saxophone clinic; Woodwind clinic; Recital
Platti/Rousseau *Sonata in G*
de Fesch/Jones *Sonata in F*
Chopin/Rousseau *Largo*
Dubois *Dix Figures a Danser*

1976

No date
Japan Band Director's Clinic
Clinic

January 13
University of North Carolina-Greensboro; East Wind Quintet
Heiden *Intrada*
Dubois *Les Trois Mousquetaires*

January 24
Indiana University-South Bend Wind Ensemble; Kenneth Geoffroy, conductor
Creston *Concerto, op. 26*
Kreisler *Liebesleid*

January 31
Cudahy, Wisconsin High School Concert Band, Jazz Ensemble; Larry Osterburg, conductor
Cimarosa/Rousseau *Larghetto and Allegro*
Gershwin/Hermann *Porgy and Bess Medley*
Speak Low (Special ensemble)
Spera *Patty* (Jazz ensemble)

February 16
Armstrong State College Concert Band; Stephen Brandon, conductor
Cimarosa/Rousseau *Introduzione and Allegro*
Lawrence *Contentment*
Gershwin/Hermann *Porgy and Bess Medley*

February 19
Indiana University Jazz Ensemble; Gene Hunn, conductor
Spera *Patty*
Shanklin *Chief's Blues*

March 7
University of Mississippi Symphonic Band; Luther Snavely, conductor
Cimarosa/Rousseau *Concerto*
Puccini/Hermann *Tosca Fantasy*
Gershwin/Hermann *Porgy and Bess Medley*

March 19
Westerville, Ohio High Schools Orchestra; Sidney Townsend and John Fryar, conductors
Cimarosa *Concerto* (II, III, IV)
Milhaud *Scaramouche*
Jazz Selections
Bernstein *Selections from West Side Story*

March 28 and 29
Wartburg College Band; Robert Lee, conductor
Badings *Concerto*

April 5
Indiana University Contemporary
Chamber Ensemble; Keith Brown,
conductor
Milhaud *La Création du monde*

May 15
Thornwood, Illinois High School Varsity
Band and Concert Band; Paul Jankowski,
conductor
Cimarosa/Rousseau *Larghetto and Allegro*
Shapiro, Bernstein *Harlem Nocturne* (Varsity Band)
Puccini/Hermann *Tosca Fantasy*
Gershwin/Hermann *Porgy and Bess*

June 19
Iowa State University: National Band Association; Bloomington, Minnesota, Medalist Band; Louis Witt, conductor
Puccini/Hermann *Tosca Fantasy*
Lawrence/Newsom *Contentment*

October 9
Western Illinois University: Illinois Saxophone Conference Clinic

November 11
Rosemount High School Band; Art Smith, conductor
Lefebvre *Andante and Allegro*
Gershwin/Hermann *Porgy and Bess Medley*

November 12
Mariner Concert and Symphonic Bands
Puccini/Hermann *Tosca Fantasy*
Gershwin/Hermann *Porgy and Bess Medley*

November 21
Riverside City College Wind Ensemble; Roger Erickson, conductor
Cimarosa/Rousseau *Concerto* (I, II)
arr. by Hermann *Stella by Starlight*
Gershwin/Hermann *Porgy and Bess Medley*
Puccini/Hermann *Tosca Fantasy*

1977

February 10
Ohio Northern University Symphonic Band; Alan Drake, conductor
Cimarosa/Rousseau *Larghetto and Allegro*
Gershwin/Hermann *Porgy and Bess Medley*

February 16
North Central High School Concert Band, Symphonic Wind Ensemble, Jazz-Rock Ensemble; Samuel Rhinesmith and Douglas Warner, conductors
Newsom *Contentment*
arr. by Hermann *Stella by Starlight* (Concert Band)
Lefebre *Andante and Allegro*
Gershwin/Hermann *Porgy and Bess Medley* (Symphonic Wind Ensemble)
Garner *Misty*
arr. by Newsom *Summer of '42*
arr. by Wheeler *Around Midnite*
Shanklin *Chief's Blues*

March 25 and 26
Central Missouri State University: North American Saxophone Alliance South Central Congress; Wesley True, piano
Clinic (25 and 26)
Debussy/Rousseau *Rapsodie*
Cimarosa *Concerto*
Glazounov *Concerto*
Linn *Quartet* (Goacher, Lansing, Bamber)

March 27
Indiana University-South Bend Wind Ensemble; Kenneth Geoffroy, conductor
Creston *Concerto, op. 26*

April 1
Norfolk, Virginia: Navy School of Music All-Eastern Band Instrumental Clinic, Clinic "Teaching Techniques"

November 12
Pfeiffer College; Fumiyoshi Maezawa,

Jean Lansing, Dennis Bamber
CPE Bach/Cunningham *Rondo*
Bozza *Andante et Scherzo*
Pascal *Quartet*
Arma S*ept Transparences*
Tchaikovsky/Mule *Andante*
Paich *Toccata in F*

1978

February 28
Hilchenbach, Germany: Siegerland-Orchester; Rolf Agop, conductor
Glazounov *Concerto*
Debussy *Rapsodie*

March 3
Northwestern University: American Bandmasters Association VanderCook College of Music Symphonic Band; Richard Brittain, conductor
Puccini/Hermann *Tosca Fantasy*

April 22
Rochester, Minnesota John Marshall High School Symphonic Winds, Jazz Ensemble; Larry Kolpek, conductor

April 24 and 25
Springfield, Illinois Symphony Orchestra; Harry Farbman, conductor
Creston *Concerto, op. 26*

July 23
Shell Lake, Wisconsin; Pauli Worth, piano
Dubois *Concertstück*
Debussy/Rousseau *Rapsodie*
Creston *Concerto, op. 26*
Derr *I Never Saw Another Butterfly* (with Norma Rousseau)
Haydn *Concerto in C*

November 7
Florida Southern College; Fumiyoshi Maezawa, alto, Kenneth Fischer, tenor, and Dennis Bamber, baritone
CPE Bach/Cunningham *Rondo*
Bozza *Andante et Scherzo*

Arma *Sept Transparences*
Dubois *Concertstück* (with Rita Fandrich)
Haydn *Concerto in C (I, II)*
Tchaikovsky *Andante*
Paich *Toccata in F* (with John Watkins, Judy Alexander)

November 14
Anthony-Seeger Campus; Fumiyoshi Maezawa, alto, Jean Lansing, tenor, Dennis Bamber, baritone
CPE Bach/Cunningham *Rondo*
Pascal *Quartet*
Tchaikovsky/Mule *Andante*
Mozart/Sibbing *Quintet (Allegro)* with George Wolfe
Carisi *Yamaha Suite*
Paich *Toccata in F* with Michael Davis, Tim Hays

November 15
University of Notre Dame; Fumiyoshi Maezawa, Jean Lansing, Dennis Bamber, Norma Rousseau, Nick Medich, Terry Engemann
CPE Bach/Cunningham *Rondo*
Bozza *Andante et Scherzo*
Pascal *Quartet*
Scarlatti/Hemke *Sonata No. 44*
Zajac *Five Miniatures*
arr. by Rousseau *He's Gone Away*
Paich *Toccata in F*

December 1 and 2
Anchorage, Alaska Symphony Orchestra; Maurice Dubonnet, conductor

1979

January 13
Washington, DC: U.S. Navy Band Saxophone Symposium; Pauli Worth, piano
Dubois *Concertstück*
Creston *Concerto, op. 26*
Haydn *Concerto in C*
Derr *I Never Saw Another Butterfly* (with Norma Rousseau)

February 2
Ohio Music Education Association,
Toledo Concert Band; Samuel Szor,
conductor
Creston *Concerto, op. 26 (II, III)*

February 3
Ohio Music Education Association
Conference, Toledo
Clinic

February 14
Eau Claire, Wisconsin
Clinic

February 16
Minneapolis: Minnesota Music
Educators Association Convention
Bloomington Medalist Concert Band;
Earl Benson, conductor
Cimarosa/Rousseau *Larghetto and Allegro*

March 4 and 5
Arizona State University: North
American Saxophone Alliance
Symposium; Janice Meyer and Walter
Cosand, piano
Clinic; Recital
Dubois *Concertstück*
Creston *Concerto, op. 26*
Haydn *Concerto in C*

April 7–9
Susquehanna (Pennsylvania) University
Workshop

April 8
Susquehanna (Pennsylvania) University
Symphonic Band; James Steffy,
conductor
Creston *Concerto, op. 26*

April 29
University of Kansas Symphonic Band;
Robert Foster, conductor
Creston *Concerto, op. 26*
Cimarosa/Rousseau *Larghetto and Allegro*

June 30
Northwestern University: World
Saxophone Congress VI
Lecture-Demonstration "Singing with
the Saxophone"
Bach *Ich hatte viel Bekümmernis* from
Cantata #21 (with Norma Rousseau)
Gershwin *Porgy and Bess Medley*
Traditional *Irish Tune from County
Derry* (unaccompanied)

July 26
Shell Lake, Wisconsin; John Radd, piano
Bozza *Aria*
Bach *Sonata in E-flat*
Bach *Seufzer, Thranen, Kummer, Noth*
(with Norma Rousseau)
Bolling *Jazz Suite (I)* (with Lisa-Marie
Rousseau, Kevin Bents, Joseph
Rousseau)

October 30
Southwest State University, Minnesota
Symphonic Wind Ensemble; Rollin
Potter, conductor
Cimarosa/Rousseau *Larghetto and Allegro*
Hagen/Reed *Harlem Nocturne*

November 30–December 2
University of Minnesota Wind Ensemble
Tour; Frank Bencriscutto, conductor
Cimarosa/Rousseau *Larghetto and Allegro*
Bencriscutto *Concerto Grosso* (with
Cheri Moquist, Mike Krikava, Bill Ford,
and Rad Wakefield)
Gershwin/Hermann *Porgy and Bess Medley*

December 3
St. Francis, Minnesota High School
Concert Band and Jazz Ensemble;
Richard Foley, conductor
Reed *Ballade*
Creston *Concerto, op. 26 (III)*
arr. by Newsom *Summer of '42* (with
Jazz Ensemble)
Garner *Misty*

December 4
Kellogg Concert Band Ensemble; Lee Lueck, conductor
Gershwin/Hermann *Porgy and Bess Medley*
arr. by Hermann *Stella by Starlight*

1980

January 18
Towson (Maryland) State University: American Single Reed Workshop; Frederick Minger, piano
Bach *Sonata in E-flat*
Hába *Partita*
Creston *Concerto*

February 8
Augusta (Kentucky) College; Joseph Rezits, piano
Heiden *Sonata*
Cilea/Rousseau *Sonata in D*
Tcherepnine *Sonatine Sportive*
Brahms/Rousseau *Sonata in F minor*

February 15
Bellingham: Washington Music Educators Association Conference
Clinic "Sax Techniques"

February 16
Bellingham: Washington Music Educators' State Conference, Sehome High School Concert Band; Ray Blank, conductor
Badings *Concerto*
Cimarosa/Rousseau *Larghetto and Allegro*

April 13
Indiana University Symphonic Wind Ensemble; Frederick Ebbs, conductor
Glazounov *Concerto*

April 27
Bloomington, Indiana Symphony Orchestra; Keith Brown, conductor
Milhaud *Scaramouche Suite*

July 18
St. Mary's College; Joseph Rezits, piano
Heiden *Sonata*
Saint-Saëns/Teal *Sonate*
Tcherepnine *Sonatine Sportive*
Brahms/Rousseau *Sonata in F minor*

July 20
Shell Lake, Wisconsin; Joseph Rezits, piano
Saint-Saëns/Teal *Sonate*
Heiden *Sonata*
Derr *I Never Saw Another Butterfly* (with Norma Rousseau)

1981

January 25
Kokomo, Indiana Symphony Orchestra; Benjamin Del Vecchio, conductor
Glazounov *Concerto*

March 14
Butler County, Pennsylvania Symphony Orchestra; Paul Chenevey, conductor
Glazounov *Concerto*

April 5
University of Wisconsin-Eau Claire Symphony Band; Karel Husa, guest conductor
Husa *Concerto*

April 7
Bloomington, Indiana Jazz Festival
Spera *Patty*
Hagen *Harlem Nocturne*

May 19
Grand Rapids, Michigan Symphonic Band; William Root, conductor
Cimarosa/Rousseau *Larghetto and Allegro*
Gershwin/Hermann *Porgy and Bess Medley*

June 13
Indiana University; Paul Borg, piano
Hába *Partita*
Brahms/Rousseau *Sonata in F minor*
Bach/Rousseau *Sonata in E-flat*

Bach *Quia respexit humilitatem* (with Norma Rousseau)
Bach *Seufzer, Thränen, Kummer, Not*

June 14
Indiana University; Charles Webb, piano
Bassett *Music for Saxophone and Piano*
Debussy/Rousseau *Rapsodie*
Bonneau *Caprice en forme de valse*
Saint-Saëns/Teal *Sonata*
Villa-Lobos *Fantasia*

July 12
Shell Lake, Wisconsin; Charles Webb, piano
Bassett *Music for Saxophone and Piano*
Debussy/Rousseau *Rapsodie*
Bonneau *Caprice en forme de valse*
Saint-Saëns/Teal *Sonata*
Villa-Lobos *Fantasia*

1982

January 4
Indiana University Hoagland Carmichael Memorial Ceremony

February 5
Indiana University; Kari Miller, piano
Orrego-Salas *Quattro Liriche*

February 9
Denfeld, Minnesota High School Concert Band and Stage Band; Gerald Klun, conductor
Cimarosa/Rousseau *Larghetto and Allegro*
Gershwin/Hermann *Porgy and Bess Medley*
Hagen *Harlem Nocturne*
Arr. by Newsom *Summer of '42*
Garner *Misty*

February 12
Mary College; Marylynn Fletcher, piano
Glazounov *Concerto*
Creston *Sonata, op. 19*
Heiden *Sonata*

February 14
Bemidji State (Minnesota) University Wind Ensemble and Symphony Band; Gavin Rhodes Lewis, conductor
Glazounov *Concerto*
Gershwin/Hermann *Porgy and Bess Medley*

April 6
Indiana University Concert Band; Wilbur England, conductor
Husa *Concerto*

April 25
Philharmonic Orchestra of Indianapolis; Benjamin Del Vecchio, conductor
Cimarosa *Concerto*
Milhaud *Scaramouche*
Ibert *Concertino da camera*

July 9
Nuremberg, Germany: World Saxophone Congress XCIII
Munich Radio Orchestra, Werner Albert, conductor
Feld *Concerto* (premiere)

July 21
Leeds, England Institute Gallery Clinic

October 14
Košice, Czechoslovakia State Philharmonic; Stanislav Macura, conductor
Feld *Concerto*

November 8
Laxenburg Castle, Austria; Claus Christian Schuster, piano
Heiden *Sonata*
Orrego-Salas *Quattro Liriche*
Debussy/Rousseau *Rapsodie*
Bach/Rousseau *Sonata in E-flat*

1983
No date
Janáčkova, Czechoslovakia Philharmonic Orchestra
Feld *Concerto*

January 20
Missouri Music Educators Association
Central Missouri State University
Concert Band; Russell Coleman, conductor
Creston *Concerto, op. 26*

February 8
Olivet Nazarene (Illinois) College; Kari Miller, piano
Heiden *Sonata*
Orrego-Salas *Quattro Liriche*
Debussy/Rousseau *Rapsodie*
Bach/Rousseau *Sonata in E-flat*

April 12 and 14
Santiago, Chile Orquesta Filarmonica; Juan Pablo Izquierdo, conductor
Debussy *Rapsodia*
Glazounov *Concierto*

July 29
Minnesota Orchestra; Leonard Slatkin, conductor
Milhaud *The Creation of the World*

October 21
Vienna: Schubert-Saal; Hans Graf, piano
Creston *Sonata, op. 19*
Hindemith *Sonata*
Debussy/Rousseau *Rhapsodie*
Bach/Rousseau *Sonata in E-flat*
Villa-Lobos *Fantasia*

October 28–30
Göteborg, Sweden Brass and Woodwind Center
Saxofon-Seminarium

November 4 and 5
Vienna: Yamaha Music Center
Clinics

November 7
Paris: Salle Alfred Cortot; Odile Delangle, piano

1984
January 18
Indiana University; Kari Miller, piano
Orrego-Salas *Quattro Liriche*

February 10
Helsinki, Finland: Sibelius Akatemia; Kari Miller, piano
Muczynski *Sonaatti*
Denisov *Sonaatti*
Debussy/Rousseau *Rapsodia*
Feld *Soprano Saxophone Sonaatti*
Bach *Sonaatti in E*

May 8
Osaka Orchestra
Haydn *Concerto in C*
Milhaud *Scaramouche Suite*

May 26
Tokyo (first by American); Hans Graf, piano
Heiden *Solo*
Orrego-Salas *Quattro Liriche*
Debussy/Rousseau *Rapsodie*
Feld *Elegy*
Bach/Rousseau *Sonata in E Major*
Villa-Lobos *Fantasia*

July 8
Indiana University; Kari Miller, piano
Milhaud *Scaramouche*
Fox *S.A.X.* (with Jean Lansing, Kenneth Fischer, Randall Smith, Ralph Burton)
Feld *Elegy*
Haydn *Concerto in C*
Kaufmann *Meditation*
Dubois *Les Trois Mousquetaires* (with Jerry Sirucek, Earl Bates, Sidney Rosenberg)

July 22
Shell Lake, Wisconsin; Kari Miller,
piano
Milhaud *Scaramouche*
Glazounov *Concerto*
Fox *S.A.X.* (with Kenneth Fischer,
Donald Adams, Randall Smith, Ralph
Burton)
Feld *Elegy*
Bach *Sonata in E*

September 23
Indiana University; Charles Webb, piano
Kaufmann *Meditation*

September 27
University of Michigan: An Evening of
Music in Remembrance of Larry Teal;
Deborah Moriarty, piano
Brahms/Rousseau *Sonata in F minor (II)*

1985

February 9
Ithaca College; Mary Ann Covert, piano
Orrego-Salas *Quattro Liriche Brevi*
Debussy/Rousseau *Rapsodie*
Feld *Elegy*
Haydn/Rousseau *Concerto in C*
Master Class

February 10
Capital University; Kari Miller, piano
Debussy/Rousseau *Rapsodie*
Feld *Elegy*
Haydn *Concerto in C*
Diemente *Diary, Part II* (with James
Carroll)
Creston *Sonata, op. 19*

February 14
Doane (Nebraska) College Concert
Band; Hubert Brown, conductor
Lefebvre *Andante and Allegro*
Gershwin/Hermann *Porgy and Bess
Medley*
Spera *Patty* (with Jazz Ensemble)

April 23
Anchorage, Alaska Youth Symphony;
Karl Haas, guest conductor
Ibert *Concertino da camera*

May 17
Northmont (Clayton, Ohio) High School
Symphonic Band; Reginald Richwine,
conductor
Creston *Concerto, op. 26*
Puccini/Hermann *Tosca Fantasy*
Hagen/Reed *Harlem Nocturne*

June 27
Washington, DC: World Saxophone
Congress
U.S. Navy Band; Ray Cramer, conductor
Feld *Concerto*

June 29
University of Maryland: World
Saxophone Congress VIII
Master Class

June 30
Indiana University; Kari Miller, piano
Muczynski *Sonata, op. 29*
Denisov *Sonata*
Feld *Soprano Saxophone Sonata*
Bach *Sonata in E*

July 25
Indianapolis Symphony Orchestra;
William Curry, conductor
Ibert *Concertino da camera*
Debussy *Rhapsody*

July 28
Shell Lake, Wisconsin; Kari Miller,
piano
Muczynski *Sonata, op. 29*
Denisov *Sonata*
Feld *Soprano Saxophone Sonata*
Mozart *Concerto in C*

September 20
Bristol, England: Avon Schools
Symphonic Wind Band; David James,
conductor
Grundman *Concertante*

October
Lyon, France; Kari Miller, piano
Muczynski *Sonate, op. 29*
Denisov *Sonate*
Debussy/Rousseau *Rapsodie*
Feld *Soprano Saxophone Sonate*
Bach *Sonate in E*

October
London; Kari Miller, piano
Muczynski *Sonata, op. 29*
Denisov *Sonata*
Debussy/Rousseau *Rapsodie*
Feld *Soprano Saxophone Sonata*
Bach *Sonata in E*

October 2
Helsinki, Finland: Sibelius-Akatemia; Kari Miller, piano
Muczynski *Sonata, op. 29*
Denisov *Sonata*
Debussy/Rousseau *Rapsodie*
Feld *Soprano Saxophone Sonata*
Bach *Sonata in E*

October 16
Prague: Palác Kultury; Symphony Orchestra; Petr Vronsky, conductor
Feld *Concerto*

December 3
Indiana University; Kari Miller, piano
Heiden *Sonata*

1986

February 11
McMaster (Ontario) University; Kari Miller, piano
Muczynski *Sonata, op. 29*
Denisov *Sonata*
Feld *Soprano Saxophone Sonata*
Bach *Sonata in E*

February 19
Weber (Utah) State College, Bonneville High School Bands; Thomas Root, conductor
Cimarosa/Rousseau *Larghetto and Allegro* (with Weber State College Band)

Bencriscutto *Serenade*
Gershwin/Hermann *Porgy and Bess* (with combined bands)

February 27–March 1
Madison, Wisconsin: College Band Directors National Association North Central Division Conference
Indiana University Symphonic Band Tour; Ray Cramer, conductor
Feld *Concerto (III)*

March 11
Florida Southern College Concert Band; James Slutz, conductor
Vivaldi/Lang *Concerto in B-flat* (with Andy Cleaver)
Glazounov/Intravaia *Concerto*
Puccini/Hermann *Tosca Fantasy*
Hagen/Reed *Harlem Nocturne*
Gershwin/Hermann *Porgy and Bess Medley*

March 15
Concordia (Minnesota) College Orchestra; J. Robert Hanson, conductor
Vivaldi *Concerto for Two Saxophones* (with Gail Hall)
Glazounov *Concerto*

March 25
Pittsburg (Kansas) State University Master Class; Recital with Kari Miller, piano
Muczynski *Sonata, op. 29*
Denisov *Sonata*
Debussy/Rousseau *Rapsodie*
Feld *Soprano Saxophone Sonata*
Bach *Sonata in E*

April 13
Indiana University Symphonic Band; Ray Cramer, conductor
Feld *Concerto (III)*

April 25
Memphis State University Concert Band; James Courtney, conductor
Creston *Concerto, op. 26*

April 27
Tulsa Junior College Community
Orchestra and Band; Jerrold Lawless,
conductor
Villa-Lobos *Fantasia* (with orchestra)
Debussy *Rapsodie*
Cimarosa/Rousseau *Larghetto and
Allegro* (with band)
Hagen/Reed *Harlem Nocturne*
Gershwin/Hermann *Porgy and Bess
Medley*

April 30
Adams (Colorado) State College Concert
Band and Jazz Ensemble; Stephen
Brandon, conductor
Cimarosa/Rousseau *Larghetto and
Allegro*
Heiden *Diversion*
Lieb *Short Ballet*
Gershwin/Hermann *Porgy and Bess
Medley*
Hagen *Harlem Nocturne* (with Jazz
Ensemble)
arr. by Muffet *Summer of '42*
Garner *Misty*

May 25
Nagoya, Japan; Hans Graf, piano
Heiden *Solo*
Orrego-Salas *Quattro Liriche*
Debussy/Rousseau *Rapsodie*
Feld *Elegy*
Bach/Rousseau *Sonata in E major, BWV
1035*
Villa-Lobos *Fantasia*

May 28
Shohbi, Japan; Hans Graf, piano
Heiden *Solo*
Orrego-Salas *Quattro Liriche*
Debussy/Rousseau *Rapsodie*
Feld *Elegy*
Bach/Rousseau *Sonata in E major, BWV
1035*
Villa-Lobos *Fantasia*

May 30
Musashino, Japan
Master Class

July 9
Bilborough, England
Master Class

July 12
Birmingham, England: Clarinet and
Saxophone Society
Master Class

July 13
Birmingham, England: Clarinet and
Saxophone Society; Miriam Brickman,
piano
Feld *Élégie*
Brahms/Rousseau *Sonata in F minor*
Hagen *Harlem Nocturne*
Creston *Sonata, op. 19*
Haydn *Concerto in C*
Gershwin/Hermann *Porgy and Bess
Medley*

September 13
Indiana University; Anton Weinberg,
clarinet
Hymas *Duet on a Theme by Gershwin*

September 19
Carleton (Minnesota) College
Convocation Address: "Everything You
Ever Wanted to Know About Sax"
Master Class

October 3
Indiana University
Carmichael Songs (with ensemble)

October 6
Indiana University Percussion Ensemble;
Eugene Rousseau, guest conductor
Husa *Concerto* (Sigurdur Flosason,
soloist)

October 17
Indiana University; Karl Haas
commentator/piano, Paul Biss, violin,
James Tocco, piano, Charles Webb,

piano, Anton Weinberg, clarinet
Saint-Saëns/Rousseau *Le Cygne*
Diemente *Diary, Part II* (with Kenneth Fischer)
Fox *S.A.X.* (with Tridib Pal, Frank Bongiorno, Stuart Brottman, and Dennis Sizemore)
Debussy/Rousseau *Beau Soir*
Webern *Quartet*
Rachmaninoff/Rousseau *Vocalise*
Bach/Rousseau *Sonata in E Major*

October 19
Indiana University; Josef Gingold, violin, Karl Haas, piano
Beethoven

November 11
University of Minnesota-Morris Concert Band; Charles Henry Smith, guest conductor
Heiden *Diversion*
Gershwin/Hermann *Porgy and Bess Medley*

December
Bloomington, Minnesota Medalist Concert Band;
Heiden *Diversion*

1987

January
Texas Wesleyan University Wind Ensemble; Stephen Ehrich, conductor
Creston *Concerto, op. 26*

January 29
Indiana University; Leonard Hokanson, piano, Helga Winold, cello
Beethoven *Trio, op. 11*
Hindemith *Sonata*
Brahms *Trio in A minor, op. 114*

April 12
Yale Concert Band; Thomas Duffy, conductor
Husa *Concerto*
Gershwin/Hermann *Porgy and Bess Medley*

June 7
Tokyo: Japanese Band Association, Yale University Band; Karel Husa, conductor
Husa *Concerto*

June 21
Indiana University; Kari Miller, piano; Kenneth Fischer, Stuart Brottman, and Tridib Pal
CPE Bach *Rondo* from *Quartet*
Pascal *Quatuor*
Loeillet/Hornibrook *Trio*
Fox *Three Diversions*
Handel/Rousseau *Sonata in G minor*

September 26
Morioka, Japan
Handel/Rousseau *Larghetto and Allegro*
Debussy/Rousseau *Rhapsodie*
Hába *Partita*
Rachmaninoff/Rousseau *Vocalise*
Saint-Saëns/Rousseau *The Swan*
Ravel *Pièce en forme de habanera*
Creston *Sonata, op. 19*
Loeillet/Hornibrook *Trio Sonata*

September 28
Sapporo, Japan
Handel/Rousseau *Larghetto and Allegro*
Debussy/Rousseau *Rhapsodie*
Hába *Partita*
Rachmaninoff/Rousseau *Vocalise*
Saint-Saëns/Rousseau *The Swan*
Ravel *Pièce en forme de habanera*
Creston *Sonata, op. 19*
Loeillet/Hornibrook *Trio Sonata*

October 2
Akashi, Japan
Handel/Rousseau *Larghetto and Allegro*
Debussy/Rousseau *Rhapsodie*
Hába *Partita*
Rachmaninoff/Rousseau *Vocalise*
Saint-Saëns/Rousseau *The Swan*
Ravel *Pièce en forme de habanera*
Creston *Sonata, op. 19*
Loeillet/Hornibrook *Trio Sonata*

October 4
Izumo, Japan
Handel/Rousseau *Larghetto and Allegro*
Debussy/Rousseau *Rhapsodie*
Hába *Partita*
Rachmaninoff/Rousseau *Vocalise*
Saint-Saëns/Rousseau *The Swan*
Ravel *Pièce en forme de habanera*
Creston *Sonata, op 19*
Loeillet/Hornibrook *Trio Sonata*

October 12
Czechoslovakia; Leonard Hokanson, piano
Creston *Sonata, op. 19*
Hába *Partita*
Hindemith *Sonata*
Lukáš *Legend*
Mácha *Pláč saxofonu*
Kabeláč *Suite*
Feld *Soprano Saxophone Sonata*

November 9
Indiana University Jazz Ensemble; David Baker, conductor
Spera *Blues for Mr. Mellow*

1988

February 9
New York City: Merkin Concert Hall; Harvey Sollberger conductor
Fox *Shaking the Pumpkin* (with Aleck Karis, piano, Raymond Des Roches and Joseph Passaro, percussion)

March 4
University of Central Arkansas Symphonic Wind Ensemble; Russell Langston, conductor
Heiden *Diversion*
Haba *Partita*
Gershwin/Hermann *Porgy and Bess Medley*

March 5
University of Central Arkansas North American Saxophone Alliance Regional Conference
Master Class

April 5
Indiana University Symphonic Wind Ensemble; Ray Cramer, conductor
Heiden *Fantasia Concertante* (premiere)

May 15
Izumo, Japan
Bach/Rousseau *Sonata in E-flat*
Bencriscutto *Serenade*
Debussy/Rousseau *Beau Soir*
Pergolesi/Rousseau *Nina*
Haydn/Rousseau *Concerto in C*
Denisov *Sonata (II)*
Fauré/Rousseau *Aprés un Reve*
Heiden *Diversion*

May 28
Akashi, Japan
Bach/Rousseau *Sonata in E-flat*
Bencriscutto *Serenade*
Debussy/Rousseau *Beau Soir*
Pergolesi/Rousseau *Nina*
Haydn/Rousseau *Concerto in C*
Denisov *Sonata (II)*
Fauré/Rousseau *Aprés un Reve*
Heiden *Diversion*

August 12
Kawasaki, Japan: World Saxophone Congress IX
Tokyo Metropolitan Symphony Orchestra; Kazushi Ono, conductor
Heiden *Fantasia Concertante*

September 10
Indiana University; Charles Webb, piano
Gershwin/Hermann *Highlights from Porgy and Bess*

November 20
Indiana University Big Band; David Baker, conductor
Ellington *Satin Doll*
Carmichael/Baker *Medley*
Giuffre *Four Brothers*
Monk/Baker *'Round Midnight*
Herman/Bishop *Woodchopper's Ball*
Green/Shanklin *Body and Soul*
Spera *Blues for Mr. Mellow*

Legrand/Newsom *Summer of '42*
Desmond/Wolpe *Take Five*
Gershwin/Wallarab *Porgy and Bess Medley*
Dorsey/Flosason *Oodles of Noodles*
Kern/Cobine *Medley*
Flosason *In Memoriam*
Carmichael/Rousseau *Stardust*
McDonald & Hanley/Rousseau *Back Home in Indiana*
Hagen/Rousseau *Harlem Nocturne*

December 15, 16, and 18
Japan
Bencriscutto *Serenade*
Debussy/Rousseau *Rapsodie*
Hába *Partita*
Haydn/Rousseau *from Concerto in C*
Heiden *Diversion*

1989
January 21
University of Akron; Kari Miller, piano
Bach/Rousseau *Sonata in E*
Heiden *Diversion*
Ravel/Rousseau *Pièce en forme de Habañera*
Haydn/Rousseau *Concerto in C (Allegro spiritoso)*
Gershwin/Hermann *Porgy and Bess Medley*

April 9
Bloomington, Indiana Camerata Chamber Orchestra; Keith Brown, conductor
Haydn/Rousseau *Concerto in C*

April 20
Concordia (Minnesota) College; Pauli Worth, piano
Muczynski *Sonata, op. 29*
Kabeláĉ *Suite*
Heiden *Fantasia Concertante*
Hadyn/Rousseau *Concerto in C*
Villa-Lobos *Fantasia*

May 19
Japan Band Clinic
Special Lecture

July 12 and 15
Indianapolis Symphony Orchestra; Raymond Leppard, conductor
Debussy *Rapsodie*
Milhaud *Scaramouche Suite*

July 24
Indiana University; Kari Miller, piano, Fritz Magg, cello
Heiden *Fantasia Concertante*
Kabeláĉ *Suite*
Milhaud *Scaramouche*
Beethoven *Trio, op. 11*

July 25–27
Indiana University
Master Class

July 30
Shell Lake, Wisconsin; Kari Miller, piano, Fritz Magg, cello
Heiden *Fantasia Concertante*
Kabeláĉ *Suite*
Milhaud *Scaramouche*
Beethoven *Trio, op. 11*

November 15
Salem, Oregon Concert Band; Timothy Siess, conductor; Willamette University Band, Martin Behnke, conductor
Cimarosa/Rousseau *Larghetto and Allegro* (with Willamette University Band)
Gershwin/Hermann *Porgy and Bess*
Badings *Concerto* (with Salem Concert Band)

1990
1990–1991 Columbia Artists Community Concerts; Kari Miller, piano
Heiden *Sonata*
Debussy/Rousseau *Rapsodie*
Milhaud *Scaramouche*
Bach/Rousseau *Sonata in E*
Saint-Saëns/Rousseau *Sonata, op. 166*

Gershwin/Hermann *Porgy and Bess Medley*

April 23
Baylor University Wind Ensemble;
Michael Haithcock, conductor
Feld *Concerto*

April 28
Anderson, Indiana Symphony Orchestra;
Richard Sowers, conductor
Glazounov *Concerto*
Milhaud *Scaramouche*
Massenet/Rousseau *Meditation from Thaïs*
Gershwin/Hermann *Medley from Porgy and Bess*

May 8
Vienna: Mozart-Saal; Haydn Trio
Orrego-Salas *Partita, op. 100*
Debussy/Rousseau *Rapsodie*

June 16
Hong Kong
Bach/Rousseau *Sonata in E-flat*
Debussy/Rousseau *Beau Soir*
Gershwin/Hermann *Porgy and Bess Medley*
Saint-Saëns/Rousseau *The Swan*

July 14–22
Sandbach, England: Brereton International Music Symposium
Saxophone Course with Jean-Yves Fourmeau

August 17–20
Yatsugatake, Japan
Saxophone Seminar with Fourmeau Quartet

August 22
Japan
Clinic and Concert
Glazounov *Concerto*
Dubois *Divertissement*
Gershwin/Hermann *Medley from Porgy and Bess*

September 4–21
Munich Allgemeine Rundfunk Deutschland International Flute Competition
Juror

October 2
Indiana University
Eaton *Five Miniatures for Tenor Saxophone*

October 28
Germany: Bernhard Heiden 80th birthday celebration; Leonard Hokanson, piano
Heiden *Sonata*

1991

January 21–February 2
Japan tour

January 27
Shizuoka, Japan
Heiden *Sonata*
Kabeláč *Suite*
Rachmaninoff/Rousseau *Vocalise*
Saint-Saëns/Rousseau *Sonata, op. 166*
Saint-Saëns/Rousseau *Le Cygne*
Ravel/Rousseau *Pièce en forme de Habañera*
Puccini/Hermann *Tosca Fantasy*

February 1
Tokyo; Mariko Hattori, piano
Feld *Alto Saxophone Sonata* (premiere)

February 7, 8, and 9
Indianapolis Symphony Orchestra;
Raymond Leppard, conductor
Milhaud *La Creation du monde*

February 22
Kansas City, Missouri: College Band Directors National Association Convention
Soloist

February 27
University of Wisconsin-Platteville; Kari Miller, piano
Heiden *Sonata*

Debussy/Rousseau *Rapsodie*
Milhaud *Scaramouche*
Bach/Rousseau *Sonata in E*
Saint-Saëns/Rousseau *Sonata, op. 166*
Gershwin/Hermann *Porgy and Bess Medley*

March 1–3
Luther College Dorian Festival Recital
Soloist with Luther College Band

March 16
Otrava, Czechoslovakia
Soloist with orchestra

March 20
Prague, Czechoslovakia: Jaromir Klepáĉ, piano; Amy Barber and Lubor Krása, percussion; Václav Mazáĉek, conductor
Muczynski *Sonata, op. 29*
Kabeláĉ *Suite*
Heiden *Diversion*
Feld *Alto Saxophone Sonata*
Fox *Shaking the Pumpkin*

March 31
Indiana University: Bernhard Heiden 80th birthday celebration; Leonard Hokanson, piano
Heiden *Sonata*

April 13
Eugene, Oregon Adult Band Festival: Salem Community Band; John Skelton, conductor
Gershwin/Hermann *Porgy and Bess Medley*
Heiden *Diversion*

May 16–29
Japan tour

June 1
La Sierra (California) University Wind Ensemble; Barbara Favorito, conductor
Heiden *Diversion*
Puccini/Hermann *Tosca Fantasy*
Gershwin/Hermann *Porgy and Bess Medley*
Hagen/Reed *Harlem Nocturne*

July 12
Lambach, Austria: Heinz Medjimorec, piano
Bach/Rousseau *Sonata in E*
Saint-Saëns/Rousseau *Sonata, op. 166*
Debussy/Rousseau *Rapsodie*
Milhaud *Scaramouche*
Gershwin/Hermann *Suite from Porgy and Bess*

July 15–August 24
Salzburg, Austria: Mozarteum International Summer Academy Saxophone Course (first ever)

1992

January 11
Japan
Heiden *Fantasia Concertante*
Muczynski *Sonata, op. 29*
Milhaud *Scaramouche*
Saint-Saëns/Rousseau *Sonata, op. 166*
Massenet/Rousseau *Meditation from Thaïs*
Dubois *a la Parisienne*
Gershwin/Hermann *Medley from Porgy and Bess*
Kreisler/Rousseau *Schoen Rosmarin*
Puccini/Hermann *Tosca Fantasy*

February 25
Indiana University Symphonic Wind Ensemble; Frederick Fennell, guest conductor
Bruch/Kimura *Kol Nidrei*

May 9
University of Massachusetts, Amherst: 10th Annual New England Saxophone Symposium, Kari Miller, piano
Muczynski *Sonata, op. 29*
Feld *Alto Saxophone Sonata* (North American premiere)
Saint-Saëns/Rousseau *Sonata, op 166*

May 28–June 8
Japan tour

July 12
Indiana University Chamber Recital with Alfred Prinz

July 26
Shell Lake, Wisconsin Recital

July 27–31
Shell Lake Saxophone Workshop

August 3–21
Salzburg, Austria: Mozarteum Saxophone Course

August 24–September 1
Japan tour

September 2–29
Munich: Allgemeine Rundfunk Deutschland International Clarinet Competition
President of the Jury

September 30–October 3
Prague, Czechoslovakia
Recording of Feld's music

October 17
Wakefield District College: Second British Saxophone Congress; Jaromir Klepáč, piano
Heiden *Fantasia Concertante*
Debussy/Rousseau *Rapsodie*
Muczynski *Sonata, op. 29*
Feld *Alto Saxophone Sonata*
Saint-Saëns/Rousseau *Sonata, op 166*
Massenet/Rousseau *Meditation from Thaïs*
Dubois *À la Parisienne*

1993

January 17–26
Japan tour

March 10–17
Europe tour

March 15
Vienna Hochschule für musik; Peter Schmidl, piano
Saint-Saëns/Rousseau *Sonata, op. 166*
Feld *Alto Saxophone Sonata*
Tull *Concerto da Camera* (with brass ensemble)

May 23
Prague, Czechoslovakia Spring Festival
Solo Recital

May 27–June 8
Japan tour

July 1–13
Europe tour

July 4–11
Brereton, England: International Summer Symposium

July 25
Shell Lake, Wisconsin
Solo Recital

July 25–30
Shell Lake, Wisconsin
Saxophone Workshop

August 2–14
Salzberg, Austria: Mozarteum Saxophone Course

August 4
Salzburg, Austria: Mozarteum; Jaromír Klepáč, piano
Recital (first ever)
Heiden *Fantasia Concertante*
Debussy/Rousseau *Rapsodie*
Muczynski *Sonata, op. 29*
Feld *Alto Saxophone Sonata*
Saint-Saëns *Sonata, op. 166*

August 22–26
Yatsugatake, Japan
Saxophone Seminar with Fourmeau Quartet

August 23
Yatsugatake, Japan
Saint-Saëns *Sonata, op. 166*
Bernstein *West Side Story Medley*

August 27
Yatsugatake, Japan
Concert with Iwan Roth, Jean-Yves Fourmeau, Nobuya Sugawa, and Masato Kumoi

November 14
Bloomington, Indiana Camerata Orchestra; Keith Brown, conductor
Creston *Concerto, op. 26*
Massenet *Mediation from Thaïs*

1994

February 7
Interview on National Public Radio

February 24
Royal Northern (England) College of Music
Master Class; Recital

February 25
University of Salford, Manchester (England)
Master Class; Recital

February 26
Leeds (England) College of Music Saxophone Day
Master Class; Recital

February 27
Dublin (Ireland) College of Music
Master Class; Recital

March 4–6
Livorno, Italy: Mascagni Conservatory
Master Classes–"Teaching Music"

March 8
Paris Conservatory
Master Class

April 6–8
Cincinnati: Indiana University Symphonic Band Spring Tour, Music Educators National Conference National Convention; Ray Cramer, conductor
Creston *Concerto, op. 26 (II, III)*

April 21
Indiana University Symphonic Band; Ray Cramer, conductor
Creston *Concerto, op. 26 (Allegro)*

April 23
Indiana University Recital

May 21–23
Portland and Salem, Oregon
Master Classes

May 24
University of Oregon Wind Ensemble Soloist

June 12
Shell Lake, Wisconsin; Yuki Homma, piano
Glazounov *Concerto, op. 109*
Muczynski *Concerto, op. 41*
Haydn *Concerto in C Major*

June 12–17
Shell Lake, Wisconsin
Saxophone Workshop

July 17–30
Salzburg, Austria: Mozarteum
Saxophone Course

July 22
Ossiach, Austria: Budapest String Soloists
Glazounov *Concerto*

July 23
St. Florian, Austria: Budapest String Soloists
Glazounov *Concerto*

July 31–August 7
Brereton, England: Saxophone Course
Recital

August 18–20
Montréal: Canadian Imperial Bank of Commerce National Music Festival Juror

August 26
University of California-Sacramento
Seminar

September 12–14
Bloomington, Indiana
Recording with Winds of Indiana;
Frederick Fennell, conductor

September 30 and October 1
Muncie, Indiana: Music Teachers
National Association Convention
Master Class; Recital with Joseph Rezits,
piano
Cilea *Sonata*
Saint-Saëns *Sonata, op. 166*

October 23
Indiana University Recital; Leichen
Foster, Thomas Walsh, and Shirley
Diamond
Pascal *Quatuor*
Fox *Hear Again in Memory*
Feld *Alto Saxophone Sonata*
Saint-Saëns *Sonata, op. 166*

November 16
Austin Peay (Tennessee) State University
Wind and Percussion Exchange
Master Class; Recital with Anne Glass,
piano
Arban/Berry *Carnival of Venice*
Saint-Saëns *Sonata, op. 166*
Bernstein/Rousseau *Selections from West Side Story*

December 1–10
Japan tour

December 16
Chicago: Midwest Band Clinic
VanderCook College Symphonic Band
Heiden *Diversion* (Charles Menghini, conductor)
Hagen/Reed *Harlem Nocturne* (Alfred Reed, conductor)

1995
January 30
Washington, DC: Kennedy Center; U.S.
Army Band; Col. Bryan Shelburne,
conductor
Heiden *Diversion*

March 12–14
University of North Texas
Master Class; Recital

May 12–14
Fischoff Chamber Music Competition
Juror

June 26–28
Indiana University Saxophone Master
Class

July 22–28
London, England

July 31–August 12
Salzburg, Austria: Mozarteum
Saxophone Course

August 24–30
Yatsugatake, Japan: Hamamatsu
International Wind Instrument Academy
and Festival

September 27–October 3
Mainz, Germany: Villa Musica
Chamber music classes

October 1
Carlsberg, Germany: Bürgerhaus
Heiden *Intrada*

October 3
Pirmasen, Germany: Carolinensaal
Heiden *Intrada*

October 28
Chicago: VanderCook College of Music
Clinic

November 17–24
Europe tour

November 21
Budapest Strings
Glazounov *Concerto*

1996

February 4
Indiana University Symphonic Band,
Ray Cramer, conductor
Feld *Concerto*

February 15
Indiana University; Alfred Prinz,
clarinet, Monte Bedford, oboe, Kim
Walker, bassoon
Prinz *Ballade for Clarinet, Alto
Saxophone, and Piano* (premiere)
Dubois *Les Trois Mousquetaires*

March 24–April 2
Japan tour

March 30
Performance with Tokyo Bach Band

April 12
Olivet Nazarene University Concert
Band; Harlow Hopkins, conductor
Heiden *Diversion*
Puccini/Hermann *Tosca Fantasy*
Gershwin/Hermann *Porgy and Bess
Medley*
Hagen/Reed *Harlem Nocturne*

April 13
Bloomington, Indiana Pops Orchestra;
Ray Cramer, conductor
Gershwin/Hermann *Suite from Porgy
and Bess*
Carmichael *Stardust*

April 15
Indiana University Percussion Ensemble;
Wilber England, conductor
Denisov *Concerto Piccolo*
Gershwin/Cobine *Summertime* (with
Albert Cobine, harmonica)
Gershwin *Porgy and Bess Medley*

May 10–12
Dublin, Ireland
Master Classes; Recital

May 28–29
University of Georgia Master Class; Kari
Miller, piano; Kenneth Fischer,
saxophone
Debussy/Rousseau *Rapsodie*
Muczynski *Sonata, op. 29*
Feld *Alto Saxophone Sonata*
Lamb *Six Barefoot Dances*
Saint-Saëns *Sonata, op. 166*

June 9
Shell Lake, Wisconsin; Andrey
Kasparov, piano
Creston *Sonata, op. 19*
Massenet/Rousseau *Méditation from
Thaïs*
Loeillet/Hornibrook *Trio* (Jeremy Burke,
tenor saxophone)
Saint-Saëns *Sonata, op. 166*
Milhaud *Scaramouche*

June 10–14
Shell Lake, Wisconsin
Saxophone Workshop

July 8–10
Indiana University Saxophone Master
Class

July 28–August 10
Salzburg, Austria: Mozarteum
Saxophone Course

August 25–29
Hamamatsu, Japan: International Wind
Instrument Academy and Festival

August 26
Hamamatsu, Japan: Recital
Savari *Quintet* (with Jean-Yves
Fourmeau and Nobuya Sugawa, soprano;
Masato Kumoi, alto; Jiro Akamatsu,
tenor; Eugene Rousseau, baritone)
Loeillet *Trio* (with Masato Kumoi and
Hiroshi Nagao, piano)

November
Japan tour

1997

February 5
Indiana University; James Strain, marimba, Harvey Phillips, tuba
Heiden *Four Fancies*

February 13–16
Budapest, Hungary
Recording with Budapest Strings

February 24–26
Paris Conservatory
Master Classes

April 6
Indiana University: Frederick Fox Festival; Daniel Michalak, piano, Bruce Hamilton and Robert Patterson, percussion, Scott Stewart, conductor
Fox *Shaking the Pumpkin*
Fox *Hear Again in Memory*

April 25
Central Methodist (Missouri) College; Charles Wells Memorial Concert
Soloist with Band

May 7–10
Vienna, Austria
Recording with Haydn Trio

June 20–30
Tour of Prague and Moravia

July 1–11
Tokyo College of Music
Master Classes

July 27–August 9
Salzburg, Austria: Mozarteum Saxophone Course

August 21–29
Hamamatsu, Japan: Wind Instrument Festival

October 20
Indiana University; Don Freund, piano; Pat Harbison, trumpet; Otis Murphy; Thomas Walsh; Steven Stusek
Freund *Sky Scrapings* (premiere)
Carisi *Yamaha Suite*

December 6
Bloomington, Indiana Pops Orchestra; John Canfield, conductor
Berlin/Cobine *White Christmas*

1998

February 18
Indiana University; Thomas Robertello, flute, Kim Walker, bassoon, Bruce Bransby, bass
Koechlin *Épitaphe de Jean Harlow*
Bentzon *Racconto*

March 27
Northwestern University: North American Saxophone Alliance Conference
Master class

April 6
Indiana University; Thomas Robertello, flute, Nicholas Daniel, oboe, Susan Bicknell, clarinet, Karen Paradis, bassoon, Myron Bloom, horn
Heiden *Intrada*

May 11–27
Japan tour
Recitals, Master Classes, Research and Development at Yamaha

June 4–12
Mainz, Germany: Villa Musica
Chamber music classes

June 9, 10 and 11
Bad Kreuznach Römerhalle; Bacharach Burg Stahleck; Traben-Trarbach Parkschlößchen
Saint-Saëns *Sonata, op. 166*

June 13
Dortmund, Germany Conservatory
Recital, Master Class

June 20 and 21
Bloomington, Illinois: Yamaha Young Performing Artists
Recital, Lecture

June 23–24
Chicago: VanderCook College of Music
Clinics

August 10–22
Salzburg, Austria: Mozarteum
Saxophone Course

October 31–November 9
Dinant, Belgium: Adolphe Sax
International Competition
Juror

November 21 and 23
Cedar Rapids, Iowa Symphony; Peter
Perret, guest conductor
Marcello *Concerto in D minor*
Milhaud *Scaramouche*

1999

January 17
Indiana University; James Hayden
Johnston, conductor
Marcello *Concerto in d*

February 27–March 5
University of Nebraska (Omaha,
Lincoln, Kearney)
Artist in Residence

March 15
Recital with Zagreb Saxophone Quartet
Fox *S.A.X.*

March 23
Hilchenbach-Dahlbruch, Germany:
Südwestfälischen Philharmonie; David
Stern, conductor
Glazounov *Concerto, op. 109*
Creston *Concerto, op. 26*

March 24
Mittwoch, Germany: Südwestfälischen
Philharmonie; David Stern, conductor
Glazounov *Concerto, op. 109*
Creston *Concerto, op. 26*

April 14
Grand Rapids, Michigan Chamber Music
Society; Kari Miller, piano
Stein *Quintet* (Steven Brook, David
Wheeler, violins; Barbara Corbato, viola;
Karen Krummel, cello)
Orrego-Salas *Partita, op. 100*
Yuyama *Divertimento* (David Hall,
marimba)
Beethoven *Trio, op. 11*
Eychenne *Cantilène et Danse*

April 16
Michigan State University; Kari Miller,
piano
Freund *Skyscrapings*
Fox *Hear Again in Memory*
Debussy/Rousseau *Rapsodie*
Feld *Alto Saxophone Sonata*
Saint-Saëns *Sonata, op. 166*

April 18
Central Michigan University; Kari
Miller, piano
Bach *Sonata in E Major*
Debussy/Rousseau *Rapsodie*
Feld *Alto Saxophone Sonata*
Saint-Saëns *Sonata, op. 166*

April 24
University of North Texas
Master Class

April 25
University of North Texas
Bach *Sonata in E Major*
Debussy/Rousseau *Rapsodie*
Feld *Alto Saxophone Sonata*
Loeillet/Hornibrook *Trio* (Eric Nestler,
tenor saxophone)

April 27
National Public Radio's Karl Haas
"Adventures in Good Music"—
"It's All in the Genes"

May 6–9
Fischoff Chamber Music Competition
Juror

June 20–22
Ashland, Oregon: American Band
College

June 24–26
Indiana University Saxophone Master Class

July 23–27
Hamamatsu, Japan Wind Instrument Festival

late July–early August
Salzburg, Austria: Salon Concert
Fox *Hear Again in Memory*

late July–early August
Salzburg, Austria: Mozarteum Saxophone Course

August 8
Shell Lake, Wisconsin
Recital

August 8–13
Shell Lake, Wisconsin
Saxophone Workshop

October 15
Carleton (Minnesota) College
Recital

October 15–17
Shell Lake, Wisconsin
Saxophone Class with Zagreb Quartet

October 17
Clarke (Iowa) College
Recital

October 21–25
Dinant, Belgium: Adolphe Sax International Competition
Juror

November 3 and 4
University of Wisconsin-Eau Claire Concert Band
Soloist

November 6
Bloomington, Indiana Pops Orchestra
Soloist

No date
Tokyo: Musashino Wind Ensemble; Ray Cramer, conductor

2000
January 28 and 29
Blue Springs, Missouri
Clinic and Soloist

February 18–21
Prague: Martinů Hall; Feld 75th birthday celebration
Feld *Quintet* (premiere; with Pražák Quartet)

April 26
Henderson (Arkansas) State University Wind Ensemble
Concerto
Recital; Kari Miller, piano
Debussy/Rousseau *Rapsodie*
Fox *Hear Again in Memory*
Smith *Sonata No. 1*
Feld *Alto Saxophone Sonata*
Saint-Saëns *Sonata, op. 166*

April 30
Tulsa, Oklahoma Community College Orchestra and Community Band; Jerrold Lawless, conductor
Mozart *Concerto in C Major* (with orchestra)
Puccini/Hermann *Tosca Fantasy*
Feld *Festive American Fantasy* (premiere; solo saxophone, chorus, band, orchestra)

June 18 and 19
Bloomington, Illinois: Yamaha Young Performing Artists
Soloist, Master Class

June 24 and 25
Vancouver (British Columbia) Community College
Master Class

July 5–9
Montréal, Canada: World Saxophone Congress
Master Classes; Soloist

July 17–29
Salzburg, Austria: Mozarteum
Saxophone Course

August 6–11
Shell Lake Saxophone Workshop

August 31
Featured on "Adventures in Good
Music" by Karl Haas for NPR

October 15
Clarke (Iowa) College; Kari Miller,
piano
Bach/Rousseau *Sonata in E*
Fox *Hear Again in Memory*
Debussy/Rousseau *Rapsodie*
Feld *Alto Saxophone Sonata*
Saint-Saëns/Rousseau *Sonata, op. 166*

October 28
Zagreb, Croatia
Recording with Zagreb Saxophone
Quartet

November 4
University of Wisconsin-Eau Claire
Master Classes; Clinic; Soloist

November 11
St. Paul, Minnesota "Saxophone Day"
Clinic, Master Class

December 15 and 16
Chicago
Three clinics

2001

January 7
Minnesota Orchestra Young Artist
Competition
Juror

January 19 and 20
Alabama Music Educators Association
Convention
Clinic; Soloist with University of
Alabama-Tuscaloosa Wind Ensemble;
Gerald Walker, conductor
Heiden *Diversion*
Carmichael *Stardust*

January 26–28
Montreal
Master Classes

February 2
Minneapolis: MacPhail Center for the
Arts
Master Class

February 10
Park Rapids, Minnesota
Solos, Clinics

February 13
Wilnar, Minnesota
Soloist with University of Minnesota
Symphonic Wind Ensemble, Craig
Kirchhoff, conductor

February 14
Minneapolis
Soloist with University of Minnesota
Symphonic Wind Ensemble, Craig
Kirchhoff, conductor

February 18
St. Paul, Minnesota: Grand Symphonic
Winds; Matthew George, conductor
Creston *Concerto, op. 26*

February 22
Minneapolis
Soloist with University of Minnesota
Symphonic Wind Ensemble, Craig
Kirchhoff, conductor

February 26
Indiana State University
Master Class; Concert with Frederick
Fennell, conductor

March 6
Hilchenbach, Germany: Jaromír Klepác,
piano
Debussy/Rousseau *Rapsodie*
Massenet/Rousseau *Meditation*
Brahms/Rousseau *Sonata in F Minor, op.
120, no. 1*
Bach *Sonata in E Major*
Saint-Saëns *Sonata, op. 166*

March 8
Tongren Brussels, Belgian Air Force
Band; Alain Crepin, conductor
Heiden *Diversion*
Crepin *Saxflight*
Gershwin/Hermann *Porgy and Bess Medley*

March 2–13
Interviews with François Daneels

March 14–18
Saxophonist with Minnesota Orchestra

March 22–25
Arizona State University
Master Classes; Recital; Laura Loewen, piano
Bach *Sonata in E major*
Fox *Hear Again in Memory*
Debussy/Rousseau *Rapsodie*
Feld *Alto Saxophone Sonata*
Saint-Saëns *Sonata, op. 166*

March 31
University of Central Florida
Master Classes; Recital; Laura Loewen, piano
Bach *Sonata in E major*
Fox *Hear Again in Memory*
Debussy/Rousseau *Rapsodie*
Feld *Alto Saxophone Sonata*
Saint-Saëns *Sonata, op. 166*

April 4
Indiana State University
ER Big Band Concert
Satin Doll; Carmichael Medley; Take Five; Porgy and Bess Medley; Woodchopper's Ball; Stardust, Back Home Again in Indiana; others

April 6 and 7
Indianapolis: Bands of America Honor Band
Clinics; Soloist with Col. Arnald Gabriel, conductor
Heiden *Diversion*
Gershwin/Hermann *Porgy and Bess Medley*

April 27 and 28
University of Massachusetts
Master Class; Recital (Feld)

May 5
Park Rapids, Minnesota Band
Heiden *Diversion*
Take Five and *Angel Eyes* (with dance band)
Smith *In a Gentle Rain*

May 25 and 26
Zagreb, Croatia
Recording with Zagreb Saxophone Quartet

May 28–June 7
Teramo, Italy: Instituto Braga
Master Classes

June 1
Teramo, Italy: Instituto Braga; Piero D'Egidio, piano
Bach *Sonata in E Major*
Debussy/Rousseau *Rapsodie*
Feld *Alto Saxophone Sonata*
Saint-Saëns *Sonata, op. 166*

June 22–24
Vancouver (British Columbia) Community College
Recital; Master Classes

July 6–18
Japan tour: Toyko, Kyushu, Kagoshiwa, Sasebo, Takasaki
Tokyo, Musashino Wind Ensemble; Ray Cramer, conductor

July 29–August 3
Shell Lake, Wisconsin
Saxophone Workshop

August 13–24
Salzburg, Austria: Mozarteum
Saxophone Course

September 5–16
Munich International Saxophone Competition
Adjudicator

September 27–29
University of Minnesota
International Saxophone Master Classes

October 4
Fond du lac, Wisconsin
Recital; Laura Loewen, piano

November 5–8
University of Connecticut
Master Classes; Recital

2002

February
Recording with Belgian Air Force Band

February 5
Brussels, Belgium Conservatory
Master Class; Recital

March 6 and 7
Stillwater, Minnesota Junior High School

March 8–10
University of North Texas
North American Saxophone Alliance Conference

May 9–11
University of Iowa: Iowa Bandmasters
Master Class; Clinics

June 21–23
Vancouver (British Columbia)
Community College
Master Class; Recital

June 29 and 30
Ashland, Oregon: American Band
College

July 10–12
Schladming, Austria

July 15–26
Lugano, Switzerland: Ticino Musica
Master Classes; Recital

July 22
Salzburg, Austria: Mozarteum; Cordula Hacke, piano, Barbara Ann Martin, voice
Heiden *Sonata*

Hindemith *Sonata*
Heiden *Solo*
Derr *I never saw another Butterfly*

July 23
Lugano, Switzerland: Ticino Musica;
Ulrich Koella, piano
Feld *Alto Saxophone Sonata*
Saint-Saëns *Sonata, op. 166*

July 29–August 6
Salzburg, Austria: Mozarteum
Saxophone Course

August 11–16
Shell Lake, Wisconsin
Saxophone Workshop

September 27–29
University of Iowa: Voxman 90th birthday celebration; Marcelina Turcanu, piano
Gershwin/Hermann *Porgy and Bess Medley*
Weber *Polacca*/Mozart *Concerto, K. 622*/*Happy Birthday*

October 17–19
University of Minnesota
International Saxophone Master Classes

November 10
Bloomington, Minnesota Medalist Gold Medal Band
Soloist

December 19
Chicago: Midwest Clinic
Soloist with Bloomington, Minnesota Medalist Gold Medal Band

2003

March 8
Frankfurt, Germany: Yamaha Saxophone Festival
Solos with Big Band; Phil Woods, Nobuya Sugawa

March 11
Hilchenbach, Germany
Soloist

March 28–30
University of North Texas
Guest Professor

April 12
Concordia College Band; Russell Pesola, conductor
Muczynski *Concerto, op. 41*

April 14 and 15
University of North Texas
Guest Professor

April 25 and 26
Coleman Chamber Music Competition
Juror

May 8–10
Fischoff Chamber Music Competition
Juror

July 9–13
Minneapolis: World Saxophone Congress XIII

July 21–August 2
Lugano, Switzerland: Ticino Musica Saxophone Course; Recital

August 11–23
Vienna, Austria: Mozarteum Saxophone Course

October 14
DePauw (Indiana) University Percussion Ensemble
Concert

October 19
University of Minnesota
Tanya Remenikova, cello; Alexander Braginsky, piano
Brahms *Trio, op. 114*

October 23–25
University of Minnesota
International Saxophone Master Class

2004

January 9
Fairfax (Virginia) University: U.S. Navy Band Saxophone Symposium; Ralph Gambone, conductor
Heiden *Diversion*
Puccini/Hermann *Tosca Fantasy*

February 19
University of Minnesota Wind Ensemble; Craig Kirchhoff, conductor
Dahl *Concerto*

April 15
University of Minnesota: Music Educators National Conference
Encore Wind Ensemble; Jerry Luckhardt, conductor
Heiden *Diversion*

April 19–29
European Tour

May 1
University of North Carolina-Greensboro: North American Saxophone Alliance Biennial Conference
Altissimo clinic, Master class

May 16–30
Japan Tour

June 22–24
Vancouver (British Columbia) Community College
Master Class; Recital

July 19–31
Lugano, Switzerland: Ticino Musica Saxophone Course; Recital

August 2–14
Salzburg, Austria: Mozarteum Saxophone Course

October 14–16
University of Minnesota
Master Class

November 20 and 21
University of Minnesota Marching Band Indoor Concerts

No date
Japan Band Clinic
Master Class

2005

August 7
Shell Lake, Wisconsin; Cameron Hofmann, piano
Feld *Alto Saxophone Sonata*
Creston *Concerto, op. 26*

October 20–22
University of Minnesota
Master Class

October 30
University of Connecticut; Zagreb Saxophone Quartet
Kechley *Tsunagari*

December 4, 8, 10, and 11
Minneapolis: VocalEssence Orchestra; Philip Brunelle, conductor
Bennett *Seven Country Dances (I, VI, VII)*

2006

February 15
Iowa City, Iowa: North American Saxophone Alliance Conference
University of Iowa Symphony Orchestra; William LaRue Jones, conductor
Larsen *Song Concerto* (premiere)

February 17
University of Iowa: North American Saxophone Alliance Conference; Johnson County Landmark Jazz Ensemble
Guiffre *Four Brothers* (with Bennie Wallace, William Ford, Kenneth Tse)

March 22
University of Minnesota Percussion Ensemble; Fernando Meza, conductor
Denisov *Concerto Piccolo*

July 5
Ljubljana, Slovenia: World Saxophone Congress XIV
Slovenian Philharmonic Orchestra; David Itkin, conductor
Baker *Lamentations (pour la fin du monde)* (premiere)

2007

January 29–February 1
University of Georgia
Artist in Residence; Master Classes; Soloist with University of Georgia Orchestra
Larsen *Song Concerto*

February 18 and 19
Ithaca College
Master Classes; Recital

February 20 and 21
University of North Carolina-Wilmington
Master Classes; Recital

April 13 and 14
North Dakota State University-Fargo: North American Saxophone Alliance Regional Conference
Master Classes; Soloist with band

April 21–May 21
Sicily, Zagreb, Prague
Master Classes

April 24
Trapani, Sicily: Palazzo della Vicaria; Walter Roccaro, piano
Muczynski *Sonata, op. 29*
Debussy/Rousseau *Rapsodie*
Fox *Hear Again in Memory*
Saint-Saëns *Sonata, op. 166*

May 5
Bari, Italy: two concerts with Bari Symphony Orchestra; Giovanni Pelliccia, conductor
Nicodemi/de Federicis *Adagio*
Marcello *Concerto in D Minor*
Creston *Concerto, op. 26*
Gershwin *Summertime*

June 22 and 23
Vancouver (British Columbia) Community College
Master Class; Recital

August 5
Shell Lake, Wisconsin; Cameron
Hoffman, piano
Recital

August 6–10
Shell Lake, Wisconsin
Saxophone Workshop

September 18–22
Conservatório Dramático e Musical de
Tatui, "Dr. Carlos de Campos", Brazil
Master Classes; Recital; Soloist with
band

November 4
Bloomington, Indiana
Founders' Day Concert with Tridib Pal

November 20
University of Minnesota Wind
Ensemble; Craig Kirchhoff, conductor
Milhaud *La creation du monde*

November 28
Park Ridge, Illinois Civic Orchestra;
Edgar Muenzer, conductor
Ibert *Concertino da camera*
Carmichael/Gillespie *Stardust*

2008

March 1 and 2
Arkansas Symphony Orchestra; David
Itkin, conductor
Tomasi *Concerto*
Baker *Lamentations (pour la fin du monde)*

March 12
University of Minnesota Campus
Orchestra; Andy McMahan, conductor
Gershwin/Rousseau *Porgy and Bess Medley*

April 19
Ludwigsburg, Germany Symphonic
Band
Pops concert

April 22–24
Piacenza, Italy; Cameron Hofmann,
piano
Master Classes; Recital

April 25 and 26
Teramo, Italy; Cameron Hofmann, piano
Master Classes; Recital

May 11
Shell Lake, Wisconsin
Annual Gala with University of
Wisconsin — Eau Claire Jazz Ensemble

June 20–22
Vancouver (British Columbia)
Community College
Master Classes; Recital

June 25 and 26
Luther (Iowa) College
Master Classes; Recital

July 21–24
West Texas A&M University
Recital — Tomasi *Concerto*, etc.
Performance with Directors' Band

August 10–14
Shell Lake, Wisconsin
Recital; Saxophone Workshop

September 13
Abilene, Texas Philharmonic Orchestra;
David Itkin, conductor
Tomasi *Concerto*

October 3–5
University of North Carolina-Greensboro
Rousseau Celebration

October 23–25
University of Minnesota
International Saxophone Master Class

November 5
Bluffton (Ohio) College; with Zagreb
Saxophone Quartet

November 15
Las Vegas, Nevada Philharmonic; David Itkin, conductor
Tomasi *Concerto*

December 7
Bloomington, Indiana Camerata Orchestra
Tomasi *Concerto*

2009

January 31
Wausau, Wisconsin High School Band Festival
Recital; Cameron Hofmann, piano
Performance with Lawrence Conservatory Wind Ensemble

February 1
University of Wisconsin-Stevens Point
Lecture; Recital

March 8
Bloomington, Minnesota Medalist Concert Band; Jerry Luckhardt, conductor

March 9 and 10
Stillwater, Minnesota Junior High Bands Residency; Concerts with several bands

March 13 and 14
Minneapolis: Minnesota Sinfonia
Marcello *Concerto in D minor*
Glazounov *Concerto*

April 9–12
University of Idaho: North American Saxophone Alliance Regional Conference
Master Classes; Soloist with band
Heiden *Sinfonia Concertante*
Gershwin/Hermann *Porgy and Bess Medley*

May 18–20
Perugia, Italy Conservatory
Teach; Recital

May 22 and 23
Milano, Italy Conservatory
Master Classes; Recital

May 26–28
Vienna, Austria University of Music
Master Classes

May 30 and 31
Prague, Czechoslovakia
Recording

June 19–21
Vancouver (British Columbia) Community College
Master Classes; Recital

June 23 and 24
Ashland, Oregon: American Band College
Clinics; Soloist with band

July 2
Nova Gorica, Slovenia
Master Class

July 3–5
Nova Gorica, Slovenia International Competition
Juror

July 7–12
Bangkok: World Saxophone Congress XV
Master Class

July 13–19
Hong Kong International Saxophone Symposium
Master Classes
Soloist with NeoWinds; Tom Lee, conductor
Heiden *Diversion*
Recital; Amy Sze, piano
Debussy/Rousseau *Rapsodie*
Muczynski *Sonata, op. 29*
Hindemith *Konzertstück* (Kenneth Tse, alto saxophone)
Beethoven *Trio, op. 87* (Kenneth Tse, soprano saxophone and Thomas Liley, alto saxophone)

July 21
Tokyo
Master Class

August 9–13
Shell Lake, Wisconsin
Solos; Saxophone Workshop

October 9 and 10
Prague
Recording

October 22–24
University of Minnesota
International Saxophone Master Class

November 6 and 7
Fond du Lac, Wisconsin
Master Class; Recitals

2010

February
University of Georgia
Master Class

March 6
University of Georgia: North American
Saxophone Alliance Biennial Conference
Performance and Eulogy at Kenneth
Fischer Memorial
Debussy/Rousseau *Rapsodie*

March 26–28
Recording with University of North
Texas Symphony Orchestra; David Itkin,
conductor
Larsen *Song Concerto*
Baker *Lamentations (pour la fin du monde)*
Tomasi *Concerto*

August 8–12
Shell Lake, Wisconsin
Recital; Saxophone Workshop

October
Fond du Lac, Wisconsin
Windhover Center for the Arts
Soloist with Lighthouse Big Band

APPENDIX E
SAXOPHONE STUDENTS OF EUGENE ROUSSEAU

Dates refer to the academic year during which study began. Therefore, the list is not a roster of all students for each year, which consistently numbered more than twenty at Indiana University and ten at the University of Minnesota. The list is as complete as possible, with apologies for any omissions.

Indiana University

1964–65
Adler, David
Anderson, David
Atkins, Carl
Bell, Sandra (Linkimer)
Campbell, Gary
Chamberlin, John
Da Grade, Marvin
Danielson, Gerald
Drost, Michael
Gay, Marvin
Gorin, Thomas
Graver, Blanche
Greene, James
Hopkins, Harlow
Kurz, Louis
Luell, David
Mancino, Pasquale
Meyer, Thomas
Miedema, Harry
Myers, Patricia
Sapp, James
Saunders, Ralf
Smith, Terry
Smith, Ray
Spring, Douglas
Stevenson, Gerald
Teitsworth, Nancy (Greenwood)
Ulichny, Arthur
Wagner, Gary
Wilson, Janice

1965–66
Bamber, Dennis
Bell, Keith

Goldman, Rudi
Jansen, Harold
Leudders, Jerry
McGlothlin, Robert
Margoni, Daniel
Sidener, Whitney
Taylor, Mary
Todenhoft, Charles

1966–67
Barkhymer, Lyle
Brown, Jo Ann
Conrad, Jon
Cooper, Evan
Gee, Harry.
Hardymon, Donna (Poynor)
Harmer, Theodore
Jordan, Bruce
Nifong, Bruce
Peterson, George
Reed, John

1967–68
Bayer, Brandon
Busenberg, Mark
Diehl, Douglas
Flanagan, Joseph
Hores, Robert
Haupert, Gary
Krall, Barbara

1968–69
Arthur, Susan
Chesebro, Robert
Clark, Roger
Hutchcroft, Kim
Newlin, Patricia
Rones, Arthur

Rose, Bonnie (Bayer)
Teulle, Charles

1969–70
Anderson, John
Bundy, Barbara
Dashiell, Jeffrey
Crawford, Thomas
Downs, Kenneth
Focht, Richard
Gerry, Michael
Gilbertson, Carl
Grissom, Cassandra
Gudmundsson, Jon
Gyurko, Shirley
Kaiser, James
Kinghorn, Gene
Kluesner, Dean
Knauer, Douglas
Koontz, Thomas
Lang, Roxanne
McLure, Steven
Rosenberg, Roger
Scott, John
Smith, Donald
Squires, Michael
Van Lenten, Lance
Wehner, Richard
Williams, Lawrence

1970–71
Devito, Dominic
Duncan, Danny
Ford, Robert
Grant, Donald
Hunn, Gene
Riddles, David
Weece, Randall
Wolfe, George

1971–72
Alfonsetti, Louis
Beckie, Donald
Cameron, Thomas
Cory, Michael
Delman, Stanley
DiClemente, Michael
Giese, Craig
Giordano, Stephen
Rosen, Kenneth
Smith, Marilyn (Wesloski)

1972–73
Amsden, Robert
Biancosino, Anthony
Branter, David
DeMartinis, Paul
Gianacopulos, Kay
Imboden, Gregory
Lacy, Edwin
Milton, Sheri
Minghelli, Edward
Riedel, Arthur
Weinberger, Bruce

1973–74
Carroll, James
Fischer, Kenneth
Lamke, Andy
Lansing Jean
Levine, Samuel
Maezawa, Fumiyoshi
Maezawa, Kyo
Novacheoff, Mark
O'Hara, William

1974–75
Adgate, Steve
Beers, Thomas
Craig, Allan
Goacher, Stephen
Kosich, George
Lang, Carl
Marsh, John
Niceley, Gregg
Noble, Gregory
Oppenheim, Richard
Robinson, James

Sears, William
Shambly, Archie
Spies, Susan
Thompson, Willie
VanFleet, Jim
Younge, Shelley

1975–76
Downer, Phyllis
Farrelly, James
Fedie, Jessie (Abraham)
Marino, Laurie (Sears)
Meredith, Alice
Shanklin, Richard

1976–77
Burdack, Joachim
Cory, Michael
Davis, William
Fiegle, Brian
Fumusa, Joseph
Krejci, Mathew
Newman, Laura
Scott, John
Sperl, Gary
Wildhack-Nolan, Patrick

1977–78
Bennett, Matthew
Crittenden, Richard
McClure, Mark

1978–79
Butler, Hunt
Chapman, Roger
Feller, David
Hoshino, Tadashi
Jacobson, Michael
Marolf, Dane
Martin, William
Mroczkowski, David
Nield, Kathleen
Petrich, Mary
Stout, Karen
Yohe, Cindy

1979–80
Bowerly, Daniel
Brinley, Robin

Cook, Terrance
Czanderna, Kani
Faidley, Janice
Fiske, Michael
Frascotti, Robert
Kataoka, Katsui
Kelton, Christopher
Liley, Thomas
Mayer, Tansie
Pal, Tridib
Ronkin, Bruce
Schmidt, David
Snyder, William
Stusek, Steven

1980–81
Babick, Tod
Ewell, Ralph
Hester, Michael
Hinkle, Greg
Hopkins, Mark
Jamsa, Jonathan
Jennings, Dwight
Kessler, Mike
Molitor, Stephen

1981–82
Burton, Ralph
Dong, Dale
Finney, Eric
Finnsson, Karen
Hodges, Richard
Kay, David
Loy, Susan
Mitchell, Jeffrey
Nabb, David
Saddler, Augustus
Smith, Randy

1982–83
Bixler, David
Broeker, Neil
Brottman, Stuart
Dircksen, Eric
Haines, Laura
Halstead, Kevin
McCourry, Gary
Milne, David

Nolan, Julia
Ohata, Michael
Olliver, Donna
Purkhiser, Beth
Stitzer, Gail

1983–84
Adams, Donald
Anthony, Jeffrey
Ducharme, Jean
Flosason, Sigurdur
Graham, Mark
Maeda, Donna
Patchen, Jeffrey
Romines, Jay
Susevich, Randolph

1984–85
Ellison, Anne (Kelton)
Rhynard, Donald
Sizemore, Dennis
Stump, David
Vines, Sally
Wilkins, Ashby

1985–86
Bongiorno, Frank
Bowen, Ralph
Bryan, Carolyn
Gullion, Thomas
Miller, Gregory
Sander, Craig
Wagenblast, Scott
Weremchuk, George
Yonekura, Takashi

1986–87
Cupples, Audrey
Guanajuato, Edward
Hirayama, Akitetsu
Hochkeppel, William
LaMonica, Michael
Nestler, Eric
Parr, Bruce
Reed, Donald
Showalter, Laura
Towell, Gordon

Vernon, Farrell
Walsh, Thomas
Wen, Andy

1987–88
Bjorkman, Leichen (Foster)
Logoteta, Steven
Tucker, Bradley
Walker, Christopher

1988–89[151]
Baker, Lynn
Barbour, Jennifer
Butler, Lannie
Cummings, Julia
Deloughery, Paul
Goodman, Christopher
Grieser, Brian
Hahn, Erik
Horlacher, Karen
Hyzer, Gary
McKnight, Jeffrey
Maugans, Stacy
Nishimoto, Daina
O'Riordan, Kirk
Powers, Ann
Schaefer, Derek
Schattschneider, Adam
Spence, William
Stewart, Scott
Watkins, Mark
Williams, Stacee
Wipf, Stefan

1989–90
Andriese, Timothy
Deja, Richard
Hudgins, Shannon
Kolber, Todd
Nickolas, Paul
Riggins, Dennis
Rogers, Jason
Saunders, David
Shapiro, Jason

[151] Probably includes students taught by graduate assistants.

Taggart, Deanne
Vasileff, David

1990–91
Alford, Danny
Bier, William
Burdge, Barbara
DeHaas, Pablo
Hardin, Angela
Howrey, Brian
Jacobs, Douglas
Levy, Erwin
Potter, Keith
Renzi, Matthew
Schatz, Amy
Schlemmer, Paul
Sremec, Dragan
Vanderlinden, Matthew

1991–92
Benfield, Kevin
Colb, Jonathan
Diamond, Shirley
Duncan, Preston
Fisher, David
Gargrave, Eric
Jones, Robert
Kerscovitz, Mark
King, Keith
Olges, Jennifer
Valerio, Javier

1992–93
Brakel, Timothy
Isoda, Hideki
Pay, David
Viener, John

1993–94
Carter, Robert
Case, Greg
Fallek, Hayden
Tse, Kenneth

1994–95
Barclay, Parry
Berman, Brian
Burke, Jeremy
Campbell, Chris

Dutton, Christopher
Freeman, David
Gifford, Nathan
Klevay, Michael
Murtfeldt, Ryan
Tiscione, Stephen

1995–96
Choate, Kathryn
Green, Heather
Hollandsworth, Matthew
Lippy, Colin
Murphy, Otis
Nagata, Mitsuyo
Proehl, Raymond
Richardson, Dustin
Snyder, Jeffrey

1996–97
Dusdieker, Anna (Duke)
Gausch, Marta
Welker, Adrienne

1997–98
Anderson, Chris
Armentrout, Wade
Cartwright, Jay
Dessena, Maria
Drabek, Nathan
Duke, Michael
Glanton, Emily
Graham, Nichole
Paulo, Gary
Pettit, Jack
Temme, Steven

Tuck, Tag
Vance, Michael
Wellons, Rebecca
Yarbro, Steven

1998–99
Iyengar, Anil
Jones, Patrick
Hartman, Karl
Mlinarcik, Geoffrey

1999–2000
Bowers, Corey
Corbin, Katherine
Eaton, Michael
Juliá, Albert
Rhoades, Lisa
Weber, Gregory

In addition, at different times six Visiting Scholars spent a period of months at Indiana University to observe the teaching of Eugene Rousseau:

Cooper, Elburn
Currie, Alan
Greene, Philip
Ishiwata, Yushi
Kawrza, Johannes
Kitayama, Atsuyasu

Teacher of Saxophone
Teacher of Saxophone
Edinburgh Academy of Music
Kunitachi College of Music
Conservatorium für Musik
Shizuoka University

Portland, Oregon
England
Scotland
Japan
Klagenfurt, Austria
Shizuoka, Japan

University of Minnesota

2000–01
Groh, David
Hanich, Kristen
Jensen, Jamie
Jones, Patrick
Lippy, Colin
Melody, Brian
Pemberton, Elizabeth
Robison, Tim
Rude, Matt
Schuelka, Matt
Schmitz, Steve
Wytko, Anna Marie

2001–02
Andersen, Jessica
Miller, Kyle

Rodesch, Brian
Sedki, Michael

2002–03
Egger, Phil
Flink, Adam
Groh, David
Jenkins, David
Martin, Jessica
Page, Stephen
Tremmel, Matt
Uldall, Jennifer
Ukiya, Sayo

2003–04
Hanson, Michael
Miller, Kyle
Prindiville, James

2004–05
Bamford, Curtis
Kelly, Will
Parvey, Jason
Young, Colin

2005–06
Hahn, Markus
Holgers, Angela
Killam, Linden
Mortensen, Melinda
Zayas, Jose

2006–07
Brobston, Andrew
Cummins, John
Dromgold, Allison
Duncan, Preston

Duren, Andrew
Fisher, Megan
Franz, Chris
Martinez, Ricardo
Snydacker, Thomas
Wright, Scott

2007–08
McCarthy, David

2008–09
Braybrooks, Sally
Edington, Erin
Hopkins, Lucas

2009–10
Devereaux, Nelson
Fabus, Jason
Rhoades, Lisa

Rottle, Jamie
Schaller, Ted

Fall 2010
Nath, Jonathan
Wrenn, Greg

APPENDIX F

FAMILY OF EUGENE ROUSSEAU

Joseph Rousseau (son) — b. September 24, 1965, Bloomington, Indiana
Lisa-Marie Rousseau (daughter) — b. June 18, 1962, Iowa City, Iowa

Eugene Rousseau — b. August 23, 1932; Blue Island, Illinois
Married August 15, 1959 to:
Norma Rigel [Rousseau] (wife) — b. December 14, 1936; Cedar Rapids, Iowa

Earl Rousseau (brother) — b. August 18, 1920
Lucille Rousseau (sister) — b. February 8, 1918
                                  d. March 1998

Joseph Philias Eugene Rousseau (father) — b. November 10, 1895, Spalding, Michigan
                                                 d. September 2, 1975

Married December 6, 1917 to:
Laura Schindler [Rousseau] (mother) — b. November 24, 1894
                                   d. February 21, 1970; Antigo, Wisconsin

Edwin Napoleon Rousseau (uncle) — b. August 13, 1902
                                 d. September 5, 1990
Alvinn Raimont Evaris Rousseau (uncle) — b. September 1, 1904
                                 d. October 3, 1988
Elmirz Isabel Rousseau (aunt) — b. June 13, 1899
                                 d. July 14, 1995
Marian (Marie) Anne Rousseau (aunt) — b. May 23, 1901

Katherine Schindler (maternal grandmother) — b. Germany

Philias Rousseau (grandfather) — b. May 22, 1864, Lowell, Massachusetts
                                 d. November 13, 1941, Iron River, Michigan
Married June 13, 1892 to:
Cora Robinson [Rousseau] (grandmother) of Powers, Michigan —
                                 b. April 6, 1877, Michigan
                                 d. September 21, 1925, Antigo, Wisconsin

Jean Rousseau (paternal great-grandfather) — b. Angers, France; probably immigrated
                                 through the port of Boston

Peter Robinson (maternal great-grandfather) — b. Canada

Harriet Jarvis [Robinson] (maternal great-grandmother) — b. Wisconsin

NOTES

The notes below are related to the teaching chapters. All unattributed quotations, concepts, and anecdotes are verified by Eugene Rousseau.

IMS – International Music Supply presentation (Des Plaines, Illinois)
IUMC – Indiana University Master Class (summer saxophone workshops)
IUSC – Indiana University Studio Class (saxophone academic studio classes)
MN – University of Minnesota (Eugene Rousseau International Saxophone Master Classes)
MW – The Midwest Clinic presentation (Chicago)
SL – Shell Lake, Wisconsin Arts Center (Eugene Rousseau Saxophone Workshops)
UK – University of Kansas presentations
VC – VanderCook School of Music presentation (Chicago)

11: TONE PRODUCTION

PAGE
103 "The air is the soul of the sound," IUMC July 11, 1984.
103 "The air stream is very similar," IUMC June 14, 1982.
103 The concept of warm air, IUSC February 3, 1981.
103 Rousseau has described the embouchure, IUMC June 13, 1983.
103 The lower lip is often too smooth, IUMC June 14, 1982.
103 The corners of the mouth must be, IUMC June 17, 1981.
103 "think of the inside of the mouth," IUMC June 18, 1981
103 "the generation of the tone does not," IUMC June 18, 1983.
103 The amount of mouthpiece in the mouth, UK July 5, 1977.
103 Too little mouthpiece and reed in the mouth, IUMC June 15, 1983.
103 "The embouchure is everything between", SL August 9, 2005.
104 He has no objection to the use of tape, IUMC July 10, 1984.
104 The embouchure is the same for all, IUMC June 14, 1982.
104 Rousseau warns players not to be afraid, IUSC October 26, 1979.
104 he cites singer Thomas Hampson, VC October 28, 1995.
105 "The embouchure is solid," IUMC June 14, 1983.
105 Rousseau is adamant that the jaw, IUMC June 14, 1982.
105 "verify the tone from time to time," IU July 8, 1983.
105 Sometimes a student will have difficulty, IUMC June 13, 1983.
105 "A student will automatically find," IUMC June 24, 2000.
105 "Remember to keep a whole-note sound," IUMC June 17, 1981.
106 Another matter of difficulty, IUMC June15, 1983.
106 Incidentally, Rousseau says that Selmer, IUSC November 26, 1979.
106 Rousseau observes that almost every classical, IUMC June 23, 2000.
106 The optimum position of the reed, MW December 17, 1994.
107 "To make good music is challenging enough," IUMC June 15, 1982.
107 One especially useful tool is to bend, IUMC June 14, 1982.

107 "While it can enhance the tone," IUMC July 9, 1984.
107 "more a change of intensity than of pitch," IUMC June 17, 1981.
107 "The vibrato should be introduced," IUMC June 26, 1999.
107 Vibrato is produced through the use, IUMC July 10, 1984.
108 If a student's vibrato is very slow, IUMC July 10, 1984.
108 On the other hand, the width of the vibrato, UK April 28, 1979.
108 The vibrato and non-vibrato notes must be, IUMC June 18, 1981.
108 If vibrato is used on a relatively short note, IUMC June 19, 1981.
108 "Don't use vibrato on every note," UK July 5, 1977.

12: TUNING AND INTONATION

109 Tone production and intonation are closely related, IUMC June 18, 1981.
109 the saxophone sounds best when it is played, IUMC June 23, 2000.
109 Rousseau provides three not necessarily, IUSC February 11, 1980.
109 Two pitches should be used to tune, IUMC June 15, 1982.
109 "The instrument is made," UK July 5, 1977.
109 "the larger the instrument," IUMC June 17, 1981.
109 Note that the soprano often tends, IUMC July 12, 1984.
109 Another strategy to tune, MN October 23, 2003.
109 Some very old saxophones are marked, IUMC June 15, 1983.
109 In addition, Rousseau believes it is possible, IUMC June 13, 1983.
110 Intonation adjustments are done primarily, IUMC June 14, 1983.
110 High A is sharp, IUMC June 16, 1983.
110 Mule always used the right hand, IUSC February 11, 1980.
110 Middle D (piano) is sharp, IUSC February 11, 1980.
110 Soprano F-sharp (forte) is flat, IUMC July 12, 1984.
110 Soprano F-sharp (piano) is sharp, IUMC July 12, 1984.
111 If the low C is flat, IUMC June 15, 1982.
111 If a note is sharp in both octaves, IUMC July 9, 1984.
111 Selmer's middle C may have a hole, IUSC February 11, 1980.
111 On an associated issue, UK July 5, 1977.
111 Soprano saxophones have two bore constructions, IUMC June 26, 1999.
111 The different bore constructions, MN October 15, 2004.
111 Nonetheless, Rousseau believes we have learned, IUMC June 24, 1999.
111 "a well-constructed saxophone," IUSC November 17, 1980.
111 "Your reed is tired," SL August 9, 2000.

13: TECHNIQUE

112 "Let the saxophone," IMS December 16, 2000.
112 "The fingers should," IUMC June 24, 2000.
112 An exception occurs, MW December 17, 1994.
112 "Hit it right," MW December 17, 1994.
112 The left thumb, IUMC June 24, 2000.
113 "the saxophone technique," IUMC July 10, 1984.

113 He recommends that, IUSC February 3, 1981.
113 "One can build," IUMC June 16, 1981.
113 This suggestion is in line, IUMC July 10, 1984.
113 Rousseau has spoken of, MN October 13, 2006.
114 "The speed of," IUSC February 3, 1981.
114 "The frequency of," IUMC June 18, 1981.
114 In addition, Rousseau, IUSC October 26, 1979.
114 The fingering, which, MN October 24, 2003.
114 "The saxophone differs," IMS December 16, 2000.
114 The fingering was suggested, SL August 14, 2002.
114 Another fingering which IUSC October 26, 1979.
115 Rousseau's preference, IUMC July 10, 1984.
115 Another strategy, learned, SL August 7, 2000.
115 Rousseau also advises, IUMC June 15, 1982.
115 Another tactic which, SL August 7, 2000.
115 "Spring tension affects," IUMC June 14, 1983.
115 "much more than," IUMC June 15, 1981.

14: ARTICULATION

116 this action should be, IUMC June 15, 1982.
116 "Touch the tip," MW December 17, 1994.
116 And further, ONU April 24, 1992.
116 "clarify certain notes," IUMC June 14, 1983.
116 a soft "t", IUSC February 3, 1981.
116 In fact, Rousseau, IUSC February 3, 1981.
116 Using the tongue, IUMC June 16, 1982.
116 Articulation is presented, IUMC June 15, 1982.
116 Rousseau advocates checking, IUMC June 14, 1983.
116 "an accent is," IUMC June 15, 1982.
116 "don't interpolate," IUMC June 18, 1982.
117 "the tongue is a valve," VC October 28, 1995.
117 To develop rapidity, IUMC June 14, 1983.
117 "Get your basic tone," MW December 17, 1994.
117 "Some problems," IUMC June 14, 1983.
117 "Use the left hand," IUMC June 15, 1982.
117 "Don't use the tongue," IUMC June 15, 1983.
117 "You can't tongue," VC October 28, 1995.

15: HIGH TONES

118 "From low B-flat," IUMC June 15, 1983.
118 "One can start," IUSC April 28, 1980.
118 A related strategy, SL August 13, 2002.
119 "Most people turn," IUSC April 28, 1980.
119 Rousseau recommends three, IUSC November 24, 1980.

119 "One of the acoustical peculiarities," IUMC June 15, 1982.
120 Rousseau offers four, IUSC January 27, 1981.
120 "Often the jaw," UK April 28, 1979.
120 "As one plays higher," IUSC November 24, 1980.
120 "By the time," IUMC July 12, 1984.
121 "Sometimes one must," IUMC June 15, 1982.
121 "you can get." IUMC June 17, 1981.

16: THE OTHER SAXOPHONES

122 "If you play one," IUMC June 14, 1982.
122 "if you play more," VC October 28, 1995.
122 The shape of, IUMC June 24, 2000.
122 "Each instrument has," SL August 14, 2002.
122 The soprano, for example, SL August 14, 2002.
122 more resistant, IUMC June 16, 1981.
123 "The soprano is not," UK April 28, 1979.
123 Be certain that the weight, IUMC June 24, 1999.
123 The shorter levers, SL August 11, 2005.
123 "Don't put too much," SL August 12, 2002.
123 The straight soprano, IUMC June 16, 1983.
123 The soprano saxophone seems, IUMC June 16, 1983.
124 The tenor shares, IUMC June 16, 1983.
124 The low octave vent, IUMC June 18, 1982.
124 "You'll never regret," VC October 28, 1995.
124 A harness is also possible, IUMC June 24, 2000.
124 One must remember, SL August 9, 2000.
124 "You will never," VC October 28, 1995.

17: PERFORMANCE

125 For a performance, IUMC June 13, 1983.
125 The stand should be, IUMC July 9, 1984.
125 Make certain that, IUMC June 14, 1983.
125 All music should be, SL August 15, 2002.
125 "memorization is," IUMC June 15, 1981.
125 Remember that a performance, IUMC June 25, 1999.
125 "Be in good physical," IUMC June 14, 1983.
125 Rousseau suggests several, IUMC June 24, 1999.
125 It's important to keep, IUMC June 17, 1982.
126 "When you come on stage," IUMC June 14, 1982.
126 Know where the piano pitch, IUMC July 12, 1984
126 "make us want," IUMC June 24, 1999.
126 "launch the piece," SL August 1, 2001.
126 "Breaths should be," IUMC July 9, 1984.
126 "Sometimes it's necessary," IUMC June 15, 1983.

126 "We all know," IUMD June 14, 1982.
126 "remember that there are," MN October 24, 2003.
126 "much music is played," IUMC June 16, 1982.
126 "Be certain to quietly," IUMC June 14, 1982.
126 "Have enough bricks," IUMC June 14, 1983.
127 Regarding unaccompanied pieces, IUMC July 19, 1983
127 "There are only five," IUMC June 24, 2000.
127 "Even if we don't want," IUMC June 24, 1999.
127 "all music is played," IUMC June 24, 2000.
127 He cites Andres Segovia, IUMC June 24, 1999.

BIBLIOGRAPHY

BOOKS
Busoni, Ferruccio. "Sketch of a New Esthetic of Music," in *Three Classics in the Aesthetic of Music*, trans. by Th. Baker. New York: Dover Publications, 1962.
Horwood, Wally. *Adolphe Sax: His Life and Legacy*. Baldock, England: Egon Publishers, 1983.
Liley, Thomas. *A Brief History of the World Saxophone Congress, 1969-2000*. Minneapolis: University of Minnesota Press, 2003.
Logan, George M. *The Indiana University School of Music: A History*. Indiana University Press, 2000.
McCathren, Donald. *The Saxophone Book*. Kenosha, Wisconsin: G. Leblanc Company, 1954.
Runyon, Santy. *Suggestions for Woodwind Players*. N.p., n.d.
Slonimsky, Nicholas, ed. *Baker's Biographical Dictionary*. 6th ed. New York: Schirmer, 1978.

DISSERTATIONS AND THESES
Hall, Gail. "Eugene Rousseau: His Life and the Saxophone." DMA diss., University of Oklahoma, 1996.
Gronseth, Joel. "The World Saxophone Congress and its Impact on the Profession." MM diss., Bowling Green State University, 1996.
Jones, Patrick. "Interpreting Selected Works for Saxophone-based Performer-Composer Relationships." DMA diss., University of Minnesota, 2004.

ARTICLES
Aderman, Darrell. "Eugene Rousseau Comes to Shell Lake." MS, 2007.
Deffayet, Daniel. "Saxophone Study at the Paris Conservatory." Trans. by Brian Minor. *World Saxophone Congress Newsletter*, Vol. I, No. 3 (Winter 1971): 3.
Delangle, Claude. "Interview with the Legendary Marcel Mule on the History of Saxophone Vibrato," trans. by Huguette Brassine. *Australian Clarinet and Saxophone*, March 1998: 5–11.
Dickson, Harvey. "Eugene Rousseau gives respect to saxophones." *(Lakeland, Florida) Ledger*, March 16, 1986.
Flynn, Courtney. "Alvin Mistak, 1930–2007: Longtime maestro at Evanston High." *Chicago Tribune*, February 27, 2009.
Holgate, Max. "Some thoughts on the soprano saxophone." *Clarinet and Saxophone*, Vol. 12, No. 1 (March 1987): 37–38.
Indiana University School of Music. "Rousseau marks milestone." *Music Alumni Notes*, Vol. 18, No. 1 (Winter 1992): 5.
"Traugott Rohner, 1906–1991", *Instrumentalist*, October 1991: 2.
Interview from National Public Radio's "Morning Edition" reprinted in *Indiana Alumni Magazine*, September/October 1988.
Jacobi, Peter. "Music making news through special concerts." *(Bloomington, Indiana) Herald-Times*, February 4, 1996. p. D4.
Keel, Greg. "Eugene Rousseau." *Saxophone Journal*, Vol. 12, No. 3 (Fall 1987).

Kelton, Christopher. "Meet Eugene Rousseau: Saxophone Performer and Professor." *Instrumentalist*, Vol. 38, No. 2 (September 1983): pp. 9–16.
Mills, Bart. "Sax player makes classic choice." *(Lima, Ohio) News*, February 7, 1993.
Murtfeldt, Ryan. "Rousseau solos with IU group." *Indiana Daily Student*, April 15, 1996.
Phillips, David. "Saxophonist carves niche in classical music." *Indiana Daily Student*, Vol. 120, No. 66 (June 19, 1987).
Roberts, Richard J. "Eugene Rousseau: Master of the Saxophone." *Arts Indiana*, Vol. 10, No. 8 (November 1988).
Stabler, David. "Critic's Choice." *The Oregonian*, November 20, 1992.
Summerour, Jenny. "World-famous professor to play his classical sax." *(University of Georgia) Red & Black*, Vol. 103, Issue 143 (May 29, 1996).
Summerwill, Lyn. "Eugene Rousseau." *Clarinet & Saxophone,* Vol. 17/1 (March 1992).
Walters, Gordon. "Saxophonist takes classical twist to Big Band sound." *(Terre Haute, Indiana) Tribune-Star*, February 27, 1982.

REVIEWS
Anthony, Michael. "Diverse 'Sommerfest' moves from whimsical to the sublime." *Minneapolis Star and* Tribune, August 2, 1983.
Concert review, *Indianapolis News.* "ISO offers French celebration" May 13, 1989.
Concert review, "Trompetenstoß und Triowonne." *Weiner Zeitung*, May 12, 1996: 5.
Doisy, Marcel. Record review, *La Revue des Disques*, May 1972: 16.
Gibson, David. *Steps to Excellence* review. *Saxophone Journal*, September/October 1988.
Hudební Rozhledy. Prague, October 1985: 43. (Review of Feld *Concerto*).
Hume, Paul. Recital review, *Washington Post*, November 7, 1966: 16.
Hunt, Judith. "Guest conductor, saxophonist made good concert even better." *Anchorage Daily News*, April 25, 1985.
Jacobi, Peter. "Rousseau's new CD offers brilliant, soulful selections." *(Bloomington, Indiana) Herald-Times*, October 12, 1997: D4.
Jacobi, Peter. "Saxophone recital a summer treat." *(Bloomington, Indiana) Herald*-Telephone, June 22, 1987.
Jacobi, Peter. "Weekend music flows." *(Bloomington, Indiana) Herald-Times,* April 16, 1996: D4.
Maylan, Richard. Recital review, *London Times*, January 23, 1967: 17.
Plotinsky, Anita Heppner. "Rousseau's saxophone recital unusual event well received." *(Bloomington, Indiana) Herald-Times*, July 15, 1984.
Recital review, *Clarinet and Saxophone*, Vol. 17/4 (December 1992).
Recital review, *Journal Musical Français*, January 1968: 12.
Recital review, *Music News from Prague*, October 1987: 16.
Recital review, *Music News from Prague,* February-March 1988.
Recording review, *Blue Note Journal*, February 1989: 32.
Recording review, *Clarinet and Saxophone*, Vol. 17/4 (December 1992).
Recording review, *Gramophone*, August 1972: 19.
Recording review, *Saxophone Journal*, May 1996: 75.
Rosenzweig, Miriam. "Eugene Rousseau: Saxophonist Par Excellence." *Indiana Alumni Magazine*, September/October 1988.
Seebohm, Andrea. Recital review, *Vienna Express*, February 2, 1967: 21.

Shupp, E.E., Jr. Record review, *New Records*, April 1972: 42.
Strongin, Theodore. Recital review, *New York Times*, January 7, 1965: 18.
Underwood, James. "Rousseau's sax superb." *(Bloomington, Indiana) Herald-Telephone*, November 10, 1987.
Viola, Joe. *Saxophone Vocalise* review. *Saxophone Journal*, Vol. 20, No. 6 (May/June 1996).

NEWSPAPERS
Daily Iowan, September 27, 2002.

INTERVIEW
Hall, Marion. Interview with Eugene Rousseau and author. Bloomington, Indiana, June 2004.

RECORDINGS
Mule, Marcel. *"Le patron" of the Saxophone*. Clarinet Classics CC0013.

LETTERS
Copland, Aaron. Letter to Rousseau, March 6, 1961.
Creston, Paul. Letter to Rousseau, March 15, 1968.
Fisher, Albert (*Original Amateur Hour*). Email to author, June 19, 2009.
Hopkins, Harlow. Letter to author, December 2, 1986.
Schott, Robert. Letter to Rousseau, April 7, 1986.

ELECTRONIC RESOURCES
Pfleger, Karl. *On-Line Cumulative Learning of Hierarchical Spars n-grams*. Computer Science Department, Stanford University.

Abbott Northwestern Hospital
http://www.abbottnorthwestern.com/ahs/anw.nsf/page%20/history

Almeida, Antonio de
http://www.naxos.com/conductorinfo/5.htm

Ancia Saxophone Quartet
http://www.anciaquartet.com/members.htm

Angers, France
http://en.wikipedia.org/wiki/Angers

Blue Lake, Illinois
http://en.wikipedia.org/wiki/Lake_Chicago

Brecker, Michael
www://john-robert-brown.com/michael-brecker.htm

Central Missouri State University
http://www.cmsu.edu

Chicago Musical College
http://ccpa.roosevelt.edu/music/history.htm

Conservatoire de Paris
http://en.wikipedia.org/wiki/Conservatoire_de_Paris
http://idrs.colorado.edu/Publications/Journal/JNL14/JNL.14.Conr.html

Cortese, Glen
http://www.oregonmozartplayers.org/season/cortese.asp

Crepin, Alain
http://www.alaincrepin.be/GR/EN/biografie.htm

Ebbs, Frederick
http://www.indiana.edu/~bands/ebbs.html

Ferguson, Donald
http://special.lib.umn.edu/findaid/ead/univarch/Ead2/uarc00483.xml

Fulbright Scholars
http://us.fulbrightonline.org/about_programhistory.html

Guillain Barre Syndrome
http://www.mayoclinic.com/health/guillain-barre-syndrome/DS00413
http://www.ninds.nih.gov/disorders/gbs/detail_gbs.htm
http://enwikipedia.org/wiki/Guillain-Barr%C3%A9_syndrome

Herman, "Woody"
http://hometown.aol.com/_ht_a/bookviewzine/issue217.html
http://www.cduniverse.com/search/xx/music/pid/1082217/a/The+Third+Herd+1951.htm

Haugen, Ruben
http://www.stthomas.edu/music/faculty/ensembledirectors.html

G. Leblanc Company
http://www.gleblanc.comhistory/index.cfm

Leblanc "Rational Saxophone"
http://mediatheque.cite-musique.fr/mediacomposite/CMDM/CMDM000000300/saxo-
    phone_musee_04.htm

Luther College
http://luther.edu/about/
http://luther.edu.about/history.html

Macaferri, Mario
http://www.lutherie.net/mario_en.html

Mozarteum (Salzburg)
http://www.moz.ac.at/english/soak/history.shtml

Noble, Weston
http://www.fabm.com/WestonNobleRetirement.html

Pascucci, Vito
http://www.jsonline.com/story/index.aspx?id=163424
http://www.bandusa.com/directors_pages/DirectorsHistory/9.2003/VitosDeath/Vitos
    Death.html

Paynter, John
http://www.bands.org/public/resourceroom/JPP.asp

Prague Conservatory
http://www.prgcons.cz/eng/history.asp

Preucil, William
http://www.preucil.org/enrollmentforms/Flyer%202009%20web.pdf

Rousseau, Eugene
http://www.music.umn.edu/directory/facProfiles/RousseauEugene.php

Shell Lake Arts Center
http://www.chronotype.com/newarticle.asp

Ted Mack's Original Amateur Hour
http://www.originalamateurhour.com

University of Minnesota School of Music
http://artsquarter.umn.edu

Voxman, Himie
http://www.uiowa.edu/~musicsax/Voxman.html
http://www.news-releases.uiowa.edu/2003/april/040303voxman-award.html
www.dailyiowan.com/home/index.cfm?event

Yamaha Music Corporation
http://www.global.yamaha.com/about/history.html

Carolyn Bryan email, March 19, 2007.
Michael Hester email, March 11, 2007.
Christopher Kelton email, March 10, 2007.
Susan Loy email, February 7, 2007.
Susan Loy email, February 8, 2007.
Kate Newlin email, February 12, 2007.
Kenneth Tse email, March 25, 2007.
George Weremchuk email, March 3, 2007.
Anna Marie Wytko email, August 31, 2008.

INDEX

Abbott Northwestern Hospital (Minneapolis), 72-73.
Aderman, Darrell, 77, 78, 79.
Aiello, Elmer, 78.

Bain, Wilfred, 40, 41, 42, 43, 50, 68.
Bamber, Dennis, viii.
Belgian Air Force Band, 74-75.
Beneš, Hana, 59-60.
Bichurin, Mark, 44-45.
Bjorkman, Leichen, 81.
Brecker, Michael, 103.
Brodie, Paul, 51, 78.
Bryan, William Lowe, 42.
Burmeister, Arthur "Benny", 6

Campbell, Charles Diven, 42.
Composers: Baker, Claude, 76; Feld, Jindřich, 60, 78; Heiden, Bernhard, 51-52; Larsen, Libby, 76; O'Ricrdan, Kirk, 82.
Conductors: Almeida, Antonio de, 60; Crepin, Alain, 74, 75; Ebbs, Frederick, 24; Fennell, Frederick, 65-66; Itkin, David, 76; Jones, William LaRue, 76; Paynter, John, 12.
Cooper, Elburn, 56.
Cortese, Glen, 75.
Cortimiglia, Leo, 25-26.
Currie, Alan, 56.

Davis, Stan, 9.
Delangle, Claude, 77, 136-37.
Delvincourt, Claude, 28.
Distinguished Professorship, Indiana University, 60-61.
Dixon, James, 24.
Dorsey, Jimmy, 4.
Douglas, Basil, 52.
Douse, Kenneth, 4.
Druart, Henri, 34-35, 49.

Eck, Emil, 14, 15.
Erickson, Arnie, 25.
Étoile Music, 80.

Ferguson, Donald, 68.
First World Saxophone Congress (Chicago), 51-52.
Fischer, Kenneth, viii.
Foster, Dean, 81.
Frederick, Horace, 4.

Freedman, Albert, 9.
Friedman, Claire, 32.
Fuchs, Wenzel, 61.

Gallodoro, Alfred, 5.
Ganz, Rudolph, 10.
Glotin, Albert, 81.
Greene, Philip, 56.

Hartman, Karl, 67.
Haugen, Ruben, 70-71.
Haydn Trio of Vienna, 66, 78, 132.
Hemke, Frederick, 12, 38, 78, 136.
Herman, Woodrow "Woody", 8-9.
Hervig, Richard, 25.
Hochschule für Musik (Vienna), 61.
Hodges, Johnny, 107.
Hooks, John, 16.
Houvenaghel, Charles, 30, 56-57.

Ingham, Richard, 56.
Instituto G. Braga (Italy), 62.
Ishiwata, Yushi, 56.
Isoda, Hideki, 80-81.

Jacobs, Arnold, 107.
Jankowski, Paul, 6, 7, 21.
Jansen, Elda, 3, 131.
Jenner, Lyle, 3.
Jones, Merrill, 39.

Kawakami, 58.
Kawrza, Johannes, 56.
Kell, Reginald, 117.
Kimpton, Jeffrey, 68, 69, 71, 74.
Kitayama, Atsuyasu, 56.

Lacour, Guy, 132.
Leblanc, Léon, 30, 34, 49.
Leudders, Jerry, 55.
Living Legends, 66.
Lombardo, Guy, 4.
Luckhardt, Jerry, 68, 71.
Luper, Albert T., 24.
Luyben, Robert, 39.
Maccaferri, Mario, 81.

McCathren, Donald, 14, 104.
Maezawa, Fumiyoshi, viii, 56.
Markle, Roy, 78.
Mayer, Robert, 13-14.
Meron, Sam, 9.
Merrill, Barzille Winfred, 42.
Midwestern Music and Art Camp, vii, viii.
Mistak, Alvin, 21-22, 24.
Mozarteum (Salzburg), 61, 62.
Mule, Marcel, vi, 6, 26-27, 28-29, 31-35, 51, 81, 99, 103, 111, 114, 115, 131.
Myers, David, 68, 71.

Neilson, James, 50, 133.
New Budapest String Quartet, 72.
Noble, Weston, 19.
Nouax, Michel, 58.

Oberg, Paul, 68.
Oberhoffer, Emil, 68.

Pascucci, Vito, 14, 29-30, 56, 58, 64.
Paul Kuentz Chamber Orchestra, 53.
Pemberton, Roger, 45.
Pianists: Fuerstner, Carl, 44, 49-50, 137-48; Graf, Hans, 64-65; Hall, Marion, 47, 49; Hokanson, Leonard, 63, 64; Klein, Leonard, 44, 45; Klepáč, Jaromír, 72; Medjimorec, Heinz, 78; Miller, Kari, 135; Rezits, Joseph, 46.
Pitluck, Sherman, 44.
Portnoy, Bernard, 79-80.
Prague Conservatory, 62.
Pressler, Menahem, 133.
Preucil, William, 45-46.

Rascher, Sigurd, vii, 5, 51, 77, 114.
Recordings: Coronet *Eugene Rousseau Plays the Saxophone*, 47; Coronet The *Virtuoso Saxophone*, 47; Delos *Saxophone Colors*, 64-65; Delos *Saxophone Vocalise*, 65; Deutsche Grammophon *Saxophone Concertos*, 52-55; Jeanné *Brahms*, 72; Jeanné *Brahms/Mozart Quintets*, 72, 115; RIAX *The Undowithoutable Instrument*, 66; RIAX *Tsunagari*, 71.
Rees, Dick, 71.
Reviews: *Blue Note Journal*, 64-65; Doisy, Marcel, 53; *Gramophone*, 53-55; Hume, Paul, 46; *Journal Musical Français*, 49-50; *London Times*, 48; Maylan, Richard, 48; *Music News from Prague*, 63-64; *New Records*, 55; *New York Times*, 45; *La Revue des Disques*, 53; Rozhledy, Hudebni, 63; *Saxophone Journal*, 65; Seebohm, Andrea, 48-49; Shupp, E.E., Jr., 55; Strongin, Theodore, 45; *Vienna Express*, 48-49; *Washington Post*, 46.
RIAX, 80

Rohner, Traugott, 14.
Roth, Iwan, 31, 77.
Rousseau Music Products, 79.
Rousseau, Cora, 2.
Rousseau, Earl (brother), 2.
Rousseau, George Philias, 1-2.
Rousseau, Jean, 1-2.
Rousseau, Joseph Eugene (father), 2, 3, 7, 135.
Rousseau, Joseph Eugene (son), 22, 79.
Rousseau, Laura (Schindler) (mother), 2, 3.
Rousseau, Lisa-Marie (daughter), 22, 40, 72.
Rousseau, Lucille (sister), 2.
Rousseau, Norma (Rigel) (wife), 16, 19, 20-21, 29, 36, 40, 49, 59-60, 72.
Runyon, Santy, 104.

Sanders, Robert L., 42.
Schilke, Renold, 56.
Schindler, Katherine, 2.
Schott, Robert, 134.
Schuessler, Roy, 68.
Scott, Carlyle, 68.
Sharrow, Leonard, 15.
Shell Lake Arts Center, v, viii, 77-79.
Simpson, Wilbur, 14.
Slattery, Tom, 78.
Sremec, Dragan, 71.
Stowell, Jerry, 14.
Stusek, Steven, 82.

Teal, Laurence, 23, 38, 51, 77, 78, 136.
Ticino Musica (Switzerland), 62.
Tse, Kenneth, 82.
Turchen, Abe, 9.

Ultan, Lloyd, 68.

Voxman, Himie, 21, 22, 23, 24, 25, 26, 40, 64.

Waterhouse, William, 133.
Webb, Charles, 41, 68, 78.
Wells, Charles, 39.
Wells, Herman B, 42, 68.
Wells, Jack, vii.
Wiley, Russell L., vii, viii.
Wingert, George, 39.
Winold, Allen, 44, 45.

Winter, Paul, 45.
Wolff, Karen, 68.
Wollam, Abe, 78.
Woods, David, 69.
Woods, Phil, 144.
World Saxophone Congress XIII (Minneapolis), 74-76.
Wytko, Joseph, 77, 136.

Xenakis, Iannis, 44.

Yamaha Corporation, 56, 57-59.

Zagreb Saxophone Quartet, 70, 71, 77.
Zahler, Noel, 68, 71.